THE PRAIRIES ON FIRE:
Lincoln Debates Douglas, 1858

To Stan Morris,
Very best wishes!
Go State!

Richard D. Schwartz

To the memory of my father.

ISBN: 1453692320
ISBN-13: 9781453692325

TABLE OF CONTENTS

PROLOGUE

"The Battle of the Union Is To Be Fought in Illinois"

On seven days in seven Illinois towns in the summer and autumn of 1858 Republican Abraham Lincoln debated Democratic Senator Stephen A. Douglas in a race for Douglas's Senate seat. Lincoln's performance in the seven encounters and in the six-months-long campaign won him national acclaim, garnering him speaking invitations throughout the free states the very next year. He then became a serious if not front-running candidate for the 1860 Republican presidential nomination. Without the Douglas-Lincoln debates (for that would have been the billing at the series' outset in August), Lincoln would never have attained the stature to filch that nomination from New York's William Henry Seward. Republican electoral victory might still have followed, and with it secession, but America would have lived the crisis of the 1860s without Lincoln in the White House.

It is literally impossible to imagine the Abraham Lincoln of history and myth without these seven encounters. And yet the debates suffer in both the scholarly and popular minds. Historians have tended to disparage the debates as repetitive and overrated. Meanwhile, the declining number of Americans who have even heard of the debates tend to recall Lincoln debating Douglas for the presidency, which never happened. 1

This book speaks to the latter audience. Someone wanting to read about the debates could select from respected academic treatises by scholars such as Allen Guelzo, Harry Jaffa, or David Zarefsky. Or you could read one of the excellent 300-odd page transcriptions of the seven debates edited by noted Lincoln scholars. Or your public library might have one of the two narrative histories written thirty or more years ago. All have served important functions. Why add another book to this syllabus?

For today's citizen reader, the Lincoln-Douglas debates present a "teachable moment." We fret about our political culture with its negative campaigning, its media bias, its appeals to divisive religious, racial, and ethnic "wedge issues." All showed themselves in 1858, however; we are not the first generation of Americans to endure these. At the same time, Illinoisans of 1858 offer modern-day Americans a lesson in the demands of democratic citizenship. They came out by the thousands to hear the two candidates, and many traveled hard miles to do so. Small Illinois towns became theaters of oratory, heckling, adversarial journalism, even fistfights; and this rough political arena spawned the greatest American statesman, sharpened physically, morally, and emotionally for the ordeal of the 1860s.

Under endless prairie skies, along the banks of America's greatest river, in perhaps the most American of settings, two men, products of typically American migrations, came before average Americans to argue a uniquely American question: did the unalienable truth that all men are created equal include people who were not white? The vast middle American outdoor theater fit the question's greatness more truly than could any lecture hall or legislative chamber or courtroom, and it is hard to imagine such a discussion occurring anywhere else on the planet in the middle nineteenth century.

Four key players made the 1858 race historic:

Abraham Lincoln: Forty-nine years old. He rises from inauspicious Kentucky roots. He will malign his own lack of education, but he reads and learns; the cadences of the King James Bible will never really leave him, and even as a busy lawyer and politician he teaches himself Euclidean geometry. He overcomes failure and heartbreak to achieve upper middle class status, a lawyer of statewide reputation, a state legislator in the 1830s and 40s; a Whig, a proponent of government aiding economic growth through "internal improvements," what we would now call infrastructure. Briefly a member of Congress at the time of the war with Mexico, he errs politically by introducing a resolution calling on Democratic President Polk to identify the actual "spot" on American soil upon which "invading" Mexican forces first spilled American blood. Lincoln and many of his countrymen know that the land in question was claimed by both nations, but the stunt does not enhance the voters' opinion of the freshman congressman. By the late 1840s, his political profile reduced, he devotes his energies primarily to a budding law practice.

When Douglas pushes the Kansas-Nebraska Act through Congress in 1854, Lincoln dives back into politics over the possible introduction of slavery into the northern Plains. He contends that the extension of slavery beyond the slave states violates America's "ancient faith," that all men are created equal. He misses narrowly in a bid for the Senate seat not held by Douglas in 1855, as the former Democrat-turned Republican Lyman Trumbull surges from behind to take it. With the Whigs no longer in existence, Lincoln professes not to know which political party he belongs to, but by the next year he has cast his lot. In 1856, delegates to the first Republican national convention place his name in nomination for vice president, but he does not have the votes. As 1858 approaches, and with Douglas increasingly vulnerable after a public break with the Buchanan administration over the fraudulent, pro-slavery "Lecompton constitution" for the would-be state of Kansas, Lincoln and his many Republican friends leave nothing to chance, working to assure him the nomination of the Illinois Republican party as their first, last, and only choice for Senator.

Accepting the nomination on June 16, he begins his quest quoting the words of Jesus, a wise choice given the growing evangelical presence in Illinois. He contends that since "a house divided against itself cannot stand," the nation cannot forever go on "half slave and half free." He asserts that the nation will in future become all free or all slave, and he asks the assembled Republicans, "Have we no tendency toward the latter condition?" He contends that Douglas and other leading Democratic politicians are engaged in a conspiracy to take slavery national, even into Illinois and the other free states. And he answers eastern Republicans such as Horace Greeley of the widely-read New York *Tribune.* Some have urged Illinois Republicans not to contest Douglas's re-election; still others wish to draft Douglas as the Republican candidate. Lincoln asserts that "a living dog is better than a dead lion," and that Douglas has never truly opposed slavery or its spread. Douglas will spend much of the six months ahead citing the House Divided speech as evidence that Lincoln is an abolitionist, which he is not.

He wears clothes badly.   He has a sharp nose and outsized jaw and cheekbones and sunken, piercing eyes; he is clean-shaven. People either laugh with or at him, and sometimes it seems as though audiences see in him what they want to see. Some jeer at his high-pitched Kentucky twang. And yet . . . "I must confess that 'Long Abe's' appearance is not comely," writes a New York reporter, but "stir him up, and the fire of his genius plays on every feature. His eye glows and sparkles," and "every lineament, now so ill formed, grows brilliant and you have before you a man of rare power and of strong magnetic influence." Whatever the case, that voice carries to the far reaches of crowds. Some testify that on the stump he is loose-limbed, all elbows and knees and sudden jerks. Others swear that he stands still and steady as he speaks. He holds membership in no church, but he gracefully quotes Scripture in his public speeches and private writings. Unusually gentle and generous, he suffers from occasional episodes of deep depression. Men look to him as a leader, a sort of lovable uncle, and they laugh at his jokes and yarns. In the 1940s Aaron Copland will call him a "quiet and melancholy man," but this campaign will call forth Lincoln the extrovert. His house on Eighth and Jackson, near the Illinois state capitol, is a happier place when he is home; he overindulges his sons, and gives his strong but needy wife the attention she needs. The family has known tragedy; his son Eddie is eight years dead by the time of the challenge to Douglas.

He treasures what he terms "our ancient faith," that all men are created equal. Slavery violates that faith, so slavery is wrong and must not be allowed to spread, not even one inch beyond the fifteen slave states. He assures all who will listen that he has no wish to threaten the Union's survival by advocating the abolition of slavery in the slave states. He believes that black men and women are included in "all men are created equal," but in a qualified sense. He does not advocate their political equality, and denies that he wishes to see black voters or jurors. He denies their right to "social equality," and spends substantial time assuring whites that he does not advocate interracial marriage. But he does believe that they deserve equal economic rights: blacks deserve the right to rise as he has risen; they deserve the right to enjoy the fruits of their own labor just as much as whites, all whites (up to and including the prominent senior Senator from Illinois.) Slavery completely cancels these economic rights, which Lincoln considers even more foundational to America's promise than the right to vote or to freely associate.

Lincoln aches to make an impact on his fellow Americans; he craves their respect. To take the Senate floor, to follow the great Henry Clay is his dream. He desperately wants to win this election. 2

Stephen A. Douglas: Forty-five years old at the time of the campaign, he somehow seems Lincoln's senior. Like Lincoln a migrant into Illinois, but by way of Vermont and upstate New York. This might suggest roots in the evangelical social reform movements of the period. But Douglas's passion is not social improvement; it is Jacksonian politics, which celebrates the political wisdom of the white common man. Short and squat and intense, he moves faster and more successfully into and beyond Illinois politics than does Lincoln. His ticket has been punched in the state legislature and in the Illinois Supreme Court (a position he received in part because of a shady judicial reorganization bill he sponsored, and throughout the 1858 canvass, Lincoln will teasingly refer to his opponent not as "Senator," but as "Judge.") In the '40s he serves in the U.S. House of Representatives, driving John Quincy Adams to distraction during the debates over the Gag Rule on antislavery petitions, then he moves on to the Senate. He is a leather-lunged advocate for Manifest Destiny, calling for the nation to expand, to conquer. Strongly supportive of the successful war with Mexico, his legislative acumen deftly rescues the nation in 1850 when secession threats accompany California's application for statehood.

But the 1850s have otherwise not gone well for him. Rejected as the Democratic nominee due in part to his overeager approach in 1852, he inadvertently restarts the sectional crisis in 1854 by trying to organize the Kansas and Nebraska territories with no restrictions on slavery under "popular sovereignty." He hopes that the territorial settlers can peacefully decide a question that the men in Washington cannot. Violence soon flares in "Bleeding Kansas," an antislavery Massachusetts senator is brutally caned on the Senate floor by a South Carolina congressman, and Douglas's beloved Democratic Party takes a pounding in the 1854 legislative elections in the North at the hands of opponents soon to congeal into the Republican Party. In 1856, the Democrats pass him over for James Buchanan, who has safely avoided the crisis as ambassador to Britain. Buchanan's presidential term presents Douglas with two more problems: the Supreme Court's *Dred Scott* ruling throws open all territories to slavery, denying the power of Congress to restrict territorial slavery and calling into question Douglas's popular sovereignty doctrine; and Buchanan makes support for the Lecompton constitution a test of party loyalty. When Douglas opts to lead the fight against the fraudulent Kansas constitution, he becomes a marked man within his own party, especially its southern wing.

Once slovenly and badly-behaved when in his cups, Douglas has remarried after the death of his first wife. Adele Cutts Douglas, his elegant new wife, has helped to make him more presentable. He is well-tailored and well-groomed, although he seems unable to shake his alcohol habit. An unusual little fold of skin just above the bridge of his nose, his fully-packed face and body, his gorgeous main of dark hair and his rumbling, florid style of address bespeak his intensity as a debater.

He is an early species of the Washington-based politician; his home is there, not in Illinois. He has not spent much time in the state recently, having opted for a European tour that included the Senator's polite refusal of an audience with Queen Victoria; of all foreign nations, Douglas is most suspicious of the British. Most Illinoisans have never laid eyes on their most famous fellow citizen. Douglas's two sons remain in Washington where they attend a Jesuit school. Adele will travel with him throughout the campaign. Lincoln will joke to a friend that at least *he* doesn't need his wife along to keep him sober.

He represents an updated Jacksonian democracy. He adores the Union of the states and stands upon the principle of local self-government. He believes that whites are superior to non-whites. He foresees more territorial acquisition, and this sets him aglow. At the same time he supports a transcontinental railroad and a slightly more activist government than have doctrinaire Jacksonians. As for slavery, Lincoln has it right when he charges that Douglas "don't care" about whether the people of the territories vote slavery up or down; the voting itself matters. He acts as absentee manager of a Mississippi plantation that his first wife inherited from her father, and insists that the slaves be provided for.

On July 9, after signs of reconciliation with Buchanan, Douglas invites Lincoln to sit on the balcony of a Chicago hotel as the Senator gives his first speech of the campaign before thousands of adoring citizens. Stunningly he reverses field, blistering the administration for Lecompton. He soon turns to Lincoln, for whom he publicly professes his respect and affection. Douglas then plays the race card, linking his challenger to abolition, to full racial equality, to race mixing, a taboo "tantamount to bestiality" in that time and place according to one scholar. In Latin America, "I have seen the effects of this mixture of superior and inferior races," Douglas shouts, and the result has been "degeneration, demoralization, and degradation below the capacity for self-government." He will take the low road on race throughout this campaign, and if he has a secondary target it will be the great black abolitionist Frederick Douglass, to whom he will attempt to tether Lincoln.

This seat is his to lose. But to lose it would be to lose all hope of ever gaining higher office. He confides to associates that in Lincoln the Republicans have nominated a dangerous foe; the two have known one another for decades, and have debated one another in other settings. Experience tells Douglas not to underestimate Lincoln. 3

The Press: The newspapers that will report the debates resemble today's bloggers and talk-show programs much more than they do mainstream newspapers and networks. Douglas is part owner of the Chicago *Times,* and the paper offers no claims to "balance" or "objectivity." Lincoln's strategic and tactical advisors include key figures of the Chicago *Press and Tribune,* and at Freeport, in the second debate, that paper's editor William Bross will sit with Republican leaders, applauding and calling encouragement to Lincoln. In the capital city, Douglas's friend Charles Lanphier edits the *Illinois State Register* conducting requested (and unfortunately faulty) opposition research. Springfield Republicans can count upon the local *Illinois State Journal* to support Lincoln. Nationally, Greeley's New York *Tribune* is the most influential Republican paper. Many Illinoisans subscribe to its national weekly edition, so Greeley's tepid response to Lincoln's candidacy in the early summer troubles Lincoln and his Illinois friends. James Gordon Bennett's New York *Herald* speaks for the Democrats, especially the party's southern wing. The Buchanan adminstration has its own house newspaper, the Washington *Union.*

The two great Chicago papers send so-called "phonographers" to transcribe the two contestants' words *and* the crowd reactions. Emergent technologies--the railroad, the telegraph, and the steam-driven press--mean that readers have access to the candidates' words and the newspapers' critiques soon after each debate. Newspapers from the great Eastern cities and from the South and Northwest send reporters to "cover" the debates. As Lincoln hangs in with Douglas, round-after-round, interest builds. In October, one newspaper will proclaim that, "the battle of the Union is to be fought in Illinois."

Meanwhile, smaller local Illinois presses carry the story to their readers, clipping items from the larger dailies and conducting their own battles over the campaign. As impassioned as the big-city dailies, these weeklies offer pungent hometown reactions to the candidates. 4

The people of Illinois: It is only their fortieth year of statehood, but they have risen to be the fourth most populated state in the nation. By 1860 there will be over a million of them scattered from the shores of Lake Michigan to the confluence of the Mississippi and the Ohio. They are all migrants, or the children of migrants. Kentuckians and Tennesseans have come first, into "Egypt," the southernmost region of the state which supplies surplus grain to northern Illinoisans during a brutal winter in the 1830s, as Joseph's Egypt had once sustained Israel. Theirs is culturally the most Southern region of the state, white supremacist and so supportive of President Buchanan that out of Egypt comes a third candidate, a "Buchaneer" or "Danite" challenger to Douglas in the form of Judge Sidney Breese. The central region, full of onetime Whigs still searching for a relevant party identity, has seen large migration from the lower north, the upper south, and from the German states. Candidates in statewide elections consider these central counties critical. The state's northern tier, near the Wisconsin and Iowa lines, has rapidly outstripped the other two regions in population (although the state legislature fails to reflect this.) Free-soil New Englanders and Germans work the fertile soil west of Chicago. The city itself bustles with commerce, as German immigrants bump Irish Catholic laborers—loyal Democratic voters, the Irish—and jostle onetime residents of the old northern states. Evangelical Protestants, many of them temperance folk, some anti-slavery, represent another important voting bloc, in and beyond the city. Relations between groups can be delicate;

when temperance forces in Chicago city government restrict alcohol sales in 1855, the Germans rise up in the so-called lager beer riots.

Illinoisans have long supported the Democrats, but the Kansas crisis and persistent concern over immigration combine to shake that party's hold. By 1858, after terrific efforts at coalition building, the Republicans have absorbed free-soil ex-Democrats and Whigs, as well as anti-Catholic, anti-Irish defectors from the American Party (called "Know Nothings," or, if tolerant of the German Lutherans, "Know Somethings.") Illinois Republicans include in their ranks racial progressives, but more share the Democrats' white supremacy; they oppose slavery, and territorial slavery, because of its direct threat to free labor and the white man's perceived right to rise, not out of any love for the blacks. Conservative Republicans insist Lincoln distance himself from abolitionism, and some who hear a practice run of his June 16 acceptance speech—the House Divided speech--plead that he tear it up and deliver a more moderate address. Listening to the council of his law partner Billy Herndon, Lincoln refuses. Herndon tells Lincoln that the speech will one day make him President, a stretch given Lincoln's total lack of executive experience.

Illinoisans inhabit a political culture that appears a miniature version of the nation as a whole, and this attracts the interest of politicians and newspapers North and South.

The state is overwhelmingly white--and white supremacist. State legislators and voters have placed harsh restrictions on free blacks, going so far as to ban any newly-arrived free blacks from entering Illinois. Egypt is of course the least friendly of areas for African-Americans. Union County in southernmost Illinois is so vigorous in its enforcement of the fugitive slave laws that runaways heading up the Mississippi Valley take their chances in Missouri rather than crossing into Union. The county's Democratic candidate for Congress, John Logan, is said to have hunted down runaway slaves himself. Madison County claims a rueful distinction, the 1837 Alton murder of the anti-slavery printer Elijah Lovejoy in defense of his press at the hands of an anti-abolitionist mob. Illinois has as vicious black codes as any free state.

Only adult white men will vote in this race. But women throughout Illinois, and children too, will attend the debates in large numbers. No Illinoisan will cast a direct vote for either Stephen Douglas or Abraham Lincoln. For under the United States Constitution of 1787, the Illinois state legislature (last apportioned before the founding of the Republican Party and, because of election procedures, one with a small but important number of Democrats not facing re-election in this cycle) will select the winner. The state legislators will make their choice in January, 1859. 5

"Your Position Is Dangerous to Your Success"

Only blocks from home, Lincoln introduced the rationale for his campaign on June 16 in the Illinois House of Representatives chamber to Republicans who had braved heavy rains and swollen rivers to nominate him. As a house divided could not stand, as the nation could not endure permanently half-slave, half-free, Republicans must be vigilant, for a conspiracy led by Douglas, former President Pierce, Supreme Court Chief Justice Taney, and President Buchanan (he mocked them as the four carpenters, "Stephen, Franklin, Roger, and James") stood ready to take slavery beyond the slave states, beyond even the territories, and into the free states. "We shall *lie down* pleasantly dreaming that the people of Missouri are on the verge of making their State *free*," warned Lincoln, "and we shall *awake* to the *reality* that the *Supreme* Court has made *Illinois* a *slave* state." That "second Dred Scott decision," amounting to the nationalization of slavery, would likely occur should Illinoisans return Douglas to Washington. Having dissuaded his law partner from giving the cautious, safe speech that more conservative Republicans had urged, Billy Herndon rejoiced. He predicted that the race for Senate would be "hot—energetic—deadly and the Democracy would certainly go gurgling down beneath red waves of slaughter." 6

From the balcony of Chicago's Tremont House Hotel on July 9 Douglas signaled *his* central strategy in the campaign: Dodge the issue of territorial slavery, where Lincoln's free-soil views accorded with those of many Illinoisans. Emphasize instead the question of racial equality, where his own white supremacist ideology would be viewed as sound by many Illinoisans, especially those in the central and southern districts. (And the Republicans knew this: on August 3, David Davis wrote to Lincoln, "All the Orators should distinctly and emphatically disavow <u>negro</u> <u>suffrage</u>, negro holding office, serving on juries and the like." And "For God's sake," added Davis, don't let abolitionists like Congressman Owen Lovejoy, visit Tazewell County, where "the people are nearly all from Kentucky." Davis warned Lincoln, "Let no ultra ground be broached by anyone.") 7

After inviting Lincoln to sit amid Democratic chieftains on the Tremont House balcony and after launching a rousing attack on the Buchanan administration, Douglas turned to his opponent. The Little Giant charged that in pursuit of his aims, simply a war between the North and South to be followed by a carnival of interracial sex, the "worthy gentleman" seated behind the Senator had formed "an unholy alliance" with Buchananite federal office holders, men "who have ceased to be Democrats, who belong to the allied army, whose avowed object is to elect the Republican ticket by dividing and destroying the Democratic party." Well, promised Douglas, "I shall deal with these allied forces just as the Russians dealt with the allies at Sebastopol. The Russians, when they fired a broadside at the common enemy, did not stop to inquire whether it hit a Frenchman, an Englishman, or a Turk, nor shall I stop to inquire whether my blows hit the Republican leaders or their allies. . ." 8

A rousing, defiant speech, a Douglas speech. This little cannonball of a man announced in Chicago his willingness to fight to the death to retain his Senate seat.

The next night, Lincoln responded in a rollicking performance from the same hotel balcony; the crowd took an active part in things, as when Lincoln took a swipe at Douglas's Sebastopol reference: "Why, my friend, the Judge, is not only, as it turns out, not a dead lion, nor even a living one—he is the rugged Russian bear!" 9

Aside from entertaining the crowd, Lincoln spoke more substantively. Douglas looked on slavery "as this exceedingly little thing—only equal to the cranberry laws of Indiana," but most Americans "do *not* look upon this matter as being this very little thing. They look upon it as a vast moral evil. . ." And, since Douglas had attempted to define "all men are created equal" as nothing more than the justification used by British subjects mounting a war for independence against the British Empire, Lincoln pounced. The men that waged the Revolution "were iron men, they fought for the principle they were contending for;" but now "among us perhaps half our people. . . are not descendants at all of these men, they are men who have come from Europe—German, Irish, French and Scandinavian," men who could not "trace their connection to those days by blood . . ." Douglas believes that "you Germans are not connected" with the principle of human equality. If this were in fact true, then the benefits of "all men are created equal" could be denied to substantial segments of the American populace, and not just blacks.

Arguments such as these, said Lincoln, were the sorts of arguments that kings had made from the beginning of time, and so Douglas had loosed "the same old serpent that says you work and I eat, you toil and I will enjoy the fruits of it." Lincoln shouted that, "whether it come from the mouth of a King, as an excuse for enslaving the people of his country, or from the mouth of men of one race as a reason for enslaving the men of another race, it is the same old serpent." Lincoln asked: If Douglas denies that all men are created equal in the case of blacks, then where does it stop? "If one man says it does not mean a negro, why [may] not another say it does not mean some other man?" So why waste time, Judge Douglas? "If that declaration is not the truth, let us get out the Statute book, in which we find it and tear it out! Who is so bold to do it!" 10

Some smart aleck yelled, "*me*," while others shouted, "*no one*," as Lincoln called over the din, "If it is not true let us tear it out!"

"*No*," cried voices, "*no*."

". . . let us stick to it then," Lincoln continued, as they cheered, "let us stand firmly by it then."

But what did "all men are created equal" mean in a nation of more than three million slaves? Lincoln reached to the New Testament: "It is said in one of the admonitions of the Lord, 'As your Father in Heaven is perfect, be ye also perfect.' The Savior," Lincoln shouted, "did not expect that any human creature could be perfect as the Father in Heaven. . .but He set that up as a standard, and he who did most towards reaching that standard, attained the highest degree of moral perfection." So be it with the principle of human equality: "let it be as nearly reached as we can. If we cannot give freedom to every creature, let us do nothing which will impose slavery upon any other creature." 11

The crowd applauded. Subtly, Lincoln had crept to the edge of abolitionism, without actually calling for abolition—*if we cannot give freedom to every creature, let us not impose slavery on anyone not yet enslaved.* You had to listen closely to understand what he had meant earlier in the speech, when he had said, "I have always hated slavery, I think as much as any Abolitionist." Lincoln was clever; he could sound abolitionist themes, even while denying that he was an abolitionist; he could quote Jesus Christ, even while refusing to commit to any church.

He closed. "I have only this to say, let us discard all this quibbling about this man and the other man—this race and that race and the other race being inferior, and therefore they must be placed in an inferior position—discarding our standard that we have left us. Let us discard these things, and unite as one people throughout this land, until we shall once more stand up declaring that all men are created equal." 12

It was a strong performance, full of humor and energy and grounded in the first principle of the nation, and Lincoln took pride it. In a letter asking that the exiled German revolutionary Friedrich K.F. Hecker be persuaded to address German voters in Springfield, Lincoln wrote to the great German leader Gustave Koerner that the Republican rally, "called twelve hours before it came together and got up without trumpery, was nearly as large" as Douglas's appearance, "and five times as enthusiastic." Douglas had already begun to travel from place to place on an impressive Illinois Central railroad car trimmed with bunting and posters and trailing a flat car mounting a 12-pounder cannon to announce the great man's arrival, but "it is all as bombastic and hollow as Napoleon's bulletins sent back from his campaign in Russia." He assured Koerner that "there is no solid shot, in these bombastic parades of his." Lincoln left the great city, clearly buoyed by his strong response to Douglas, a retort grounded in an unapologetic defense of the notion that the American experiment hinged in no small degree on whether "all men are created equal" included blacks. 13

But reactions to the speech made clear the excruciating choice facing the Republican. Some rejoiced at Lincoln's principled stand. "Friend Lincoln," wrote the Quaker Abraham Smith, "while some republicans—good men & true but <u>cautious</u> will say thou hast taken too high ground—(too near up to the standard of the Christianity of the day)—I am rejoiced that by thy speeches. . .thou art fairly mounted on the eternal invulnerabl bulwark of <u>truth</u> . . ." Douglas "is a cuning dog & the devil is on his side," wrote Smith, but the race was "no less than a contest for the advancement of the kingdom of Heaven or the Kingdom of Satan," one in which, "the fate of Douglas or Lincoln is comparatively a trifle." And one admirer of the Chicago speech wrote from Cincinnati that "straightforwardness and boldness will quite soon (if not now) carry even against such a man and I feel confidant that you may even succeed here against him." Lincoln's passionate endorsement of racial equality delighted those who craved a direct confrontation with the slave power. 14

Others were not so impressed and urged the candidate to drop the theme from his campaign. "I have just read your Speech delivered at Chicago," wrote the influential Coles County nativist W.M. Chambers in a confidential letter. "I have ever entertained a political hostility to Judge Douglas," and "there is no man, with my humble capacity, who can entertain, a more sincere desire to see him beaten in the coming contest than myself. . . I want some man to defeat him." But Chambers complained of "some objectionable views expressed by you in your Chicago speech," and called for "less of the favouring of negro equality." He added, "I cannot defend your positions as I understand them, and there are republicans here who are getting very shy and do not hesitate to condemn your course." Chambers minced no words: "your position is dangerous to your success." Chambers' Coles County neighbor, the Republican Augustus Chapman, filled in Lincoln on the July 23 meeting of "our secret Vigolance committee." As regarded Chambers, Chapman counseled the candidate to "say any thing to Him that will have a Tendency to Bring Him over to our side." Chapman explained, "we are making a fight on the Slave & Free white labor & not saying much about equality or any thing of that kind. . ." From Greenville, in southern Illinois, Jediah F. Alexander chimed in, "You must be full and explicit in explaining that you are not in favor of interfering in any manner, with slavery in the States, but allow them to keep it just so long as they can manage it. That the Republicans are not in favor of making the Blacks socially and politically equal with the Whites." Alexander explained, "When you get here, it is necessary that you treat these, and other questions connected with the Negro, more at length than you are in habit of doing," for "some folks are so hard of understanding, and like to hear a good thing repeated." From Mattoon in central Illinois, Hiram Tremble wrote, "Abe set your tim that you will make a speech and wee will get you an audience" so that Lincoln could give his views on "the Niger Equality which your enameys Charge upon you." 15

Perhaps inadvertently, Lincoln had in Chicago presented himself a choice. Did he detest so strongly that "same old serpent," that "you work and I eat, you toil and I will enjoy the fruits of it" that he would make human equality the foundation of his challenge to Douglas? Or did he need to downplay equality so as to win the support of white Illinoisans of the downstate regions, regions where voters supported bans on free blacks entering the state, regions runaway slaves sometimes avoided as they fled north, regions where abolitionists had been shunned, and in one instance murdered? The choice may look easy to modern readers, but was it an easy one for Lincoln?

The campaign was well underway. Lincoln spent significant time worrying over uncommitted former Whig and anti-immigrant American Party voters in the central counties and analyzing county-by-county results from the 1856 presidential election, in which former president Millard Fillmore had run as the American Party candidate. He wrote to his friend Joseph Gillespie in southwestern Illinois: "In Madison [County] alone if our friends get 1000 of the Fillmore votes, and their opponents the remainder—658, we win by just two votes. . . it behooves you to be actively working." With those central districts in mind he had already written to Senator John Crittenden of Kentucky, the influential political heir to the late Whig founder Henry Clay. He delicately noted reports that the Senator had been induced to write letters supporting Douglas and Democratic Congressman Thomas Harris in their re-election fights. "I do not believe the story," wrote Lincoln, "but it still gives me some uneasiness." Assuring the Kentuckian that he was not "fishing for a letter on the other side," Lincoln asked that Crittenden write back; "and if your purposes are as I hope they are not, please let me know. The confirmation would pain me much, but I should continue your friend and admirer." 16

On July 16 the Douglas express swung into central Illinois at Bloomington, the cars bedecked with banners proclaiming "Stephen A. Douglas, The Champion of Popular Sovereignty." There, Douglas renewed attacks first launched in Chicago on the house divided doctrine, linking his opponent to the "irresponsible agitators" in the abolitionist ranks. One day later, Lincoln, now chasing Douglas around the state, responded in nearby Springfield. "Senator Douglas is of worldwide renown," he announced. And all of "the anxious politicians of his party," expect him or "at no distant day to be the President of the United States. They have seen in his round, jolly, fruitful face, postoffices, landoffices, marshalships, and cabinet appointments, chargeships and foreign missions, bursting and sprouting out in wonderful exuberance ready to be laid hold of by their greedy hands." To great laughter, Lincoln's sad eyes panned the crowd. "On the contrary," he said, "nobody has ever expected me to be President. In my poor, lean, lank face, nobody has ever seen that any cabbages were sprouting out." To "tremendous cheering and laughter" from his neighbors, Lincoln no doubt smiled. 17

Unable to match Douglas' renown, said Lincoln, he would have to fight this battle on principle.

"I Accede, and Thus Close the Arrangement"

Lincoln's strategy of following Douglas around the state had been tried before; he and others had dogged the Little Giant's heels after the passage of the Kansas-Nebraska Act in 1854. It had irritated Douglas then, and it was beginning to annoy him now, especially since Lincoln seemed to take such delight in teasing the incumbent, a tendency that Lincoln would indulge long into the campaign. When in August, for instance, an agitated Douglas announced his willingness to trade blows with Lincoln, the Republican made the most of the comic imagery of the rotund Little Giant tussling with his strapping rival, "Did anyone in this audience hear him use such language? [Cries of yes.] . . . Did anybody here witness that warlike proceeding? [Laughter, and cries of yes.]. . .My. . . reason for not having a personal encounter with the Judge is, that I don't believe he wants it himself. [Laughter] He and I are about the best friends in the world, and when we get together he would no more think of fighting me than of fighting his wife." 18

They may not have been quite that good friends. Nor was Lincoln improving the relationship by tailing Douglas all over Illinois. At the same time, some Republicans were not so sure of the wisdom of this game of follow-the-leader either, and began agitating for a series of joint debates. On July 22, the Chicago *Press and Tribune* editorialized, "Let Mr. Douglas and Mr. Lincoln agree to canvass the State together, in the usual Western style," adding, "If Mr. Douglas shall refuse to be a party to such arrangement, it will be because he is a coward." Two days later, Lincoln himself wrote Douglas, asking, "Will it be agreeable to you to make arrangement for you and myself to divide time, and address the same audiences during the present canvass?" [19]

There followed a prickly exchange of letters as the party press disparaged the opposing candidates on the debate issue. Douglas wrote back to Lincoln on the 24th a letter that Lincoln did not receive until the 29[th.] In effect, Douglas said that this will be all but impossible, for I already have a heavy schedule until late October; and what about the Buchaneer Sidney Breese? Does he get to participate as well? He has "a common object with you" and if he is included, "he and you in concert might be able to take the opening and closing speech in each case." I am also surprised, scolded Douglas, that you waited until this late date to make this proposal, inasmuch as we have frequently crossed one another's paths.

But no matter how he might protest, the closeness of the race and the rising demands of the Republican press that the Little Giant come out and fight forced Douglas to acquiesce. [20]

Figuratively sighing, the Democrat closed:

I will, in order to accommodate you as far as it is in my position to do so, take the responsibility of making an arrangement with you for a discussion between us at one prominent point in each congressional district in the state, excepting the second and sixth districts, where we have both spoken and in each of which cases you had the concluding speech. If agreeable to you I will indicate the following places as those most suitable in the several congressional districts at which we should speak, to wit, Freeport, Ottawa, Galesburg, Quincy, Alton, Jonesboro and Charleston. [21]

There it was; Lincoln had said he wanted to debate Douglas one hundred times; he would get seven face-to-face meetings, which was seven more than Douglas wanted. In writing back, Lincoln groused that it was "hardly a fair statement" that he had gotten the advantage of closing in the Second District (centered on Chicago) or the Sixth (Springfield and Bloomington), and he disavowed with a straight face any plan for collusion with the Danites, (this despite the fact that the noted Danite speaker R.B. Carpenter of Southern Illinois received instructions from the Republican central committee.) He defended himself against Douglas's charge of tardiness in proposing the debates ("I can only say I made it as soon as I resolved to make it.") But he would accept, so long as Douglas would promptly name the dates. "As to other details, I wish reciprocity, and no more." 22

The Chicago *Press and Tribune* jeered that, "The little dodger shirks, and backs out, except at half a dozen places which he himself selects." And Springfield's *Illinois State Journal* opined that in his rejection from the oh-so-reasonable Republican request for 100 debates, Douglas was little better than "seven one-hundredths of a candidate for the Senate." 23

Serendipitously, the two candidates crossed paths in carriages near Bement, on July 29. They finalized agreements, and Douglas agreed to return to Bement and write up the specific terms, and send them to Lincoln in Monticello, the Republican's destination. In the note, Douglas laid out the schedule: Ottawa, August 21; Freeport, August 27; Jonesboro, September 15; Charleston, September 18; Galesburg, October 7; Quincy, October 13; Alton, October 15. His written proposal included these terms:

> I will speak at Ottawa one hour, you can reply, occupying an hour and a half, and I will then speak for a half hour. At Freeport you shall open the discussion and speak one hour. I will follow for an hour and a half and you can then reply for half an hour. We will alternate in like manner at each successive place. 24

Lincoln wrote back on the last day of July:

> Yours of yesterday, naming places, times, and terms, for joint discussions between us, was received this morning. Although by the terms, as you

propose, you take *four* openings and closes to my *three*, I accede, and thus close the arrangement. 25

And the Douglas-Lincoln debates lay ahead, best of seven.

Before the November 2 vote, Lincoln would give 63 speeches and Douglas 130; they would travel collectively close to 10,000 miles, the equivalent of three journeys across today's continental United States, delivering hours-long speeches, attending rallies, sleeping in strange beds, eating whatever food was offered. Robert Hitt for the Republican *Tribune* and Henry Binmore and Thomas Sheridan of the Democratic *Times* would transcribe what would amount to a modern-day 300-page book full of the words that the two men would speak in the seven debates. Both men would try to unify and mobilize their parties while fighting vigorously for the great undecided regions in central Illinois; they would attempt to navigate the rapids of the politics of religion and national origin; they would incur debts (Douglas much more so than Lincoln.) They would be cheered, mocked, heckled, and misquoted. In one Illinois town, Douglas would return to his sleek carriage after a rousing speech to find that cretins had smeared it with excrement; Lincoln would routinely see signs that portrayed him arm-in-arm with black women, a deep insult at the time. They would spend hours and hours shaking hands, listening to the locals, and anxiously plotting strategy. They would see and be seen by literally hundreds of thousands of Illinoisans whose curiosity and love of spectacle combined with a true concern over their nation's future. 26

They would all of them—candidates, reporters, and citizens--explore the meaning of the phrase "all men are created equal," engaging in something very much like a conversation on what those words meant in 1858 America. The frequent interjections from people in the crowds and the sheer volume of newspaper commentary from the Illinois press flowed into the main artery of the candidates' words creating a great rising, urgent discussion of the special American problem of race the way that the Illinois and Ohio Rivers flowed into the Mississippi. Nothing would be mentioned in the debates about homestead laws, transcontinental railroads, or tariffs; nothing, and this as the nation felt the effects of the financial panic of the previous year.

So what? Why reopen the Lincoln-Douglas debates for examination? The transcripts are available for anyone to read; respected scholarly works on the debates exist, too. Norman Corwin wrote a 1958 Broadway play, *The Rivalry* on the debates, and the 1940 film *Abe Lincoln in Illinois* includes a brief and inaccurate scene of the debates (which, in Hollywood's version of history came *after* John Brown's 1859 Harper's Ferry raid, and in which Gene Lockhart's Douglas comes off as a sort of American fascist in a page-boy.) And don't we all know—we're told this during every presidential election cycle—that the Lincoln-Douglas debates established the gold standard for American candidates' debates? 27

This book advances three reasons for returning to this oft-told story.

First, the debates are correctly credited with working an "external" change in Abraham Lincoln. His brave performance won him national acclaim and speaking engagements as far off as New York City, and thus prepared the way for his stunning rise to the presidency. But I would argue that an "internal" change was at least as important. The debates became for Lincoln a crucial voyage of discovery. Lincoln discovered during the debates that he could more than hold his own with the Democrats' very best politician before thousands of voters, many of them Douglasites. He learned that he was at his best as a candidate when he listened to "honor's voice" in his conduct and when he embraced the first principles of his nation as a critic of slavery's immorality. (He had made such appeals as early as 1854, but never under such pressure, never under such scrutiny, never in a campaign for an office that he dearly prized.) The Lincoln who sat down somewhere around 4:30 p.m. on October 15 in Alton, having said his last words in the debates, was a more confident, more self-aware, more inspiring political leader than the awkward challenger who had risen to reply to Douglas at Ottawa in middle August. I believe that a critical time in this transformation came between the Charleston debate of September 18 and the Galesburg debate of October 7. Prior to that time, Lincoln's performance was uneven. Even in "winning" some of the early debates he resorted to quips and courtroom stunts that came naturally to this prairie lawyer, occasionally asserting important truths but rarely sustaining these. During that three-week hiatus from the debates, however, Lincoln seems to have come to terms with "the better angels of his nature." Taking the incumbent down repeatedly in the battleground central counties in October, Lincoln found himself riding a wave of acclaim and support that had him thinking he could win; and the winning formula appeared to have as its base an unapologetic attack on slavery's immorality, not the sort of trimming often attributed to Lincoln in the debates. Although never perfect, although always a work in progress, the Lincoln of Galesburg, Quincy, and Alton was more recognizably the Lincoln we think we know, as was the Lincoln who through the winter of 1858-1859 kept repeating the mantra, "The fight must go on." The hard journey that Lincoln took in the summer and fall of 1858 forced his "coming of age" as a politician; by the winter of 1859 he knew better who he was as a political leader and where he fit in the political culture of his state, his party, and his nation, and that awareness strengthened him for the "fiery trial" that he would later face. 28

Second, the debates represent the best and last glimpse of Lincoln the campaigner. Lincoln never "ran" for President the way that modern politicians do. The 1858 campaign in fact shows us not one but two prominent politicians questing after office, and it helps us to better resurrect the political culture of middle-nineteenth-century America (the political culture that helped produce the bloodiest and most consequential war in our history) even as it shows us how Lincoln conducted himself before the voters. On the stump, Lincoln at his best proved the best sort of candidate for American public office, an appealing and potent mix of marathon runner, moralist, humorist, and populist. Off the stump, the Republican fretted and schemed; he also played angles, especially regarding the immigrant and nativist voting blocs. Lincoln would become one of our greatest statesmen; the 1858 race shows us the working politician whose labor enabled the statesman to one day emerge, and it shows how that candidate dealt with reversals.

Third, if the debates helped to create the Lincoln we claim to know, we need to realize that Illinoisans—the voters and the newspapermen and the local politicos and the women and the children and the two candidates themselves—played a critical role in this story. Lincoln and Douglas encountered thousands of their fellow citizens. Had those citizens declined to take an interest, there might have been no "Lincoln-Douglas Debates" as we know them. Had those thousands not stood under that giant prairie sky under scalding sun or in the face of howling winds then Lincoln and Douglas may just have well have debated by Morse code. And Illinoisans stamped their impact on the debates, heckling and applauding, jeering and shouting, laughing and brawling. The stories filed by small and large in-state newspapers helped to create this climate. The local pols who invited the two men to speak, made arrangements for their public appearances, and offered the candidates advice sustained momentum between encounters, even while supplying local political intelligence to the candidates. Lincoln and Douglas of course dominate modern accounts of the debates, which is appropriate. But the Illinoisans who crossed the prairie, crossed the river, or crossed the street to attend or to report the debates helped to make the debates, and so helped to make Lincoln and unmake Douglas. After the last debate, at Alton, a local newspaperman wrote of the scene in his town:

> By the hour of 12, the great American people had taken possession of the city. It went up and down the streets—it hurrahed for Lincoln and hurrahed for Douglas—it crowded the auction rooms—it thronged the stores of our merchants—it gathered on the street corners and discussed politics—it shook its fists and talked loudly—it mounted boxes and cried the virtues of Pain Killer—it mustered to the eating saloons and did not forget the drinking saloons—it was here, there, and everywhere, asserting its privileges and maintaining its rights. 29

One historian has written of "democracy's great gamble," that "enough citizens will make plain they know enough to grasp what newspapers, pundits, and politicians say—but also what they do not say, and should—so honest candidates can think it safe to tell hard truth and others find it risky to fake." Given that definition, Illinoisans, although imperfect when it came to racial issues, proved themselves resolute and able foot soldiers of democracy. This is an American story, but it is also Illinois' very own to celebrate. Under vast Middle American skies the people of that state took on a question fit for such a stage: what do we mean by all men are created equal? 30

Something like a perfect storm would occur for one of the contenders, as celebrity, geography, communications and transportation advances, a poorly apportioned state legislature, simmering religious and racial convictions, and party and sectional infighting would combine with his own growing confidence and moral sense, starting him down a road that would change him and change his nation. As summer heat gave way to autumn harvest and then to prairie winter, that candidate would emerge in a political sense a little more fully human, a little more the leader he really was.

The nation would have further to go.

CHAPTER ONE: "I AM YET ALIVE"

"And Not to Your Passions"

"Ladies and Gentlemen," bellowed the senior Senator from Illinois, "I appear before you to-day for the purpose of discussing the leading political topics which now agitate the public mind." With these words, Stephen Douglas began the debates in heavily Republican Ottawa, southwest of Chicago, settled by migrants from the free states and by Irish immigrants, a canal town nestled between the Fox and the Illinois rivers. 1

The crowd, which had swelled Ottawa's population from 7,000 to at least 10,000, settled under a scalding August prairie sun as Douglas began an hour's opening speech. "Agitation" was the theme: in the good old days of the second party system, Democrats and Whigs had been truly *national* parties, Douglas said. They loved to beat one another at the polls, and they differed sharply on national banking, tariffs, transportation improvements, and federal power versus states' rights. But, argued Douglas, the Whigs and Democrats "agreed on this Slavery question, while they differed on those matters of expediency to which I referred." As evidence of this, Douglas cited the Compromise of 1850, the legislative package enacted amid a severe crisis of Union driven by the acquisition of new lands after war with Mexico. Now, charged Douglas, a new and purely sectional party, the Republicans, had supplanted the Whigs. In Illinois and throughout the North, he charged, these "Black" Republicans preached an abolitionist ideology that was "agitating" public opinion and by implication threatening the Union. 2

This was to put it mildly a selective reading of history. Republicans had not invented the sectional dispute over slavery. In the 1830s and early 40s, the Whigs had divided sharply over the House of Representatives' "gag rule" on anti-slavery petitions, as crusty old John Quincy Adams joined forces with other northern Whigs against a pro-slavery coalition of Southern Whigs and Northern and Southern Democrats. Again, in 1846, a Pennsylvania Democrat named David Wilmot had ignited a fiery constitutional argument with his so-called Wilmot Proviso. Hoping to regain legislative seats for the Democrats in the North, Wilmot had proposed--before the Mexican War's conclusion--that all lands won from Mexico be free of slavery. Democrats and Whigs from the slave and free states chose up sides as the argument over western slavery became "constitutionalized." Sharply different views of Congressional power over territorial slavery emerged. And California's 1849 application for statehood sparked a severe crisis of Union. Douglas himself did much to save the day, after Henry Clay had failed to pass through Congress a grand "omnibus" compromise, bringing together northerners and southerners in the Union-saving Compromise of 1850. 3

But even then, it was hard to see in this sectional or inter-party consensus. Whigs divided sharply over the compromise. Scandalized by a rugged new fugitive slave law, so-called "Conscience" Whigs refused to support the compromise. "Cotton" Whigs, charged their erstwhile colleagues, backed the plan in search of continued profits that could be maintained only by holding the south in the Union. The rift ultimately killed the Whig Party. Meanwhile, "Free Soil" Democrats clung to the Wilmot Proviso; at the other end of the party, "fire eating" Southern Democrats aggressively pressed the "common property doctrine," which would throw all the territories open to slavery. Only through some clever legislative maneuvering did Douglas and other Union-minded members save the day. One historian has said that what happened in 1850 was not a compromise: it was an armistice. 4

But Republican agitation was Douglas's theme that broiling day in Ottawa. Until 1853-4, Douglas noted, the Whigs and Democrats had adopted common election-year platforms as regarded slavery in the territories. At the heart of those platforms, he added, lay "the right of the people of each state and of each Territory to decide their local and domestic institutions for themselves, subject only to the Federal Constitution." (This wasn't quite true either. For more than thirty years, the Missouri Compromise had barred slavery north and west of Missouri's southern border. In *that* compromise, again the work of Clay, Congress had barred slavery from the territories that lay north of Missouri's southern border and east of the Rockies.)

Now, as Douglas recounted the recent past, the crowd reacted. They applauded and hissed, wrote the anti-Douglas *Chicago Daily Press and Tribune.* Or they laughed and cheered and shouted "Hurrah for Douglas" according to the Chicago *Times,* a Democratic newspaper. These interjections by the crowd may or may not have pleased Douglas, but they certainly suggested that the audience intended to take part in the Ottawa debate. 5

And who could blame them? There were no seats, except those occupied by dignitaries on the wooden platform from which the candidates spoke. The August heat enveloped the thousands of spectators, packed tight on the treeless town square and baking in hot sun. "It would seem that the most exposed part of the City was selected for the speaking," grumbled the *Times'* correspondent. Lincoln had arrived in town the night before on a 17-car railroad train of supporters, Douglas brought a large entourage, and all morning long the crowds had swelled. Marching bands thumped out songs; local militia units paraded and drilled; vendors hawked food and drink, including alcohol. As Republicans and Democrats crowded together on the square, partisans pushed and shoved. 6

The debate started 30 minutes late, at 2:30 p.m. It took that long to get the candidates through the crowd and to the platform, the awning of which had broken when some local yahoos had earlier climbed atop and plummeted through. (Accounts of the incident play this as though it were a Hollywood movie, with town juvenile delinquents dropping into the laps of astonished city fathers; there is no mention of people being *hurt,* but if such a thing happened there had to have been injuries.) An enormous, unruly crowd had gathered by 2:30. As Lincoln looked out over the crowd he thought: *how can they hear us?* 7

The Ottawans—and their guests—had to have been awash in sweat and coated with a gritty dust. The dust stained the ornate sashes worn by local Democrats and Republicans appointed marshals to control the crowd. Seldom were so few overrun by so many as were those marshals. 8

After about three minutes, Douglas concluded his lesson in selective party history. When, wrote the *Times,* "the speaker was interrupted by loud and long continued applause." Which may in fact have been the case, although the pro-Lincoln *Tribune* jeered, "Here a number of persons began to applaud, when one strong-voiced applauder, with more enthusiasm than the rest, prolonged the strain until it ended in a melancholy howl, which produced great laughter." That melancholy howl—or that prolonged applause—induced Douglas to try to get the crowd to pipe down: "My friends," he intoned, "silence is more acceptable to me than your applause." He continued, "I desire to address myself to your judgment—to your understanding—to your consciences—and not to your passions." Douglas tried some version of this appeal in many of the debates—he seems to have been sensitive to crowd reaction—and it usually worked for about two minutes before people got back into the act. 9

And well they should have. Many had taken pains to get to Ottawa; many others would travel great distances to attend the other six debates, some from out of state. They rode trains (which were quite a bit more dangerous in those days than today.) They came by riverboat and canal boat and oxcart and wagon and, of course, by foot. Men, women and children had prepared for the debate in Ottawa as would the locals in six other towns. They built the speakers' platforms, played in bands, marched with local militia units, organized and took part in parades, prepared food; some acted as auxiliary speakers before or after the main event. Ottawa Republicans and their Democratic counterparts, "spurred by a fierce resolve to outdo the enemy in numbers, noise, and display" planned for weeks to aid their man, as would the citizens of the other debate sites. They had earned the right to react to the candidates' words, and Douglas's admonitions to quiet down cut little ice with them. 10

Douglas immediately introduced another theme that he would carry with him all over Illinois. His Senate colleague, the Republican Lyman Trumbull, had in 1854 conspired with Lincoln to "abolitionize" the Illinois Democratic and Whig parties, in order to claim the state's two Senate seats for themselves. Douglas did not say, nor did he imply a simple truth: that 1854 would have been an ideal time to attempt such a scheme, for that was the year that witnessed enactment of Douglas's own Kansas-Nebraska Act. Instead, he explained how the conspiracy worked. 11

Douglas knew that American voters have a taste for conspiracy in their politics. Historians have shown us how conspiracy fears influenced the thinking of Americans at the time of the Revolution, during the Federalist era, in Andrew Jackson's presidency. Lincoln himself had electrified his own party only one month earlier at Springfield by sounding the alarm of a slave power conspiracy threatening to bring slavery into the free states. 12

But Douglas's use of the assumed Trumbull/Lincoln conspiracy was only a means to an end. By linking his opponent to this 1854 scheme, Douglas could link him to something far more damaging: a series of resolutions, seven in all, that Douglas claimed had been adopted by the Illinois Republican party in Springfield in the same year. With these resolutions, Douglas would present his opponent to the white voters of Illinois (and their wives and children) as a dangerous radical, an abolitionist.

William Lloyd Garrison or Frederick Douglass would have applauded many of these resolutions, adopted at what Senator Douglas called "the first Mass State Convention ever held in Illinois by the Republican Party." The delegates, he shouted, intended to "'restore Kansas and Nebraska to the position of free territories . . .to repeal and entirely abrogate the fugitive slave law; to restrict slavery to those states in which it exists; to prohibit admission of any more slave States into the Union; to abolish slavery in the District of Columbia; to exclude slavery from all the territories . . .and to resist the acquirements of any more territories unless the practice of slavery therein forever shall have been prohibited.'"

These were abolitionist resolutions; they did everything but call for the end of slavery in the slave states (although it is important to note that they did not go *that* far.) Republicans cheered each statement as Douglas read it, and Douglas, showing an early tendency to interact with his audience, could not help but comment on that.

"Now, gentlemen, you have cheered—you Republicans have cheered every one of these propositions," called Douglas, "and yet I venture to say that you cannot get Mr. Lincoln, your candidate, to come out and say he is now for each one of them."

The Democrats in the crowd laughed and applauded their man; someone yelled, *"Hit him again!"*

Which Douglas did, using for the first time his party's race-baiting nickname for the opposition. He explained that, "when you were not aware for what purpose I was reading these resolutions, you cheered them as good Black Republican doctrine, and yet my object in reading them is to put the question to Abraham Lincoln this day, whether he now stands, and will stand by each article of that creed, and carry them all out."

Douglas had spent the last eight years on the floor of the US Senate, fencing with the Websters, the Clays, the Calhouns, as well as newer arrivals such as James Henry Hammond and Charles Sumner. These men played it hard, and now Douglas would give Lincoln a taste of what awaited him should he somehow get to the Senate floor. More to the point, Douglas would force on his foe a choice: endorse the 1854 resolutions to hold your northern Illinois free-soil base, or deny the resolutions, in order to reach out to the central Illinois districts that would decide the election.

Douglas spoke without extensive notes. He did carry with him "reference materials." Among these was a small notebook. Douglas had glued Lincoln's House Divided speech into the notebook, as well as other items that he planned to quote. These may have included the fruits of some eleventh-hour opposition research that the senator requested from a close friend, Charles Lanphier, editor of the Illinois *State Register*, a pro-Douglas Springfield newspaper. On August 15, Douglas had written to Lanphier for information pertaining to an 1856 attack speech given by Democrat Thomas L. Harris in the U.S. House of Representatives. Harris's speech had made heavy use of the same anti-slavery resolutions that Douglas cited in Ottawa. "I desire to know the time and place at which that convention was held, whether it was a mass meeting or a delegate Convention, and whether Lincoln was present and made a speech," Douglas instructed Lanphier. "This information is very important and I want it immediately. Please consult Major Harris, hunt up the facts and write to me instantly directed to Ottawa. I must have it before next Saturday." Considering the prominent place that these resolutions played in Douglas's performance in Ottawa and in many other venues, he sought this material from Lanphier on the late side. In an era before telephones, faxes or Fed Ex, audio or videotape or the personal computer, Douglas was shaving it fairly close to write Lanphier a mere seven days before the showdown. The haste with which Lanphier had to work would cost Douglas over time. 13

"I desire to know," Douglas now shouted, "whether Mr. Lincoln to-day stands pledged as he did in 1854, in favor of the unconditional repeal of the Fugitive Slave Law." He then let loose more questions for his opponent, all in the form of demands: *I desire him to answer* if he's pledged to vote against new slave states, even if the people of that state want slavery; *I want to know* if he pledges to vote against the admission of a new state with such a Constitution as its people have drafted; *I desire to know* if he's pledged to abolish slavery in Washington; *I desire to know* if he's pledged to abolish the interstate slave trade; *I desire to know* whether he's pledged to prohibit slavery in all of America's territories; *I desire him to answer* whether he is opposed to the acquisition of new territory if it may be open to slavery.

The crowd's cheering these propositions wasn't enough for Douglas: "I want him to answer." Although the transcripts don't indicate it, one assumes that Douglas must have come down hard on the word "*him,*" and he would probably have turned or pointed to Lincoln.

For Douglas was executing the game plan. Put the challenger on the defensive, associate him with the radical abolitionists by ignoring the more moderate 1858 Republican platform. Overwhelm him early, and keep him in an explanatory posture. Above all, be conscious of the battleground counties where this election would be won or lost: the central counties in this large state. There, voters tended to be Unionist, reasonably conservative in most things political and suspicious of slavery, but suspicious of abolitionists as well. They also tended to be white supremacist, which made them about like most white Americans of their age. (Lincoln came from that area, from Springfield in Sangamon County, and the county's voters had gone 1,483 to 418 in favor of a provision in the 1853 state constitution forbidding free blacks to enter the state.) Douglas knew that Ottawa would not be critical to his re-election hopes; it was Republican territory. But he also expected that further south, Illinoisans would read Douglas's questions and Lincoln's answers, and they would vote for state legislators based in large part on Lincoln's soundness, his moderation. And those legislators would choose the winner in the 1858 Senate race. 14

Douglas would also try to cut Lincoln off in the race for the center. The senator crowed, "I want Abraham Lincoln to answer these questions in order that when I trot him down into Lower Egypt I may compel him to repeat the same." Douglas would use this line a couple of times in the first two debates, which were in the Republican north; "Egypt" was deep Southern Illinois, the home of migrants from Kentucky and other slave states, and Douglas knew he himself would do well there even with pro-Buchanan "Danite" candidates in the field. (In Egypt, in fact, Lincoln could afford to be frank on these resolutions; he could write off these counties. But he needed those central counties, and Douglas knew it.) "My principles," proclaimed the Senator, "are the same everywhere." And then, just in case anyone missed the point: "I desire to know whether Mr. Lincoln's principles will bear to be transplanted from Ottawa to Jonesboro." Douglas thus set Lincoln up for another attack: that the Republican would take different positions in front of different audiences in different regions of Illinois.

Returning to the 1854 platform, Douglas contended that it was made to "destroy the old Whig and Democratic parties, and transfer each of their members, bound hand and foot, into the Abolition party, under the direction of Giddings and Chase." (Although white abolitionists Joshua Giddings and Salmon P. Chase were anathema to many conservative Illinoisans, when the pro-Douglas *Times* ran its official transcript of the debates editors stuck in the name of the black abolitionist Frederick Douglass for good measure, hoping to further worry those swing voters in central Illinois.) 15

Douglas then turned to another historical topic: Abraham Lincoln. "I mean nothing personal, disrespectful, or unkind to that gentleman. I have known him for nearly twenty-five years." Douglas noted that both had migrated to the state. He explained that he himself had been "a humble school teacher in the town of Winchester" and Lincoln "a flourishing grocery keeper in the town of Salem."

The crowd laughed and applauded at that last line, for Douglas was needling Lincoln; a "grocery" in those days didn't traffic in fruits and vegetables, milk, and meats; it was a frontier saloon. Hence the laughter— my opponent kept a saloon in Salem! (Douglas meant New Salem.) "He was more successful in his occupation than I was in mine and thus became more fortunate in the world's goods." Here Douglas stretched the truth; by 1858, the Little Giant was both rich and famous. In contrast, Lincoln had a nice house at the corner of Eighth and Jackson in Springfield, a nice, sometimes lucrative law practice with his pal Billy Herndon, and a major financial challenge facing him as he campaigned rather than ringing up those billable hours. 16

Douglas then cracked that he had done his level best as a school teacher, and then as a cabinet maker, "but,"—and here came an example of Douglas humor—"my old bones said I succeeded better in bureaus and secretaries than in anything else." This play-on-words led Douglas into both men's early political careers. They met as young state legislators, and Lincoln, recalled Douglas, "was then as good at telling an anecdote as now. He could beat any of the boys at wrestling—could outrun them in a foot race—beat them at pitching quoits and tossing a copper, and could win more liquor than all the boys put together."

The crowd got quite a laugh at that line, Douglas's second reference to Lincoln and alcohol. This was reasonably daring--and fairly dishonest-- given Douglas' own reputation as the life of the party, and Lincoln's lack of interest in drink. But evangelical voters abounded in Illinois, and in those central regions. Why not take a chance?

Douglas also assured the audience that their would-be Senator presided with "dignity and impartiality" at "horse races and fist-fights." Lincoln, Douglas reminded the Ottawa crowd, then served one term in the U.S. House of Representatives, where he "distinguished himself by his opposition to the Mexican War, taking the side of the common enemy, in time of war, against his own country." Douglas nicked Lincoln for having demanded in a House resolution—the "Spot Resolution"--that President James K. Polk identify the exact "spot" on American soil where the initial Mexican attacks had occurred. Douglas' quick flash of the knife came at the conclusion of an appraisal of his opponent that until then had been dismissive in an affectionate sort of way. The Little Giant would revisit the Mexican War in weeks to come.

A quick sideswipe at the career of his Senate colleague Lyman Trumbull ("the author of a scheme to repudiate a large portion of the debt of Illinois and thus bring infamy and disgrace upon the fair escutcheon of our glorious State"), and Douglas was off on two substantive lines of attack.

First, Douglas went after Lincoln's "House Divided" speech. As Douglas read Lincoln's now famous introductory remarks, Republicans in the crowd cheered, and crowed, *"Good! Good!"* Douglas heard them, as he would hear hecklers throughout the debates.

"Yes," called Douglas, "I have no doubt it is, and I am delighted to hear you Black Republicans say good."

The *Tribune* reported that this triggered more shouts of "Good! Good!" Some of the crowd laughed; the great man was reacting to this audience.

"I have no doubt that that doctrine expresses your sentiments, and yet I will prove to you, if you will listen to me, that doctrine is revolutionary and destructive of the existence of our government." Douglas explained that the founding fathers had intentionally set up a nation part slave and part free; anyone who disturbed that balance invited a war of free states against slave states.

Then Douglas moved on to the second line of attack: "We are told by Lincoln that he is utterly opposed to the Dred Scott decision and will not submit to it, for the reason, he says, that it deprives the negro of the rights and privileges of citizens." The *Times* reported laughter at the notion that anyone could hold such a position.

Douglas's deep voice "had an explosive and staccato quality and at least at the beginning of the campaign had great carrying power." The senator now pounded on. 17

"Now, I ask you, are you in favor of conferring upon the negro the rights and privileges of citizenship?"

"No, no," shouted some.

"Do you desire to strike out of our State Constitution that clause which keeps slaves and free negroes out of the State, and allow the free negro to flow in—"

"Never!"

"—and cover our prairies with his settlements." (Did Douglas emphasize "our" and "his"?)

He continued: "Do you desire to turn this beautiful State into a free negro colony--"

"No, no!"

"—in order that when Missouri shall abolish slavery, she can send us these emancipated slaves to become citizens and voters on an equality with yourselves?"

Playing on the status anxiety of laboring whites, he counseled, "[I]f you desire to make them eligible to office—to have them serve on juries and judge of your rights—then go with Mr. Lincoln and the Black Republicans in favor of negro citizenship."

Douglas then announced that, "I am opposed to Negro citizenship in any form . . .But Mr. Lincoln, following the lead of Abolition orators that came here and lectured in the basements of your churches and school houses reads the Declaration of Independence that all men are created equal, and then says, 'How can you deprive the negro of that equality which God and the Declaration of Independence awards him?'"

Douglas had a ready answer: "I do not question Mr. Lincoln's conscientious belief that the negro was made his equal, and hence is his brother."

That triggered laughter, according to the *Times*.

"But for my own part, I do not regard the negro as my equal, and I positively deny that he is my brother, or any kin to me whatever."

"Never!"

"*Hit him again!*"

Douglas was on a roll, in an awful sort of way: "I do not believe the Almighty ever intended the negro to be the equal of the white man."

"*Never, never,*" they yelled.

"If he did he has been a long time demonstrating the fact." The crowd—some of it at least—laughed and cheered at that witticism. Douglas said, "For six thousand years the negro has been a race upon the earth, and during that whole six thousand years—in all latitudes and climates wherever the Negro has been—he has been inferior to whatever adjoined him. The fact is he belongs to an inferior race and must occupy an inferior position." Members of the crowd cheered as Douglas ended his rant.

In the time remaining, the distinguished gentleman from Illinois raised two other priority items: "The question is far more important to you. What shall be done for the free negro?" In fact, Douglas spent no time on doing anything *for* blacks, other than to state that he was opposed to slavery in Illinois. He then raised a passion of his own, one that he would return to frequently in the months to come: the fact that all of this slavery agitation was getting in the way of the really important development, westward expansion. The answer to the problem was, of course, popular sovereignty. "If we still obey that principle we can go forward increasing in territory, increasing in power, in strength and glory, until the Republic of America shall be the North star that shall guide the friends of freedom throughout the civilized world."

And with that, Douglas sat down, to rousing cheers.

"The Equal of Every Living Man"

"When Mr. Lincoln arose," the *Times* smirked, "there were evident signs of a desire to applaud." The Republican *Press and Tribune* saw more enthusiasm in the crowd: "Mr. Lincoln then came forward and was greeted with loud and protracted cheers from fully two-thirds of the audience . . .It was some minutes before he could make himself heard, even by those on the stand." The *Tribune* added, "This was admitted even by the Douglas men on the platform." Even in the crackling heat, even after Douglas's fiery hour-long attack, the Republicans, including the big-city types from Cook County, cheered their man lustily. Lincoln was in friendly territory; the local congressman, Owen Lovejoy, was a noted abolitionist, and Ottawa was a Republican stronghold.

The first thing Lincoln said--probably amiably--was, "Don't take up my time." He continued his bemused tone—a tone he was comfortable with, and would try to maintain through much of the debates as a contrast to the volcanic Douglas: "when a man hears himself misrepresented a little, why, it rather provokes him, at least so I find with me, but when he finds the misrepresentation very gross, why it sometimes amuses him." The *Trib* reported that the crowd laughed.

Jocular Lincoln might be, but he had to respond to Douglas's charges, and this meant that he had to offer explanations—not what the Republicans in the crowd craved, and no way to rally the uncommitted. In 1854, "There was a call for a convention to form a Republican party in Springfield. I think my friend Lovejoy, who is with me on the stand, had a hand in it. I think that is so, and I think that if I will remember correctly that he tried to get me to it; and I would not do it. Well I believe it is also true, as I went from Springfield when the convention was in session. I did not remain, but went to Tazewell [County] court."

That was how Lincoln kicked off. He then announced that—to clear up any questions regarding his ties to abolitionism--he would read from his 1854 Peoria speech on the Kansas-Nebraska Act.

"*Put on your specs!*" sang out a voice.

"Yes, sir, I am obliged to do that. I am no longer a young man."

Specs on, he then read for approximately seven minutes from a four-year-old speech in which he disavowed any idea of what to do with the slaves after emancipation; sympathized with Southern slaveholders for not knowing what to do; and proclaimed that he did not favor making blacks the "social or political equals" of whites.

Altogether a turgid start, especially for a challenger hoping to give voters a reason to turn out of office a charismatic, controversial, powerful Senator who had taken care of Illinois through his immense influence—now compromised somewhat—in the federal government. What was Lincoln thinking?

The audience soon learned. For the first time in these debates, Lincoln spoke his mind. Laying aside the Peoria speech and his specs, he called out, "I have no purpose, directly or indirectly, to interfere with the institution of slavery in the states where it exists." He disavowed any legal right or "inclination to do so," and he shouted that, "I have no disposition to introduce political and social equality between the white and black races." He asserted "a physical difference between the two, which in my judgment will probably forever forbid their living together" in a state of "social and political equality." And since "there must be a superiority somewhere, I as well as Judge Douglas, am in favor of the race to which I belong having the superior position."

These words surprise and disappoint us today, accustomed as we are to seeing in Lincoln a singular sensitivity to racial injustice and a strong opposition to slavery. He *won't* interfere with slavery where it exists, in the slave states? He *doesn't* think blacks and whites are equals, or ever can be equals? And what about this "physical difference" that Lincoln seems to think favored the white man? (A quaint notion for all of us who live in post-Jackie Robinson America.) And what really baffles us is that Lincoln says 'I'm with Douglas on this one'—*Douglas?*

You are almost ready to throw in the towel on Lincoln, even this early in the debates, and then a more generous view emerges. Nonetheless, Lincoln shouted, "I hold that because of all of this"—did he mean "despite" all of this?—"there is no reason at all furnished why the negro after all is not entitled to all that the declaration of independence holds out, which is 'life, liberty, and the pursuit of happiness'. . . ."

The *Tribune* reported loud cheers on that last line.

As the cheers died, Lincoln continued, ". . .and I hold that he is as much entitled to as the white man. I agree that the negro may not be my equal and Judge Douglas' equal in some respects—certainly not in color, and in intellectual development, perhaps—but in the right to the bread which his own hand earns, *he is my equal, and Judge Douglas' equal, and the equal of every living man.*"

The Republicans in the crowd erupted when Lincoln finished that line. The *Times* reported cries of "Bully for you," and "all right." The *Trib*—its transcript italicized the last line--reported great applause. After all those minutes of reading from an old speech, the tag line, an applause line, meant to punctuate this segment, must have hit this crowd like smelling salts. Lincoln had *not* endorsed racial equality, immediate abolition, or any such thing. But he had endorsed the extension of a "free labor" way of life to all people in America, including the slaves, who each day were denied the fruits of their labor, denied a chance to advance through hard work, denied what later generations would call the American Dream. 18

Even if he lacked the vision, the daring, or the creativity to know how to end the peculiar institution, Lincoln *had* spoken strongly against slavery, and for the extension of "natural rights" to all Americans, including the nearly four million black slaves. He had done so in a race for a Senate seat in a state that had adopted some of the most extreme anti-black measures of any free state and despite knowing that the "moderate" central Illinois districts would hold the key to victory. And most of the voters in those districts were in fact quite a bit less than moderate on racial issues. Lincoln had publicly proclaimed his belief: the Declaration of Independence's truths *did* apply to blacks.

Never one to spend too much time on a serious topic, Lincoln turned to "the Judge's" memory of bygone days. Douglas "is woefully at fault again about his early friend being a grocery keeper." The *Tribune* reported laughter, perhaps a release after the heavy, freighted discussion of racial equality. "I don't know if it would be a great sin if I had, but he is mistaken." Lincoln continued, "Lincoln never kept a grocery in his life." More laughter, although Lincoln had to be careful not to alienate the drinkers in the crowd, some of whom were no doubt pretty well along by 3:45 p.m. "It is true that Lincoln did work, the latter part of one winter at a little still house up at the head of the hollow." The laughter that the Republican press reported suggested that Lincoln had deflated Douglas's claim, established himself as one of the boys, and opened the way for a defense of his positions on the Mexican War, which he attempted next.

Then he rebuked Douglas's assault on the House Divided speech. "He has read from my speech at Springfield in which I say that 'a house divided against itself cannot stand.'—Does the Judge say it can?"

As the crowd laughed, Lincoln said, "I don't know," then turned to look at his opponent, who seemed to have taken no notice of Lincoln or of his question—"the judge don't seem to be attending to me just now—but I would like to know if in his opinion it can. If so," continued the Republican, "that raises a question of veracity with a somewhat higher character than myself," a line that drew some chuckles.

Moving beyond these antics Lincoln pressed on, contesting Douglas on the origins of the divided house. Far from ordaining a nation part slave and part free, the founding fathers legislated "to put off its source," and legislated "against its spread" and left "the public mind at rest in the belief that it was in the course of ultimate extinction." Indirectly, Lincoln was alluding to the Constitution's restrictions on the Atlantic slave trade and to the 1787 Northwest Ordinance, which barred slavery from the Northwest Territory.

Then came the wind-up; and Lincoln would use it repeatedly through the debates: Douglas "and those who have acted with him have placed that institution on a new basis, one that looks to the perpetuation and extension of it." Who was the real radical in this race? Who was honoring the original intent of the Founding Fathers? If we would only honor that intent, "place it where Washington, Jefferson, and Madison placed it," then "the crisis would be passed, and though the institution might be alive long, and might linger for a hundred years, yet it would be going out in God's own time, in the way that would be best for both the white and black races."

This passage is deeply unsatisfying to modern readers. First, what does Lincoln mean exactly by "placing it in the course of ultimate extinction?" Certainly, that entails barring slavery from the territories. But is that it? That would not "free" any slaves. And what about his guess that slavery's abolition might be achieved in a way mutually beneficial to both blacks and whites no earlier than 1958? Douglas would expend lots of breath all through the towns and hamlets of Illinois trying to prove that Lincoln was an abolitionist. Reading Lincoln's words, it's clear that Douglas was reaching.

A voice called out: "*You repudiate popular sovereignty?*"

Lincoln said, all right, let's talk about that. "What is popular sovereignty?"

Another voice: "A humbug."

Lincoln may have smiled at that, as he explained that popular sover-eignty "does allow the people of a territory, to have slavery if they want it, and it don't allow them to not have it if they don't want it."

The people laughed and applauded. He explained that, until a vote was taken, slaveholders could enter a territory with as many slaves as they could haul, implanting slavery in new lands. He explained, "if any one among them" wants to bring in slaves, "there is no one or number of them that can keep him from it."

The *Times* stenographer heard a lone voice in the crowd:

"*Well, you are a fool.*"

"Well," called Lincoln, "that may be, and I guess there are two of us that are that way."

The laughter that ensued led Lincoln back onto a still mysterious, sardonic defense of the House Divided speech. In Chicago, on July 9, Douglas "complimented me as a kind, amiable, and intelligent gentleman. Notwithstanding I had said this, he goes on and draws from that speech this tendency of mine to set the states at war, and to set the Negroes and white people to marrying one another."

That was how the *Times* reported it. The *Tribune* version went like this: "he. . .draws out from my speech this tendency to set the States at war with one another, to make all the institutions uniform, and set the niggers and the white people to marrying together." The *Times* quoted Lincoln as later saying, ". . .what is necessary to make the institution of slavery national? There is no danger of the people of Kentucky shouldering their muskets to bring slavery among us—there is no danger of our going there to make war on them." But the *Tribune* had it: "There is no danger that the people of Kentucky will shoulder their muskets and with a young nigger on every bayonet march into Illinois and force them upon us. There is no danger of our going over there and making war upon them." 19

Why would the Republican, free-soil paper report its man using the word 'nigger,' perhaps inserting it where Lincoln had not used it? Or for that matter, why would the Democratic, anti-black newspaper 'cleanse' Lincoln's words, expunging "nigger" and replacing it with the more genteel 'negro' when Lincoln had in fact used the slur? It could be that the "phonographers"—the stenographers—heard it differently. But it could be that either side –the *Times* on one hand, Lincoln and/or the *Tribune* on the other, offered their version with those critical central districts in mind. For many swing voters in those areas there might have been no shame in using the word nigger; in fact, in the recognizable way that whites, especially white males, have often proved that they are "one of the boys," disparaging blacks might actually *gain* you support. Hence it may not have been accidental that Democratic reporters made Lincoln seem *more* sensitive to blacks, while Republican papers might make him seem more *insensitive*.

Lincoln did or did not use the word "nigger" at Ottawa, but he probably used it on at least one occasion, as evidenced by a dispatch filed on November 28, 1860 by Henry Villard for the December 2, edition of the New York *Herald*. Historians Don and Virginia Fehrenbacher rate Villard's dispatch as one of the more reliable anecdotes in their collection of the "recollected words" of Lincoln. In the story, President-elect Lincoln tells of an "Old Zach," a Kentucky dirt farmer elected justice of the peace who must rule on the abuse of black slaves in his first case on the bench. Lincoln's Kentuckian says, "'I'll be damned if I don't feel almost sorry for being elected, when the niggers is the first thing I have to attend to.'" 20

Lincoln seems to have occasionally used "nigger" to characterize *others'* less enlightened views; in this case the language of Stephen A. Douglas in reasonably abolitionist Ottawa. On the other, that of an (imaginary) hayseed public official whose socio-economic background resembles that of Lincoln's own father and the people of Lincoln's native region, this time in front of a German-born reporter for a New York paper.

Whatever the case, Lincoln was going again for some laughs, and these at the expense of Douglas's characterization of his rival. Douglas had at Chicago complimented Lincoln, and "I was a little taken by it, it coming from a great man, and one that the world acknowledges as a great man— I do not speak that in mockery." He called, "I was not much accustomed to flattery. I was very much like the hoosier with gingerbread—he said that he loved it better and got less of it than any other man."

"Roars of laughter," reported the *Tribune*. Lincoln continued that at Bloomington, Douglas "said that I had said that I would not go into the slave states, but that I said I will go to the bank of the Ohio and shoot over among them." Then, at Clinton he said that, "'unless he shall be successful in firing his batteries, the Union cannot stand.'" Lincoln looked out over the crowd. "Now, I did not think that was the way to treat a kind, amiable, intelligent gentleman."

More roars of laughter, according to the *Tribune*.

As the senator sweated on the speakers' platform, Douglas must have made a mental note never again to say anything nice about his opponent.

As he developed the theme of Douglas's part in a conspiracy to nationalize slavery via the Kansas-Nebraska Act and the *Dred Scott* ruling, Lincoln allowed as how it looked "to outsiders, poor, simple, amiable, intelligent gentlemen,"--here the *Trib* again reported an audience falling over itself in laughter--"it looks as if it was the place left to put that Dred Scott decision in." And again he predicted a "second" *Dred Scott* ruling, or what he called "the next Dred Scott decision" that would nationalize slavery.

Democrats did not especially want to talk about Dred Scott, not in free-soil northern Illinois, and so a man in the crowd, identified disparagingly as "A Hibernian" by the *Tribune*, growled, "*Give us something besides Dred Scott!*"

Lincoln called back, "Now, no doubt you would rather hear something that don't hurt you."

He decided it was time to wind up, although he had spoken for just over an hour. Perhaps it was the heat. Or perhaps he sensed that now was the time to evoke a more recent hero, one especially popular among the old Whigs in the counties south of Republican Ottawa. "Mr. Clay—my beau ideal of a great man, the man for whom I fought all my humble life" had once said that those who opposed "ultimate emancipation" would need to return "to the hour of our own liberty and independence, and muzzle the cannon that thunders its annual joyous return; that they must blow out the moral lights around us; that they must pervert the human soul and love of liberty, and then, and not till then, they could perpetuate slavery in this country."

Lincoln called to his sweat-soaked audience that, "Judge Douglas is now, by his example and his vast influence, doing that very thing in this community."

The crowd applauded. "When he is saying that the negro has no share in the Declaration of Independence, he is going back to the year of our revolution, and to the extent of his ability, he is muzzling the cannon that thunders its annual joyous return. When he is saying, as he often does, that if any people want slavery they have a right to have it, he is blowing out the moral lights around us. When he says he don't care whether slavery is voted up or down, then to my thinking he is, so far as he is able to do so perverting the human soul and eradicating the light of reason and the love of liberty on the American continent." And, shouted Lincoln, "when he shall have succeeded in bringing public sentiment to an exact accordance with his own—when this vast assemblage goes back with these sentiments instilled into them, then it needs only the formality of a second Dred Scott decision, which he is in favor of, to make slavery alike lawful in all the states, old as well as new."

There it was. A Douglas victory would clear the way for a second Dred Scott ruling. Slavery could come to the free states, courtesy of the incumbent senator, the great man himself, Stephen A. Douglas.

"My friends," said Lincoln, "that ends the chapter; the judge can take his half-hour." And he sat down.

"I Will Yet Bring Him to Milk"

"The first point I will call your attention to," barked Douglas, is "what I said about the Republican party in 1854, and the platform that was formed on the 5th [of] October in that year, and then put the question to Mr. Lincoln whether or not he approved of each article of that platform."

"He answered that already," came a voice.

The Little Giant forged on. "I have told him that I should call for a specific answer to each of these interrogatories."

"He has answered."

"You cannot make him answer." The Republicans in the crowd smelled opportunity; they'd so far seen both candidates mix it up with the audience.

Douglas continued, "I do not charge him with being a member of the committee that reported the platform."

"Yes, you did."

"The fact that it was the platform of the Republican Party is not now denied; but Mr. Lincoln now says that although his name was on the committee, that he don't think he was there. He thinks he was in Tazewell, holding court."

Here a disturbance occurred in a crowd that had now stood for two hours in the August heat; the disruption sent Douglas back to a standard line: "I ask your silence, and no interruption." He turned back to his line of argument. "I want to remind Mr. Lincoln that he was here and I will remind him of the fact."

"You can't do it."

"He wasn't there."

Douglas was by this time having a hard time stringing together two sentences. It got so bad that Ottawa Mayor Joseph Glover, the chairman of the local Republican committee, felt compelled to intercede on the Democrat's behalf. "I hope no Republican will interrupt Mr. Douglas," he called. "The masses listened to Mr. Lincoln attentively, and as respectable men we ought now to hear Mr. Douglas, and without interruption."

Douglas then narrated his recollection of the events of October 5, 1854. After Lincoln had given a speech in the Illinois House chamber, Douglas was about to make a reply, when Ichabod Codding, a noted abolitionist, had walked onto the House floor, announcing that the "Republican Convention would meet instantly in the Senate Chamber, and called upon the Republicans to go into this very convention instead of listening to me."

Here, the *Times* noted, Lincoln interrupted, "excited, angrily:"

"Let the Judge add that Lincoln went along with them." The *Times* added: "this interruption was made in a sneaky way, as Lincoln floundered around the stand."

"Mr. Lincoln says let him add that he went along with them to the Senate chamber. I will not add that for I do not know it."

Lincoln cut in, according to the *Times*: "I do know it."

The *Times* then added: "Two of the Republican committee here seized Mr. Lincoln, and by a sudden jerk caused him to disappear from the front of the stand, one of them saying quite audibly, 'What are you making such a fuss for. Douglas didn't interrupt you, and can't you see that the people don't like it.'"

This entire exchange, reported by the Illinois Democratic party's most influential press organ, is open to suspicion. First, if Lincoln had earlier contended that he was in Tazewell County on October 5, 1854, why would he now want people to think that he was in fact in Springfield, in Sangamon County? For that matter, if Douglas wanted to place Lincoln in Springfield, with the Republicans, drawing up those abolitionist resolutions, why would he contest Lincoln's contention that Lincoln had adjourned with Codding and company to the Senate chamber? And why would Lincoln have picked this time to "flounder around the stand" when Douglas had landed arguably harder blows in his opening? Temperamentally, was the middle-aged Lincoln the kind of politician who needed to get yanked back into his seat by his supporters because he couldn't read audience sentiment?

When Lincoln put together the scrapbook that dominated historical accounts of the debates, he deleted all references to floundering about the stand, and to that jerk from behind. But his—and the *Tribune's* account of the verbal exchange—was in effect the same as was the Democrats' version. So the exchange must have happened, nonsensical though it seems. For a brief period, Lincoln reverted to appealing to his anti-slavery base, demonstrating that he supported that platform; and Douglas seems to have attempted to block Lincoln from doing so. Why is a mystery. Perhaps the searing heat, the pressure to perform, and a growing, irritated tendency to disparage one another's versions of history congealed, sending both men in directions that they had never intended. 21

At any rate, Douglas vowed, "whether he knows it or not, I intend to bring him to milk on this point . . .He was the leader of that party, and on the very day that he made his speech there in reply to me, preaching up the same doctrine of the Declaration of Independence that niggers were equal to white men—that very day this Republican Convention met there." Douglas, trying to get beyond the many interruptions that had marred his rejoinder thus far, delivered this summary in terms designed to connect with his audience. They knew what it meant to bring a cow to milk, and they knew what he meant when he used the word 'niggers.'

The Little Giant turned back to the seven questions that he had posed, and characterized Lincoln's responses:

Fugitive Slave Act repeal? "He answers by saying 'I wasn't on the committee that wrote it.'"

Restricting slavery to the slave states? "He says, 'I wasn't on the committee at the time. I was up in Tazewell.'"

Barring the admission of a new slave state, even if the people of that place want slavery? "He avoids the question."

On Douglas went to the delight of his supporters, who whooped and hollered, "Stick it to him," "Don't spare him."

Lincoln, reported the *Times*, interrupted a third time—"No, Judge"—and "disappeared suddenly, aided by a pull from behind."

Douglas vowed to continue putting these questions to his opponent, "again and again, and I want to screw it out of him." The *Times* reported immense applause for that cheerful promise.

Douglas then offered some expert analysis of his foe's debate performance thus far, and found it wanting: "He talked about everything he could think of in order to occupy his hour and a half, and when he could not think of anything more to say, in order to get an excuse for refusing to answer these questions, he sat down before his time was up, and told you so." Having dismissed Lincoln as a gifted judge of fistfights and horse races, but little more than a dodger, Douglas now raised questions about the challenger's debating skills.

Then he turned—once more today—to Lincoln's charges of a conspiracy to nationalize slavery. Strangely, he referred to himself in the third person, but not in the jocular fashion in which Lincoln liked to do so. Douglas complained that, "three times he has now repeated the charge of conspiracy on Judge Douglas, and thus turned it into a charge of moral turpitude." Douglas shouted, "I have not brought a charge of moral turpitude against him, and when he or any other living man brings one against me, instead of putting myself on the proof and disproving it, I will say it is a lie!" He added, "I have lived twenty-five years in Illinois—I have served you with all the fidelity and ability I know how—and he is at liberty to attack my public course and actions, to attack my views and conduct, but when he attacks my moral integrity by a charge of conspiracy between me and Justice Taney and the two Presidents, I repel it."

The *Times* reported enthusiastic applause, and someone yelled, *"Three cheers for Douglas!"*

"Mr. Lincoln," Douglas shouted, "has not character enough for integrity and truth . . .to arraign President Buchanan and President Pierce, and the Judges of the Supreme Court, any one of whom would not be complimented if put on a level with Mr. Lincoln." Clearly, Lincoln was a minor leaguer; how dare he assume "the unpardonable presumption . . .of putting himself up before thousands of people, and pretending to think that his *ipse dixit* [his unproved assertion] without proof, or fact, or evidence is enough to break down the character of the purest and best of living men." In the course of putting Lincoln in his place, Douglas identified Franklin Pierce, James Buchanan, Roger B. Taney and the Taney Court as "the purest and best of living men." Which may say a lot about Douglas's capacities as judge of character.

Douglas closed his half hour by warning the audience: either leave the states free to decide on slavery by themselves, in which case you will have "peace and harmony," or follow Lincoln's house divided doctrine to "sectional warfare."

On that fearful note, Douglas closed. The Ottawa debate ended.

"The Battle Fought and Won"

The crowd, which had stood and sweated and shifted and listened and applauded and heckled for three hours, cheered as Douglas finished. The *Times* reported that nearly "two-thirds of the meeting at once surrounded Douglas, and with music, cheers, and every demonstration of enthusiastic admiration they escorted him to his quarters at the hotel, where for several minutes they made the welkin ring with their cheers, and applause." [22]

Lincoln's supporters, not to be outdone, impulsively grabbed their man, hoisted him aloft on their shoulders, and cheering, carried him off in triumph. Legend has it that Lincoln's too-short pant legs—he was famously ill-tailored—rode up, exposing the white legs of his long johns. [23]

Almost immediately, the battle for public opinion began. The *Times* distinguished itself for its partisanship. Its August 22 article bore these headlines:

THE CAMPAIGN

DOUGLAS AMONG THE PEOPLE
Joint Discussion At Ottawa!
LINCOLN BREAKS DOWN!
ENTHUSIASM OF THE PEOPLE!
The Battle Fought and Won

Lincoln's Heart Fails Him!
Lincoln's Legs Fail Him!
Lincoln's Tongue Fails Him!
Lincoln's Arms Fail Him!
LINCOLN FAILS ALL OVER!

The People Refuse to Support Him!
The People Laugh at Him!
DOUGLAS THE CHAMPION OF THE PEOPLE!

Douglas Skins the "Living Dog"
THE "DEAD LION" FRIGHTENS THE CANINE
Douglas "Trotting" Lincoln Out
DOUGLAS "CONCLUDES" ON ABE 24

And you think today's media play rough. The article that followed reached peak partisanship as it described Lincoln's reaction to the "two-thirds" of the audience rejoicing at Douglas's victory as they escorted the Little Giant to his hotel:

Lincoln in the meantime seemed to have been paralyzed. He stood upon the stage looking wildly at the people as they surrounded the triumphant Douglas, and with mouth wide open he could not find a friend to say one word to him in his distress. It was a delicate point for Republicans who had witnessed his utter defeat, and who knew how severely he felt it, to offer him condolence, or bid him hope for better success again. The only thing they could say was that Lincoln ought not to travel round with Douglas, and had better not meet him anymore. When Douglas and the Democrats had left the square, Lincoln essayed to descend from the stage, but his limbs refused to do their office. During Douglas's last speech Lincoln had suffered severely; alternately burning with fever, and then chilled with shame, his respiratory organs had become obstructed, his limbs got cold, and he was unable to walk. In this extremity, the Republican Marshal called half a dozen men, who lifting Lincoln in their arms, carried him along. By some mismanagement the men selected for this office happened to be very short in stature, and the consequence was, that while Lincoln's head and shoulders towered above theirs, his feet dragged on the ground. Such an exhibition as the 'toting' of Lincoln from the square to his lodgings was never seen at Ottawa before. It was one of the richest farces we ever witnessed, and provoked the laughter of all, Democrats and Republicans, who happened to see it. 25

Democratic newspapers mocked the carrying off of Lincoln. They termed it a "funeral procession," and even the Whiggish Louisville *Journal*, which would soon make its peace with the notion of a Senator Lincoln, commented, "If they could have foreseen how he would come out in the debate, they would have borne him off before it commenced." (The pro-Lincoln Chicago *Press and Tribune* reported Lincoln's departure in different terms, with five thousand cheering Republicans hoisting their man in triumph, the Chicagoans marching happily back onto the railroad cars.) 26

In subsequent days, when the *Tribune* complained of wildly inaccurate debate transcripts published on August 23 by the rival *Times*, the Democratic paper retorted, "Anyone who has ever heard Lincoln speak, or who is acquainted with his style of speaking, must know that he cannot speak five grammatical sentences in succession." The *Times* responded to the *Tribune's* charge that Douglas himself had altered the transcripts by throwing down the gauntlet. "We brand the author of the statement, and we care not who he be, as a liar—In applying that epithet, we do it meaning it in the fullest extent of the term, and those to whom it is applicable may find us at our office." 27

No one seems to have taken up the challenge, perhaps because Republican papers were busy developing their own interpretation. On August 26, Horace Greeley's New York *Tribune*, which had once suggested that the Republicans draft Douglas, opined, "Of the two, partiality being left out of the question, we think Mr. Lincoln has decidedly the advantage. Not only are *his* doctrines better and truer than those of his antagonist, but he states them with more propriety and cogency, and with an infinitely better temper." The New York paper scolded Douglas for his use of the supposed Springfield resolutions of 1854: "It appears that no such resolutions were offered at any State Convention in Illinois, or adopted at any such Convention . . .They were, it seems, adopted at a small local meeting in Kane County." Although doubting that Douglas had intentionally misled the audience (the Chicago *Daily Press and Tribune* harbored no such doubts), the New York journal wrote, "there is no doubt that such a misrepresentation is, at least, a blunder, which must ultimately prove injurious to the party by which it is committed." Greeley's paper would add, "this discussion is worthy of study. It touches some of the most vital principles of our political system." Lincoln, Greeley would write, had at Ottawa made the race a clash "for the Kingdom of Heaven or the Kingdom of Satan." Although still crediting Douglas for his stalwart opposition to Lecompton, the New York paper lamented that "this sympathy is diminished by the manner in which he has chosen to conduct the canvass, which reminds us more of the wild and unscrupulous athlete of his earlier days than of the noble displays of last winter." 28

For his part, the wild and unscrupulous athlete seemed a little more shaken than the Democratic press reported. On August 22, one day after the Ottawa debate, knowing that Lyman Trumbull had come into the state to stump for Lincoln, Douglas wrote to former Illinois attorney general Usher F. Linder, "The hell-hounds are on my track. For God's sake, Linder, come and help me fight them." Writing in 1928, the Indiana Senator and Lincoln biographer Albert J. Beveridge wrote that Douglas sent that message via telegraph. The telegrapher, Beveridge explained, seeing an opportunity to make a buck, sold a copy of the cable to the Republicans. (Usher F. Linder came to be known, at least by Republicans, as "For-God's-Sake" Linder.) On September 7, the Chicago *Press and Tribune* would publish this fuller version of the communiqué, claiming it to be a "recent letter":

> For God's sake Linder, come up into the Northern part of the State and help me. Every *dog* in the State is after me—from the bull-dog Trumbull to the smallest canine quadruped that has a kennel in Illinois. 29

Whether or not Douglas wrote these lines, the mere fact that by September the Republican press could report them as plausible suggests that Douglas was showing signs of real concern. Douglas's later characterizations of Trumbull were nowhere near as complimentary as "bull-dog," which after all suggests toughness and resolve; but his frequent, scathing references to his Senate colleague over the course of the debates suggest that Trumbull's presence worried Douglas. For his part, Trumbull wrote to congratulate Lincoln on his "complete triumph over the little pettifogger." 30

Lincoln wrote two telling letters in the immediate aftermath of the Ottawa debate. On the 22nd, before leaving town, he reported to Urbana Republican secretary Joseph O. Cunningham, "Douglas and I, for the first time this canvass, crossed swords here yesterday; the fire flew some, and I am glad to know that I am yet alive." (Had a Democratic postmaster gotten a hold of this letter, as did that telegrapher in Beveridge's story, the *Times* would no doubt have a field day with Lincoln's wry, "I am yet alive.") 31

He also wrote to Chicago Republican leaders Ebenezer Peck and Norman Judd, asking that they meet with him on Friday in Freeport. To Peck he wrote, "Douglas is propounding questions to me, which perhaps it is not quite safe to wholly disregard. I have my view of the means to dispose of them; but I also want yours and Judd's. . . See Judd, you and he keep the matter to yourselves, and meet me at Freeport without fail." Douglas's questions—and more obviously, his taunts that Lincoln would not answer—had registered with the challenger. And with his supporters, who felt Lincoln had been too defensive. They offered free advice. The Chicago Tribune's Charles Ray enjoined Congressman Elihu Washburne, "When you see Abe at Freeport, for God's sake tell him to 'Charge Chester! Charge!' Do not let him keep on the defensive." This echoed some unsolicited advice supplied one month earlier from Cincinnati's J.H. Jordan, who led off an eight-page letter of suggestions by scolding Lincoln, "You are too easy on the Scamp! You should you must be severer on him!" Meanwhile, Henry C. Whitney urged Lincoln to repudiate the Springfield resolutions, for Douglas would otherwise "drive you from a conservative position to one or the other extreme." 32

Despite both sides' misgivings, each man could claim victory in some form. Douglas had gone into one of the most hostile of the seven congressional districts that would host debates, and his spirited attacks had thrown Lincoln at least temporarily on the defensive. He had advanced a number of arguments against his opponent that he would develop and refine all through the campaign. And he had taken a sufficiently conservative position on slavery and slavery agitation to enhance his prospects in the critical swing counties of central Illinois. By not losing the debate, the Little Giant could claim to have triumphed.

For his part, Lincoln had, after a ponderous start, begun to find his voice, raising many of the moral concerns felt by voters in this heavily Republican district, and he had vigorously insisted that Douglas was partly responsible both for the resurgence of slavery agitation and for the ominous tendency of slavery to go national. Lincoln's racial views grate on our modern sensibilities, but he probably articulated a view of race relations that was shared by a fairly sizable swath of the white men who would vote in this election. And, the *Times'* report aside, he survived his first encounter with the greatest man of the Democratic Party; he would be there to challenge Douglas at Freeport. 33

Although both men had taken ungenerous swipes at one another, one other difference had emerged in debate, and that difference fed the sharp distinction between the two men on race. Lincoln showed a more generous, more charitable spirit toward blacks. At some level, he *did* recognize in them a common humanity with himself, and with Judge Douglas, and with every living man. Would that he had taken this to its logical extension and endorsed political and social equality, voting, office-holding, intermarriage, and integration, all of the truths that we now consider to be self-evident. For whatever reasons—and those reasons were probably a combination of his native origins, the time and place in which he was then living, political ambition, and lack of imagination, he had not gotten there. But if we contrast Lincoln's statement that all blacks deserve the natural rights of the Declaration of Independence with Douglas' mean-spirited, mocking treatment of the Negro race worldwide and across time (and the reactions of some in the crowd), we see a fundamental difference in spirit; one marked by some generosity, the other marked by a total absence of generosity. One historian contended that the incumbent strained to "express a callous scorn for blacks." 34

Lincoln's friend, the Chicago lawyer and Republican politico Leonard Swett commented on the generous strain in Lincoln's political character:

He had very great kindness of heart. His mind was full of tender sensibilities; he was extremely humane, yet while these attributes were fully developed in his character and unless intercepted by his judgment controlled him, they never did control him contrary to his judgments. He would strain a point to be kind, but he never strained to breaking.

Most of the men of much kindly feeling are controlled by this sentiment against their judgment, or rather that sentiment beclouds their Judgment. It was never so with him. He would be just as kind and generous as his judgment would let him be—no more. If he ever deviated from this rule, it was to save life. 35

Swett, it should be added, was no sentimentalist. In 1866, he would write: "Any man who took Lincoln for a simple-minded man would very soon wake up with his back in a ditch." (This was the same no-nonsense attorney who successfully argued Robert Todd Lincoln's 1875 case for the commitment of Mary Todd Lincoln to an insane asylum.) To such a man, Lincoln's "kindness," his "humane" and "generous" spirit would not necessarily have been the highest of virtues. Sentiments such as these "becloud" one's judgment and make it harder to leave one's adversary unconscious in that ditch (which is after all, what lawyers and candidates *want* to achieve, if only figuratively.) In fact, Swett only noted Lincoln's generosity of spirit to approvingly note how well Lincoln kept it in check. Thinking no doubt of Lincoln's later reputation for pardoning sleeping sentries during the war, Swett characterized Lincoln's only deviation to be the saving of life. 36

In the legal and political circles in which Lincoln (and Douglas) traveled, a generous spirit did not get you much; it might even be seen as a weakness. More specifically, any generosity toward "inferior" races, especially blacks, may have been a liability. So Lincoln's impassioned claim that blacks deserved natural rights was newsworthy, not because he was a racial progressive by our standards or even by the standards of the time, but because he was an 1850s Illinois lawyer and Senate candidate. Whites—especially white politicians—in that place and in that time tended to benefit from being *ungenerous* to blacks; and Lincoln was not pointedly ungenerous, not at Ottawa at least, and not at Lewiston, only days before the Ottawa clash. There, he shouted that the "representatives in old Independence Hall, said to the whole world of men: 'We hold these truths to be self-evident: that all men are created equal; that they are endowed by their Creator with certain unalienable rights; that among these are life, liberty, and the pursuit of happiness.'" This, called Lincoln, "was the majestic interpretation of the economy of the Universe." It was the Founders' "lofty, and wise, and noble understanding of the justice of the Creator to his creatures."

The Lewiston crowd applauded.

"Yes, gentlemen, to *all* his creatures, to the whole great family of man. In their enlightened belief, nothing stamped with the divine image and likeness was sent into the world to be trodden on, and degraded, and imbruted by its fellows. . ." And if "some faction" were to "set up a doctrine that none but rich men, or none but white men were entitled to life, liberty, and the pursuit of happiness," then new generations should "take courage and renew the battle" begun by their fathers, "so that truth, and justice, and mercy, and all the humane and Christian virtues might not be extinguished from the land. . ." 37

And yet: *He would be just as kind and generous as his judgment would let him be—no more.* Deviating from that rule *might* in 1858 have cost a life: Lincoln's own political life.

Chapter Two: "The Scurviest of All Possible Heresies"

"Can the People In Any Lawful Way. . ."

Winfield Scott Stitely slipped into the lumber wagon. Hoping not to be noticed, "I squatted in front of the hay," he recalled seventy-one years later. And so young Winfield joined his unsuspecting uncle in a five-wagon train of residents from Lena Township, Illinois to Freeport on August 27, 1858. "He didn't notice me until we got to Baxter's Springs" to water the horses, Stitely wrote. To Winfield's delight "we were too far along to be sent back so I stayed in and saw the show that day." 1

Some fifteen thousand people saw the show, a surprising number of them children, both boys and girls. They came from all over the gently rolling plains, and the distances they covered and discomforts they endured testify to the zeal with which the people of far northern Illinois viewed the debate in Freeport. These foot soldiers of democracy played a major role on an afternoon which would forever redirect the career of Senator Stephen Douglas, and by implication, the career of his challenger. 2

Getting there was not half the fun, even if you did not face the added strain of trying not to be seen by your uncle. The quality of the roads, the lack of roadside amenities, and the traffic to Freeport all made the journey a pilgrimage by modern standards. "We drove that 40 miles in a lumber wagon," wrote A.H. Weir, "a good share of it was in the night." The daughter of one of the marshals from Florence and her seven siblings "went in a lumber wagon, pole springs and home-made seats," which must have left eight youngsters with sore backsides. 3

Louis Altenbern, the ten-year-old son of a German immigrant stonemason turned farmer, rose at 4 a.m. "to get an early start." They too set out from Lena, as the dawn came up over the prairie, gray daylight seeming to rise from the great city to the east, from Chicago, as the oceans of corn went from gray to green under an overcast sky. The family made good time, that great aim of all American fathers on family journeys, until they reached a place called Preston's Bottom just three miles from Lena. There, "we struck a line of oxen and horse teams and from that time on . . .had to stop every few rods and wait for the line to move. We did not reach Freeport until 11 o-clock" in the morning. Seven hours on the road to hear three hours of political talk. 4

A retired minister, O.F. Mattison, recalled in 1929 that he "rode from Mt. Morris, my home, 22 miles in a democrat wagon, so anxious was I to see and hear these champions on either side of such an absorbing political issue." Mattison was sixteen. 5

Freeport must have seemed exotic to these children of the northern Illinois plains. All the people, the bunting, the bands, the marshals, and the great hotel, the Brewster House. In 1929, local historians contacted debate eyewitnesses as the town prepared to unveil Leonard Crunelle's statue of "Lincoln, the Debater," and even in old age many had vivid memories of being a child in Freeport that momentous day. Many reported encountering Douglas or Lincoln personally, which is perhaps to be expected, human nature being what it is. Others' recollections were less the stuff of Hollywood, more that of a sort of unassuming Midwestern honesty.

Writing from Fort Worth, Texas, C.W. Macune, known as "Charley" Macune as an eight-year-old Freeport boy, reported that a lawyer friend of the family went to the Brewster House to call on the candidates prior to the debate and took Charley along. "Douglas scarcely noticed me when I was presented; he was standing and the large room was full, all standing, many of them talking and smoking." (Perhaps to clarify the unwholesome, smoke-filled-room atmosphere to his Prohibition-era audience, Macune helpfully added, "There was a large per cent of the Democratic Party in Freeport then that that were Irish or German and they were visible.") 6

Young Charley was then ushered into Lincoln's room:

> He was sitting down by a table; it was quiet, with only a few gentlemen present and our turn soon came. Lincoln lifted me up and sat me on his knee and talked to me in a kind fatherly way that completely won my heart. He never knew what a blessing he was to this widow's son. 7

Clinton Miller, who at seventy-five still lived in Freeport in 1929, reported that "while Lincoln was receiving friends at the Brewster House, a local character named Ward Robey, who was about Lincoln's size, was made to stand up beside Lincoln to see which was the taller, and homelier." If this happened, it must have been for Lincoln one of the burdens that came with being a politician in the late stages of the Age of Jackson, when leaders had to defer to the masses. Try to imagine: this tall, not-especially handsome person is brought to you, and everyone gets to decide a) who is taller and b) who is uglier. Perhaps the Robey encounter happened, perhaps it did not, but it suggests the sort of patience that candidates needed. 8

Some of the most believable accounts are among the most charming. Altenbern recalled, "I don't think I heard the debate," for "at the court house corner a big barbecue was in process. The carcasses of three beeves were being roasted over a ditch about six feet wide and six feet deep, and free sandwiches were being served. Here I remained for the barbecue. As a farm boy I was hungry after a light breakfast at four o'clock. I got in line, got my sandwich, got in again and got another until I had three when I had enough." Like the ten-year-old on his or her first trip to see big-time athletes, Louis remembered most the food. 9

Freeport was Republican country, as had been Ottawa. The local congressman, Elihu Washburne, had briefly flirted with Greeley's plan to draft Douglas as a Republican, but had thought better of it, to Lincoln's relief. (This would prove critical down the road, for Washburne was a key sponsor of a little-known West Point grad named Ulysses Grant after 1861.) Douglas arrived the night of the 26th to a 75-torch parade and stayed in the home of the local postmaster. Lincoln arrived the morning of the debate, a raw, damp August morning on the prairie. Around noon, the two men appeared briefly, arm-in-arm, waving to cheering throngs from the balcony of the Brewster House. They then parted company for final preparations and for the hand-shaking, shoulder-patting, and back-slapping that lubricates American politics. 10

The debate was due to begin at 2:00 p.m., and the local organizers seemed to have learned from the chaos at Ottawa. The debate site, in a grove near the Brewster House, was easily accessible for the two men. By this time both had begun to indulge in the sort of image-crafting that still obsesses American politicians. Douglas had planned to ride to the platform in a carriage drawn by four dappled grays. When Republicans heard this, they had quickly contacted "Uncle John" Long of nearby Lancaster Township, owner of a Conestoga wagon and six big horses. Learning of Lincoln's plan, Douglas decided to walk. 11

William Clingman remembered a rather dramatic entrance: "Lincoln and his party drove around the block from the front of the Brewster House and came up beside the grove." Clingman recalled, "Lincoln and his friends standing up in this wagon, and then jumping out and going by me to the platform." Standing up? Jumping out? It sounds a little showy for Lincoln. It may not have been safe, either. Clingman explained that John Long "had a blacksnake whip coiled around his shoulder" and when a driver wanted the horses to turn right "he gave a sharp jerk." One imagines that Lincoln sat in the front of the coach; a more self-consciously dashing politician might have tried standing. 12

The local Douglas newspaper, the Freeport *Weekly Bulletin* mocked Lincoln's entrance:

Lincoln's legs extending far beyond the length of any carriage to be found in Freeport, a large Pennsylvania wagon, old style, the dimensions of which we cannot give accurately at present, was procured to convey him to the stand to speak from. Mr. L. was placed in or near the rear of the box on a wagon, and his legs extended forward several feet, and resembled the skeleton of some greyhound. He is as queer looking as he is queer spoken. If Barnum could procure him in the style he so beautifully represented on his way to the stand from the Brewster House, then would Mr. L.'s fortune soon be made, for a more ridiculous and laughable show has never been presented to the American people. Judge DOUGLAS, like a brave soldier, firmly footed his way to the stand, where he demolished Lincoln's platform, as endorsed by the Republicans present at the discussion, so effectually, that Lincoln refused to stand fairly and squarely upon it. 13

Decked out in a stylish blue frock coat with "shiny buttons" and doe-colored trousers that at least one survivor remembered as white, a dandy cravat cinched about his neck, a ruffled shirt and a plantation-style hat—the resolute Douglas strode through the crowd. He passed banners reading "ALL MEN ARE CREATED EQUAL," "LINCOLN THE GIANT KILLER," "DOUGLAS AND POPULAR SOVEREIGNTY" and-- chillingly, in progressive Stephenson County--"NO NIGGER EQUALITY." Ahead lay the debate platform, a "crude" structure that seemed to one observer as no more than a "'pyramid of lumber.'" As at Ottawa, there were no chairs or benches for the audience, and this led to the standard pushing and shoving. Average folk who had taken the seats of local dignitaries had to be ejected from the platform itself. The Chicago *Times* enjoyed reporting that a leak in the roof of the platform "seemed confined to the spot where Lincoln stood, 'his boots glistening with the dampness.'" 14

Douglas had about made it to the platform when someone heaved a melon ride, smacking the senior senator from Illinois on the lapel of that blue coat. It was to prove a harbinger of things to come in what became a very long afternoon in Freeport for the Little Giant. 15

Lincoln led off. If at Ottawa he had failed to dispose of Douglas's seven questions, at Freeport he would respond. But first a proposal: Lincoln would answer every one of Douglas' questions, he shouted into the prairie wind, "upon condition that he will answer any number from me not exceeding the same number."

Republicans applauded.

"I shall make no objection to the judge saying 'yes' or 'no' right now, or if it suits him, to remain silent. I pause for a moment to see how it will be—"

"Answer!" someone yelled. After that, a long moment of silence.

"Well," Lincoln said, "I suppose that I may assume that the judge chooses to remain silent."

The crowd laughed and applauded in anticipation of an entertaining hour ahead.

As Lincoln was declaring, "I now say to you, my fellow citizens, that I will answer his interrogatories whether he answers mine or not," there was an interruption "of some minutes," according to the Chicago *Times.* William Bross, editor of the rival *Tribune* beckoned "a particular friend" onto the stand, creating an "interruption of some minutes" and in effect breaking Lincoln's early momentum. (*Times* transcripts of the Freeport debate seemed fixated on "Deacon" Bross's every move that day.)

But the interruption couldn't be helped; Robert Hitt, one of the two "phonographers" employed by the *Tribune* and a critical player in the Republican version of the debates, had failed to appear on time. Lincoln had earlier been worried enough about the missing reporter to ask aloud, "Where's Hitt? Ain't Hitt here yet?" And when the wayward phonographer finally arrived he had to wade through a vast crowd to get to the stand; eventually, "strong men lifted the frail, slender young man into the air and passed him along over the heads of the crowd to the platform." Lincoln and Bross breathed a little easier when Hitt arrived, but he had tested their patience. (Not that it was easy to cover these debates; Hitt's partner Horace White bemoaned, in Edwin Erle Sparks' words, "the open air, the rude platforms, the lack of accommodations for writing, the jostling of the crowds of people, and the occasional puffs of wind which played havoc with sheets of paper.") 16

Lincoln re-started. He considered the Republican party in Illinois to have been founded not at Springfield in 1854, but in Bloomington, two years later. By implication the resolutions that Douglas had introduced at Ottawa had no legitimacy in this race. Nonetheless, Lincoln would give his position on each of the seven questions.

Was Lincoln pledged to the unconditional repeal of the fugitive slave law?

"I do not now nor ever stand in favor of the unconditional repeal of the fugitive slave law."

Members of the crowd yelled back, "Good, good."

Was Lincoln pledged to block any new slave states attempting to enter the Union?

"I do not nor ever did stand pledged against the admission of any more slave states into the Union. . .I do not stand pledged against the admission of the people of that state with such a constitution as they see fit to make." Again, voices in the crowd called their approval.

What about banning slavery in the District of Columbia? Banning the interstate slave trade?

"I do not stand to-day pledged to the abolition of slavery in the District of Columbia.

"I do not stand pledged to the prohibition of the slave trade between different states."

A disappointingly conservative, legalistic set of answers thus far. Discerning listeners might have noted Lincoln's contention that he was not *pledged* to take these actions against slavery. But at this point, central counties or no central counties, Lincoln seemed headed toward another debate fizzle in the Republican north of Illinois. Had all of those people come all that way to hear the Republican candidate disavow any intention of doing anything harmful to slavery?

The pro-Lincoln *Tribune* indicated a surge in enthusiasm when Lincoln added, "I am impliedly, if not expressly pledged to the belief in the right and duty of Congress to prohibit slavery in all the United States territories." Hardly "give me liberty or give me death," but Deacon Bross pronounced it "good," according to the eagle-eyed *Times* phonographers.

Then Lincoln's tone shifted. Stepping away from the exact form of Douglas' Ottawa questions, Lincoln announced that now he would "state what I really think upon them."

First, the people of the southern states were entitled to a fugitive slave law, said Lincoln, but the 1850 law needed significant adjustments. Second, "I should be exceedingly glad to see slavery abolished in the District of Columbia," but "as a member of Congress I should not be in favor" of it unless the emancipation of Washington slaves be gradual, be by a vote of the majority of qualified D.C. voters, and be accompanied by compensation to "unwilling owners." Third, Lincoln implied that he had not fully considered banning the interstate slave trade, but if he did conclude that Congress had such power, "I should not be in favor of that power unless it should be upon some conservative principle," similar to that which Lincoln would apply to abolishing slavery in the District.

What about the unlikely scenario that a territory--from which slavery had been barred--applied in democratic fashion for slave statehood? What would Senator Lincoln do then? "I state to you freely, frankly, that I should be exceedingly sorry to ever be put in the position of having to pass upon that question. I should be exceedingly glad to know that there would not be another slave state admitted into the Union," but "I see no alternative, if we own the country, but we must admit it to the Union."

"That is the doctrine! That is popular sovereignty!" gushed Deacon Bross, reported the *Times*. The *Tribune* reported applause, but at this point Lincoln seemed more agonized then energized. Having whetted everyone's appetite for "what I really think," Lincoln had closed the gap between his views and those of Douglas; he certainly appeared to be no abolitionist. Which was of course both true *and* the strategy to topple Douglas.

Lincoln went over to the offensive.

He posed four questions. First, would a re-elected Senator Douglas support Kansas' admission if they adopted a constitution fairly, even though a bill sponsored by Congressman William English had passed Congress, mandating that Kansas could not enter until it had 93,000 free citizens? Second, could the settlers of a territory still bar slavery, or did *Dred Scott* render popular sovereignty a dead letter? Third, would the Senator acquiesce if the Supreme Court delivered the 'second Dred Scott decision' and told free states that they could not themselves bar slaveholding? Fourth, would the Senator pursue the acquisition of more territory, regardless of the consequences to sectional relations?

The second question, the one that followed the drab, technical "English bill" question, contained the poison. Lincoln asked Douglas, "Can the people of the United States territory in any lawful way, against the wishes of any citizen of the United States, exclude slavery from their limits prior to the formation of a state constitution?"

Douglas had the better part of forty-five minutes to ponder an answer to that one, but he probably did not feel pressed; he had addressed the issue many times before, on the Senate floor and on the hustings. Nor was he alone; Northerners and some fairly militant Southerners had done so, too. Hearing that question, Douglas's inner voice may have said, *question two, fine, I've dealt with this before. . .not very original on Lincoln's part; I can handle that one just fine.*

Or maybe not. Perhaps Douglas saw at once in the legendary "Freeport question" the thunderclouds gathering, over his candidacy, over his still unslaked thirst for the White House, over the Union that he adored.

The moment is one of the classic, dramatic moments of American political history: the exact moment when Lincoln belled the cat, perhaps forfeiting the Senate seat, but demolishing the Little Giant's hopes for the presidency in 1860, and thus vaulting himself into the White House. It may have been all of these things, or none of them. But chances are that it had none of the drama that we would like it to have had.

For one thing, this was not a courtroom. Douglas did not have to answer Lincoln's question; in fact was not allowed to answer, not immediately. Although the Democrat did enunciate something that historians have called "The Freeport Doctrine" that didn't come until well after 3:00 p.m.; Lincoln couldn't have asked the question much after 2:35.

For another, the Freeport audience seems to have missed it. Neither the *Times* nor the friendly *Tribune* indicates any thunderous hooting and hollering as Lincoln stuck his opponent, just some random cries of "that's it," "good," and "he won't answer," and some applause. That may have been at least in part because of the conditions at Freeport: 15 to 20,000 people, a raw day, the wind howling across the prairies in an early warning of autumn to come. Lacking any amplification but what nature provided him, Lincoln's voice probably rang out. But of that twenty thousand there were any number of people standing in line for three barbecued beef sandwiches like young Louis Altenbern; or, who admired mostly "the beautiful carriage in which Douglas rode." (Even though he did not ride in it.) Congressman Washburne confessed that due to the noise, the jostling for space, and the weather, "'the audience did not take in the vast importance of the debate.'" 17

And yet, Lincoln had warned that he would ask questions. Douglas could only ignore that second question at his peril.

Picking up on research undertaken in part by Republican newspapers, Lincoln then revealed that the so-called Springfield resolutions of 1854 were in fact resolutions adopted by free-soilers in Kane County. "I am just as much responsible for those resolutions passed in Kane County as for those passed at Springfield," declared Lincoln. "It amounts to just nothing; no more than there would be in regard to the responsibility of a set of resolutions passed in the moon." The faithful laughed and cheered.

Lincoln scolded his opponent, who was not just *any* Senator, but one of "world wide renown." The Republican could only attribute the Senator's falsification to "that evil genius which has attended him throughout his life, giving to him an apparent astonishing prosperity, such as led very good men to doubt of there being any advantage in virtue over vice."

As the Republicans roared with laughter, as the crowd cheered the challenger who had just accused his foe of possessing an "evil genius"— strong words applied to a long-time acquaintance—Lincoln closed. Returning to the theme of Douglas's role in the conspiracy to take slavery national, Lincoln picked up on Douglas's tendency to characterize Lincoln as being "altogether conscientious" in holding some outlandishly-rendered view or other. Lincoln called out, "I have no doubt '*he* is conscientious in the matter'" of nationalizing slavery. To laughter and cheers, Lincoln charged that Douglas believed it was a "good and blessed thing" to nationalize slavery. "I do hope that he will understand that in all this matter that he is conscientious in it."

Having ended by accusing the Judge of being a card-carrying member of the slave power conspiracy, Lincoln sat, to "more laughter and cheers," according to the *Tribune*. In his hour, he had revealed his timidity on taking action against slavery; adumbrated a gradualist solution to the question of emancipation that he would cling to until late in 1862, and had perhaps demagogically tied the tin can of the slave power onto his opponent's tail.

But he had also asked the Freeport question.

"That Kind and Respectful Attention"

Douglas rose to three cheers and no melon rinds. No doubt sensing that this was an unfriendly crowd, the Senator did not wait to use his customary admonition.

"The silence with which you have listened to Mr. Lincoln during his hour is creditable to this vast audience, composed of men of various—of all political parties." Having nodded to Republicans, Democrats, Danites, and Know Nothings, Douglas continued, "Nothing is more creditable to any large mass of people assembled for the purpose of hearing a political discussion than that kind and respectful attention that is yielded not only to your friends, but to those who are opposed to you in politics." Douglas's appeal is easily recognizable to anyone faced with addressing a truculent, potentially disruptive audience; he resembled a substitute teacher in front of a middle school class at period's outset appealing for cooperation.

The Little Giant soon turned to Lincoln's second question, the Freeport Question. He responded with what has grandly been called the Freeport Doctrine. Douglas first announced his exasperation: "I answer emphatically," he called, "as Mr. Lincoln has heard me answer a hundred times, on every stump in Illinois, that in my opinion the people of a territory can by lawful means exclude slavery before it comes in as a state."

Cheers and applause.

"Whatever the Supreme Court may hereafter decide as to the abstract question of whether slavery may go in under the Constitution or not, the people of a Territory have the lawful means to admit it or exclude it as they please, for the reason that slavery cannot exist a day or an hour anywhere unless supported by local police regulations furnishing remedies and means of enforcing the right to hold slaves."

What did Douglas mean by "local police regulations?" He seems to have meant territorial fugitive slave codes. If territorial legislatures failed to make it a crime for slaves to run away then slavery would not last long in any territory, even if Roger B. Taney himself came to Kansas and read the *Dred Scott* ruling personally in each prairie hamlet.

Jacksonian Democrat that he was, Douglas insisted, "Those local and police regulations can only be furnished by the local legislature," not the US Congress nor the Supreme Court, nor the White House in far-off Washington.

Then Douglas explained how it worked, in case territorial settlers did not themselves know how to subvert *Dred Scott*: "If the people of the Territory are opposed to slavery they will elect members to the legislature who will adopt unfriendly legislation to it." Unfriendly legislation? That sounded like the "personal liberty laws" adopted by a number of Northern states starting decades ago. These laws prohibited local law enforcement authorities from participating in the hunting down of fugitive slaves. In response to the tougher, more intrusive 1850 Fugitive Slave Act, states such as Massachusetts had passed provocative new personal liberty laws. These laws, produced in the climate that gave America *Uncle Tom's Cabin,* had driven pro-slavery Southerners to apoplexy. Douglas immediately added that the settlers could just as easily "adopt the legislative measures friendly to slavery."

Douglas concluded his response: "Hence, no matter what may be the decision of the Supreme Court on that abstract question, still the right of the people to make it a slave Territory or a free Territory is perfect and complete under the Nebraska bill."

There it was: the Supreme Court had ostensibly closed the question of slavery in the territories in 1857. Congress had no power to bar slavery from any territory, ruled the Court, and thus slavery could legally go into every territory of the United States. Now Douglas was reiterating his position that that hard-won Southern victory was not unconditional; democracy trumped the Court's ruling. If the people did not want slavery, they did not have to have it; and Douglas in Freeport supplied the formula by which Americans could keep slavery at bay. Only Buchaneers would have jeered Douglas' formula that day in free-soil northern Illinois.

So far, so good, at least in terms of taking the crowd out of it. Douglas had thus far complimented the audience, and he had staked out a position that indicated an interest in keeping some of the territories free. He thus far appeared very much the moderate Democrat who had broken with the administration over the fraudulent Lecompton vote, and he had gone one step further, undercutting the Taney Court. Independent-minded listeners, shifting and listening as closely as they could in the whistling prairie winds, may have at this point questioned Lincoln's characterization of the Little Giant as an agent of the slave power conspiracy, even as Douglas went on to reject as beneath contempt Lincoln's third question. If the goal was to gain northern Illinois support for re-election, the Senator was off to a promising start in Freeport.

Then Douglas came apart.

Moving to Lincoln's question on acquiring territories regardless of the potential for a worsened slavery debate, Douglas spoke from the gut. And the gut told him that Lincoln and Washburne and that fellow driving the Conestoga wagon, and probably the coward who bonked him with the melon rind weren't just Republicans. They were Black Republicans. They would block the admission of new territories if it meant more slave states. They cared more about blacks than about the nation's Manifest Destiny. Reprehensible!

"The Black Republican party," Douglas shouted into the wind, "laid down the proposition that under no circumstances would we acquire any more territory, unless slavery be first prohibited in the country. I ask Mr. Lincoln whether he is in favor of the proposition."

According to the *Times,* at this point Douglas turned to Lincoln, in the time-honored tradition of debaters and demanded, "Are you against any further acquisition of territory under any circumstances unless slavery is prohibited?"

Lincoln responded with words that must have been inaudible to the crowd.

"That he don't like to answer," Douglas called. He continued, "I ask him if he stands up to that article in the platform, and he turns around, Yankee fashion, and without answering it himself, asks me: Are you opposed to admitting a slave territory?"

Something had set Douglas's nerves on edge. Was it the very thought that anyone would ever say no thanks to new territory? Was it the way that Lincoln responded to the question, in "Yankee"- fashion? Or was it the initial rough reception—that melon rind, for instance--from a largely unfriendly crowd? Whatever the case, Douglas's performance went down-hill from there.

"I trust now that Mr. Lincoln will deem himself answered on these few points. He racked his brain so much in devising these few questions that he exhausted himself, and had not strength enough to devise another." The *Times* reported laughter on that last line.

But, continued Douglas, "as soon as he can hold a council of his advis-ers by getting Lovejoy and Farnsworth and Giddings and Fred. Douglass together, he will then frame and propound the other interrogatories."

The *Tribune* indicated that the crowd came alive at this point, cheer-ing the names of each abolitionist "adviser." The *Times* had it otherwise. According to the Democratic newspaper, the crowd cheered its approval and laughed, laughter "in which Mr. Lincoln feebly joined, saying with their aid he hoped to get seven questions, the number asked him by Judge Douglas."

Douglas's nasty little shot at Lincoln's mental "exhaustion" seemed to rouse Republicans in the crowd. Until then largely passive, Republicans cheered the name of the abolitionist "advisers" loud enough for Douglas to turn his attention away from Lincoln, from *Dred Scott*, from "unfriendly legislation." He addressed the abolitionist pockets of the audience who had hurrahed at the names of Giddings and Lovejoy and Farnsworth and Frederick Douglass.

"I have no doubt you think they are all good men," he shouted back. "Good Black Republicans."

The *Times* reported that voices shouted back, "White, White."

Douglas found this humorous. "I have reason to recollect that some people in this country think that Fred. Douglass is a very good man." He continued, "The last time I came here to make a speech, while I was talking on the stand to you people of Freeport, as I am today, I saw a carriage, and a magnificent one too, drive up and take its position on the outside of the crowd, with a beautiful young lady on the front seat." Then came the clincher. Sitting on the back seat was "Fred. Douglass, the Negro, on the back seat, and the owner of the carriage in front driving the Negro."

Laughter, amid cries of "Right," and "What have you to say against it?"

Feigning incredulity, Douglas bellowed over the din, "I witnessed this here in your town."

"What of it?" someone shouted.

"What of it?" shot back Douglas.

All I have to say is this, if you Black Republicans think that the Negro ought to be on a social equality with your wives and daughters, and ride in the carriage with your wife while the master of the carriage drives the team, you have a perfect right to do so. [Good, good, and cheers, mingled with shouting and cries of White, white.] I am told also that another of Fred. Douglass' kinsmen, another rich black Negro, is now traveling this part of the State making speeches for his friend Mr. Lincoln, who is the champion of the black man's party.

More shouts of "White men, white men."

Again, "What have you got to say against it?"

Douglas retorted, "All I have got to say on that subject is this, those of you who believe that the nigger is your equal, and ought to be on an equality with you socially, politically, and legally, have a right to entertain these positions, and of course will vote for Mr. Lincoln."

A lone voice sang out, "Down with the negro." Douglas had *some* vocal supporters in the crowd.

But having roused an unfriendly crowd, Douglas then worsened the situation. Attempting to keep alive the Springfield resolutions charge he had made at Ottawa, Douglas noted that Lincoln and his supporters had asserted that no such resolutions were adopted in Springfield in 1854. "Mr. Lincoln is great in the particular spots at which a thing is to be done." Having all but called Lincoln a miscegenationist, Douglas now insinuated that his rival was a traitor. "He thinks the platform was not adopted at the right spot, like the Mexican War, which in his opinion was unjust and infamous because the first blood was not shed on the right spot." It was a nasty little swipe that Douglas would use frequently in the debates.

Douglas returned to his theme: who cared where the resolutions were adopted, or when for that matter? Reading excerpts from anti-slavery Republican resolutions adopted in nearby Rockford in 1854 Douglas encountered more sustained cheers with each individual resolution. Again, he could not resist:

"You say that is all right," called Douglas, after reading resolutions decrying "'the continued and increasing aggressions of slavery'" that could only be resisted by the "'united political action of all good men.'"

"Now for the next," he shouted, and then read more resolutions as the cheering continued. "'To bring the Administration of the Government back to first principles; to restore Kansas and Nebraska to the position of territories; and to repeal and entirely abrogate the Fugitive Slave Law.'"

Someone hollered, "That's all right."

"That's all right you say," shot back Douglas. "Mr. Lincoln tells you he is not for it, and yet it is all right" for you "Black Republicans." Let me read you another, smiled Douglas.

"White Republicans! White! White!"

"Wait until I read it," Douglas insisted. The resolution called for the prohibition of any new slave states into the Union.

"Good," Republicans yelled, "Good."

Douglas shouted, "You answer by a loud voice that it is all right." Another resolution: total exclusion from the territories of slavery; the acquisition of no new slave states unless slavery were excluded prior to annexation.

"You think that is a good platform, don't you?" called Douglas.

"Good enough," came the response. "All right."

"Yes. All right," Republicans cheered.

Douglas reminded the crowd "you pledged yourself one to another never to vote for a man for office in the State or Federal government, who was not committed to this proposition."

A voice shouted, "Exactly," and, according to the *Tribune* that brought further cheers.

Douglas closed in: "Yes, you say, exactly, you were committed to them . . .What do you think of Mr. Lincoln who is your candidate and who is attempting to dodge the responsibility of this platform because it was not adopted in the right spot." Douglas then vowed to take the platform from district to district and "nail it to the back of all the Black Republicans throughout the state."

"White Republicans!" they shouted back, "White! White Republicans!"

The *Times* reported that at this point someone called out, "Three cheers for Douglas." Neither paper reported any hip, hip, hoorays.

"Couldn't you modify it and call it brown?" sang out a voice, to laughter.

"No," replied Douglas. "I could not modify it a little bit."

Douglas then directly questioned Tom Turner, a local Republican seated on the speaker's platform on the Republican resolution calling for no more slave states. Turner averred, "I drew these resolutions. . . They are our creed exactly."

Douglas no doubt smiled at that. "Mr. Lincoln says he would not like to be put in a position where he would have to vote on it." But, Douglas added, "I don't think there is much danger of his ever being put in a position where he will have to."

The Little Giant returned to another favorite theme, the 1854 Lincoln/ Trumbull scheme to abolitionize the parties and claim Senate seats for themselves. Recalling the surprise Trumbull victory earlier in the decade, Douglas gave his version of events: ". . .Trumbull having cheated Lincoln out of this place, Lincoln's friends made a great deal of fuss, and in order to keep Lincoln quiet they had to come forward and pledge themselves in advance in the State Convention that they would be for Lincoln and nobody else." Douglas continued, "Lincoln would be satisfied in no other way, and you Black Republicans—"

"White Republicans"

"White Republicans, sir."

'White, White."

The *Times* reported "great clamor" here. Douglas had finally lost control of the crowd. In a Republican town, Douglas had mocked roughly half the audience with a racial slur. He had done it repeatedly, and he had done it to people who had in many cases endured no small discomfort to hear him debate Lincoln. Packed tightly on the debate grounds, tired in many cases from their journeys to Freeport, standing now for well over two hours, they boiled over, and the senior Senator from Illinois could no longer make himself heard.

"I wish to remind you," Douglas bellowed above the din, "that there was not a Democrat here vulgar enough to interrupt Mr. Lincoln while he was talking."

The *Times* reported that great applause and "hurrahs for Douglas" accompanied that line.

Then, ever the needler, Douglas announced, "I know the shoe is pinching you when I am clinching Lincoln, and you are scared to death at the result."

More cheers, reported the *Times.*

Douglas continued, "I have seen these men when they make appointments for joint discussion, and then the moment their man has been heard try to interrupt and prevent a fair hearing."

Douglas growled, "I have seen your mobs before and I defy their wrath."

At this line, wrote the *Tribune*, a "considerable disturbance" broke out in the crowd. As people cheered, Douglas ordered his supporters, "Don't cheer. I need my whole time. Their object is to occupy it, so that I shall not go through with my evidence showing the double dealing of the Black Republican party."

Time was running short.

The crowd seemed to settle. Returning to Tom Turner's resolutions, Douglas told the crowd, "Every man who voted for those resolutions, with two exceptions, voted for Mr. Lincoln the next day for United States Senator," although they had been pledged "to vote for no man . . .who was not committed to this Black Republican platform as I read it at Ottawa."

Turning to Turner himself, Douglas bore in: "did you violate your pledge in voting for Mr. Lincoln, or did Mr. Lincoln commit himself before you gave the vote?"

At this, the *Times* reported, Lincoln jumped from his seat, grabbed Turner, "shook him nervously" and said, "Don't answer, Turner. You have no right to answer." (This strains credulity; Turner was a longtime Illinois political operative, and would have known how to wriggle out; moreover, were Lincoln to leap up and hiss such a direction at a local Republican favorite in front of a crowd of 15,000, it would be an admission of his own two-facedness. Would Lincoln have been so desperate, especially when Douglas had only recently come through a rough round of hazing from a pro-Lincoln crowd?)

Douglas moved to finish by artfully lampooning his opponent's answers to the seven Ottawa questions.

"He says he was not pledged to the repeal of the Fugitive Slave Law. He was not pledged to it—doesn't quite like it—wouldn't introduce a law to repeal it—thinks there ought to be some law—doesn't tell what it is and upon the whole don't know what to do."

Lincoln "will not tell you definitively whether he would vote for more Slave States and thus dissolve the Union, but he says he would not like to be put to the test." To laughter, Douglas repeated, "Well, I don't think he will be put to the test." As the laughter continued, Douglas turned serious: "I don't think the people of Illinois desire a man to represent them who would not like to be put to the test in the performance of high constitutional duty." To cries of "Good," reported the *Times*, Douglas vowed, "I will retire in shame from the Senate of the United States when I am not willing to be put to the test in the performance of my duty."

When the applause died down, Douglas launched one last attack on Lincoln's "House Divided" argument, and then his time expired. Pugnacious but wounded, he sat down.

"We Will All Pull Together"

Lincoln spoke directly to the unstatesmanlike show just concluded. "The first thing I think of saying to you is a word in regard to Judge Douglas' declaration about vulgarity and blackguardism in the crowd, that no such thing was shown by any democrat while I was speaking." In the slow twang that marked his public speeches, Lincoln continued, "Now, I only want by way of reply to say that while *I* was speaking [I] used no vulgarity or blackguardism toward any democrats." 18

"Apples of gold," said an elderly man seated on the platform, according to the *Tribune.* Even the *Times* reported great laughter and applause at Lincoln's scolding of the Little Giant. Clearly, Lincoln would not make the same mistake. He might answer hecklers. He would respond to crowd reaction. He would needle Douglas. But he would not err as had Douglas; he would not go out of his way to antagonize large segments of the audience.

On to substance. Lincoln took up Douglas's charges that the Republican candidate had supported the 1854 resolutions, and was engaged in a duplicitous attempt to be an abolitionist in northern Illinois, a conservative in the south. Reminding his audience that Republicans in the different parts of the state had adopted many resolutions since Douglas' Nebraska bill had become law, Lincoln stated that in 1856 the various regional groups came together around a common platform. (One that was more moderate, and less abolitionist than the program Douglas had tried to nail on Lincoln's back at Ottawa and again here at Freeport.) And he indicated his commitment to that platform. He shouted into the wind, "we are all bound as party men to this platform. . .if any of you expects that I shall be elected—as the Judge thinks he is quite sure I will not—if any of you think I shall do anything that is not indicated by the republican platform, and by my answers to-day, I tell you you will be deceived. I do not ask for the votes of any one that thinks I have secret pledges, that I do not speak plainly on."

Lincoln asked, "Cannot the judge be satisfied? Does the judge think that my going to Washington will not enable you to vote your sentiments?"

At this point, the *Times'* phonographers lost track of Lincoln's words, owing to "confusion" that "partly drowned" those words. The *Tribune's* reporters got it: ". . . and enable me to advocate sentiments contrary to this which I expressed when you voted for and elected me, I assure him that his fears are wholly needless and groundless. Is the Judge really afraid of any such thing?"

Lincoln let that sink in, and then intoned, "I will tell you what the judge is afraid of." Those that could hear may have leaned forward. What was the great man afraid of?

"He is afraid that we will all pull together." Republicans laughed; the *Trib* reported cries of "We will, we will."

"This is what the judge is afraid of. That is what is alarming to him more than anything else." More laughter, according to the *Trib*.

"Well, now, for my part I do hope that all of us who entertain opinions adverse to his doctrines and to that which appears to us to be the tendency to perpetuate slavery, that we will wave minor differences and pull together."

"We will," they cried, "We will." Loud cheers, reported the Republican newspaper.

Lincoln had deftly brought a largely Republican—and somewhat agitated--crowd back to the first assumptions of his campaign, the assumptions of the House Divided speech. Douglas was a conspirator in a scheme to nationalize slavery. Lincoln's third "Freeport question" had raised the issue yet again.

Although often times overlooked in the interest shown the second "Freeport Doctrine" question, question three was an attempt to keep alive the "Stephen, Franklin, Roger, and James" charge that Lincoln had made in Springfield when he accepted the nomination. Douglas dismissed it during his ninety-minute reply as frivolous. But it may have been of similar importance to the second question, as it kept alive Lincoln's charge that Douglas was a tool of the slave power conspiracy. And if there was one point on which Illinois Republicans of all stripes could "pull together," along with independents and free-soil Democrats, it was this: slavery must not be injected into the free states via the "next" Dred Scott decision. Shifting from his own distaste for Douglas' adolescent chivvying of the crowd, Lincoln neatly reminded that crowd of first principles: slavery must not be allowed to grow. 19

In only their second debate, Lincoln was beginning to show signs of exasperation with his opponent. Moving to Douglas's characterization of that same House Divided doctrine as an irresponsible fantasy, Lincoln admitted "I almost turn with disgust from the task of repeating an answer to it."

Disgusted he may have been, but Lincoln meant to have fun. Noting that the Washington *Union*, the unofficial organ of the Buchanan administration, had asserted that the logical extension of *Dred Scott* was that indeed no *state* could legally bar slaveholders from holding onto their property, Lincoln moved to further worsen relations between the Democratic candidate and Illinois "Buchaneers." Noting that Douglas had publicly repudiated the *Union* for this stance, Lincoln shouted, "I make a direct issue on that, that he did not make that charge against the editor of the *Union* alone."

Someone yelled, "What of that?"

Lincoln reiterated, "[I]t was more than the editor of the *Union* alone that he made his charges against." Douglas, Lincoln reminded everyone, had fallen out with Buchanan.

Just in case anyone failed to get it, Lincoln quoted passages from Douglas's March 22, 1858 Senate speech attacking the *Union*, interspersing his own editorial comments. The *Tribune* reported laughter and cheers as Lincoln drove the wedge deeper:

"'Mr. President[Lincoln now spoke as Douglas]—you find here several distinct propositions advanced boldly by the Washington *Union*, editorially and apparently authoritatively.'"

"By whose authority, Judge Douglas?"

"Who do you say authorized the publication of this article?" asked Lincoln of his foe. "We all know that the Washington *Union* was the newspaper at Washington considered to be the organ of the administration."

Then Lincoln turned prosecutor; his tone for the first time became like that of Douglas at Ottawa. He turned much less genial than had been the case when he had posed his four questions nearly three hours earlier. This was a Lincoln that most Americans do not know existed; think of a time when Lincoln publicly "demanded" anything.

"I demand of Judge Douglas to say by whose authority he meant to say those articles were published. If he can say that he did not mean the President and cabinet, who did he mean?" Pushing harder, Lincoln quoted Douglas's March 22 comment that the Buchanan administration had struck a "'fatal blow. . . at the sovereignty of the States of this Union, a death blow to State rights,'" principles, promised Douglas, "'upon which I will ever stand.'"

"Now," began Lincoln, "I ask him if he made all these remarks—if he was talking about the fatal blow being struck by the editor of the Washington *Union* when he did not mean anyone else was in on it. . . I would appeal to this audience, aye, to twelve Democrats, Douglas Democrats, on oath," Lincoln was back in the courtroom now, "to answer faithfully to the proposition that he made is not against the editor of the *Union* alone, but against the president, against the cabinet, against the framers of the Lecompton constitution and against all its advocates in and out of Congress. No man can examine those pages and fail to see that such was the fact."

Lincoln went for a laugh: "The Judge's eye is further south now." To cheers, noted the *Tribune*, Lincoln continued, "it was decidedly north then." Turning the tables on Douglas's contention that the Republican would say anything to get elected, Lincoln reminded his own party of the dalliance that some misguided Republicans had conducted with the man who had just an hour ago repeatedly spat the epithet "Black Republicans" at this crowd:

His hope was very much then upon the evisceration of the black republican party, and the turning of it in and making it the tail of his new kite. He knows that—he very well knows it—that he was then expecting to turn the republican party wrong end foremost, and place himself at one end of it, and thus fly the largest kind of a kite. He soon found that the despised black republicans understood and appreciated him better than that, and he has found that his security depends upon him crawling back into the ranks of the democratic party. . .

Tribune phonographers added ". . .with whom he now pretends to be at such fearful variance." The paper also reported that the crowd shouted, "Go on, go on," but that Lincoln called back over the cheers, "I cannot, gentlemen, my time has expired."

The debate ended. Lincoln had achieved much, if only because he had charged, Chester, charged. The second and third "Freeport questions" had forced Douglas to take positions that would further alienate the Buchanan Democrats who might be critical to a Douglas victory in a Democratic-controlled state legislature. The "unfriendly legislation" approach to territorial slavery threatened to negate the *Dred Scott* ruling. Meanwhile, the third question forced Douglas (and enabled Lincoln) to rehearse Douglas' attacks on Lecompton and the Buchanan administration's flirtation with the rights of slaveholders to be secure in their property in all of the states. This drove a further wedge between the Democratic standard-bearer and administration loyalists. (Republicans worked this angle vigorously, with help from the White House. Lincoln's supporters effectively bankrolled a fairly elaborate infiltration of the Democratic campaign, behind the efforts of one Dr. Charles Leib. The Buchanan White House would have been delighted to see the Little Giant turned out of office, even by a Republican.) And by returning to the House Divided theme of Douglas's role in the scheme to nationalize slavery, Lincoln gave Republicans and unaffiliated free-soilers good reason to "pull together." [20]

Lincoln had also shown something like perfect pitch regarding the audience. Douglas had begun his remarks fulsomely complimenting the audience for its good manners and had ended by denouncing pockets of the audience as blackguards. Lincoln not only would not make any such mistake, he actually used Douglas' undignified scuffle to take the high road. And in his rejoinder, he kept moving; this crowd had stood for at least two and one half hours when Lincoln rose for his second try. He had the good sense to return to first principles (Douglas is a tool of the slave power conspiracy, but he's trying to make you think he is not. Hence the showy and not-to-be-trusted denunciation of the administration and its newspaper. A denunciation no more to be trusted than Douglas's earlier feelers to the Republican party.) He even played on his height advantage, drawing laughs (according to the friendly *Tribune*) by painting amusing word pictures of little Stephen Douglas flying his new kite.

When it was over, Lincoln had if nothing else stabilized things. A poor performance in Freeport might have made it all but impossible for Illinois Republicans to "pull together." But now, on friendly ground, aided by an aggressive free-soil crowd which had endured bad weather and in some cases hard journeys to get to Freeport, Lincoln had stood up to Douglas more vigorously than in Ottawa. Rattled and jostled, Douglas could only hope that things would go better way down in Egypt land, in Jonesboro.

No one attempted to carry off Lincoln on their shoulders this time. No one had to.

"No Escape From the Coils"

"The great discussion between Lincoln and Douglas has resulted in the overwhelming discomfiture of the 'little giant'," crowed the Illinois *State Journal* on August 30. "He was completely wiped out and annihilated. To use his own vernacular, he was thoroughly 'trotted through.'" The *State Journal* added, "Lincoln 'brought him to his milk' in a most triumphant manner." 21

Taking a page from the Chicago *Times*' evisceration of Lincoln at Ottawa, the *Journal* continued, "Lincoln made a most powerful speech, and charged home upon Douglas with a vengeance which was perfectly overwhelming." For Douglas, "there was no escape from the coils which Lincoln wound around him," and the Senator's "platitudes about amalgamation and nigger equality—his only political stock in trade—were too old, too stupid to be listened to with patience." Confronted with Lincoln's brilliance, "Douglas fairly squirmed under the infliction. At the close, cheer after cheer for Lincoln rent the air, in prolonged shouts. The whole crowd seemed, with one voice, to join in the enthusiasm for 'Old Abe,' while Douglas crawled off to his quarters like a whipped spaniel." Freeport had been "a grand day for the cause—It is thought that Douglas, sick of his seven appointments, will decline to meet Lincoln in any further debate." 22

And in what had become standard in post-debate analysis, the *Journal* wagered that if Douglas would only keep talking, "every meeting will make hundreds of votes for us." Another Republican reporter wrote cheerfully that "the friends of Douglas slunk away—glad the day was over, sorry it had ever come. No more was heard of them that day while the Republicans held rousing meetings during the remainder of the afternoon and evening." 23

The Republican Chicago *Journal* disparaged Douglas's interactions with a crowd that it contended was four-fifths Republican. The Little Giant "was abusively personal" and had "sneeringly and insultingly repeated the epithet of 'Black Republicans' whereupon a general cry of 'White! White!' arose, from the insulted auditors and continued for some time, putting Douglas out of his humor. He shook his fist at the multitude," reported the *Journal*, and this reflected a contempt for the people. When the debate ended, "Lincoln freely mingled with the masses," but Douglas "was closeted the whole time with a number of aristocratic Democrats, at his hotel. He didn't care enough about 'the people' to mingle with them at all." 24

The Republican press also seized on the free-soil flavor of Douglas's "unfriendly legislation" comments to accuse him of trying to have it both ways. Wrote the Chicago *Tribune* in a posting subtitled "The Little Dodger Cornered and Caught," Douglas was "'brought to his milk'" in Freeport. "Had Mr. Lincoln waited until they had gone down to Egypt; the 'milk' doubtless would have been of a very different color and consistency; but the free soil atmosphere with which Douglas was surrounded worked wonders on his political lacteals." The paper ran side by side Douglas's Chicago speech of July 9 and his Freeport comments, hoping readers would notice "how entirely he swallowed Dred Scott in Chicago, and how he was compelled to throw him up again at Freeport." Galesburg's misleadingly-named *Semi-Weekly Democrat* disparaged southern Illinoisans when it opined that "Mr. Douglas evidently adapts his speeches to the section of the State he is in, taking it for granted that his followers in Egypt cannot or will not read the anti-slavery sentiments he may avow in the north." And the Rockford *Republican* reminded readers that "It is a hard matter to ride two ponies at one time, especially when those ponies are going at the top of their speed in opposite directions." Douglas would find it increasingly hard to "keep astride of his Northern hobby—*Squatter Sovereignty*—and at the same time keep a tight rein upon the neck of the Southern nag presented him by Chief Justice Taney." The *Republican* added that, "Douglas, evidently, about these days, is finding Jordan a hard road to travel; but he has one consolation—he will soon be relieved of his public burdens." 25

Needless to say, Democratic newspapers saw little to justify Republican euphoria. The Democratic newspaper in Freeport, the *Weekly Bulletin*, while tellingly noting the inability of the audience to hear the speakers through the driving winds, disparaged Lincoln's "vain attempts to extricate himself from the unpleasant position in which Judge Douglas' arguments had placed him at Ottawa." Raising the Mexican War to a campaign issue yet again, the Democrats noted that the challenger was "persistent in his calls for the particular 'spot' at which certain resolutions had been adopted" as in bygone days "when he was engaged in furnishing aid and comfort to the enemies of his country." The *Bulletin* called Douglas's speech "a masterly effort . . . We heard more than one Republican acknowledge that, much as they admired Mr. Lincoln, he was not a match for the "Little Giant.'" As for Douglas's dust-up with a hostile crowd, the *Bulletin* reported that "the utmost decorum was manifested throughout the discussion," outside of "the unmanly demonstrations made by some Republicans (whose partisan feelings were stronger than their sense of good manners.)" 26

Weeks after the debate, on September 16, the *Bulletin* reprinted an article on the Freeport debate that had run in the St. Louis *Republican*. (Pay no attention to the names of antebellum newspapers as clues to party affiliation.) The Missouri paper wrote that Lincoln "has of late years gone off into the wildest stretches of Abolitionism," so "there ought to be no ground for doubt in the minds of all those who love the Union." Lincoln's "distempered brain is full of strange fancies" befitting "the willing Representative of a party which is full of hatred of at least fifteen of all the States of the confederacy, and would destroy it rather than not succeed in their desire to obtain complete control of the General Government. Let Illinois be saved from the grasp of these desperate politicians, *and the Union is safe.*" 27

Still, the ever-reliable Chicago *Times* led the way in its ridicule of the Republican. A September 2 editorial likened Lincoln to one Titus Oates, who in 1678 had schemed to massacre the Protestant inhabitants of London, put the city to the torch, and establish a Catholic regime in England. Noting that both Oates and Lincoln had justified their stands by circulating conspiracy theories, the *Times* asked if anyone who had seen Lincoln in person, "will not realize the following description of Oates, which we quote from Macaulay: 'his legs uneven as those of a badger, his forehead low as that of a baboon, his purple cheeks, and his monstrous length of chin had been familiar to all who frequented the courts of law.'" 28

Sportingly, the editors added, "We intend no personal disrespect to Mr. Lincoln by quoting the description." 29

The *Times* then cautioned Lincoln and the Republicans: "after enjoying a feast such as vampyres might be supposed to delight in, Oates and all his imitators met gloomy, horrible ends . . .They lived long enough to see their falsehoods exposed, and to taste those pains which an outraged public opinion visited upon their iniquities. A like fate awaits the witnesses of the present day." 30

Perhaps; but the outraged public opinion seems to have been most keenly felt outside Illinois, in the slave states, as Douglas's answer to the second of Lincoln's questions began appearing in Southern newspapers. The Louisville *Journal*, a Whiggish, Unionist paper which had little sympathy for Douglas and the Democrats, but conceivably even less for free-soilers such as Lincoln, called Douglas's response a "silly, disgusting exhibition of ignorance and duplicity. . .the scurviest possible form of the scurviest of all possible heresies." The *Journal* hissed, "No friend to the constitutional rights of the South or to manly public dealing can or will tolerate it for an instant," for Douglas had committed "a most vile and miserable and unmitigated heresy." The Senator, "goes several lengths beyond the most intense and passionate Republican in the whole North." The Louisville paper wrote that were slavery "to be prohibited or abolished in the Territories by any legislative tribunal, let it be done by one in which the whole nation is represented, and not by one composed of the first stragglers from some over-burdened city or restless border State who happen to squat on the public domain. . ." 31

Other slave state papers joined in. Frankfort's *The Commonwealth* suggested that Kentuckians were thoroughly unimpressed: "The position of Mr. Douglas upon the question of slavery in the Territories is, if possible, more objectionable than that of Mr. Lincoln." North Carolina's Wilmington *Journal* sniffed that Douglas's Freeport Doctrine was "radically unsound. It won't begin to do for our use." Refusing to distinguish between the Republican and Democratic candidates, the *Mississippian* denounced both

Douglas and Lincoln, expressing hope that the country could be rid of "a pair of depraved, blustering, mischievous, lowdown demagogues." The paper "would have them make a Kilkenny cat fight of it, and eat each other up." Georgia's *Federal Union* opined that "The true men of the country will refuse to take either Mr. Douglas or Mr. Lincoln." The Louisville *Journal* concluded that, "Abolitionism itself, as respects the Territories, has never, in its highest fury, assumed such radical and scandalous ground as Senator Douglas took in his Freeport speech." Even William Lloyd Garrison, the most radical of abolitionists, "with all his fanatical and demoniacal hatred of slavery, has never in his whole life uttered an opinion at once so insulting and injurious to the South." The editorialist concluded that the "force of unscrupulous Northern demagoguism seems spent in this last expedient of the unscrupulous little demagogue of Illinois." 32

This last overheated reaction by old-line Whigs might be marked down to longstanding animus to the Democrats' most prominent statesman. But coming from a border state Unionist newspaper, not one from the cotton South, the editorial carried ominous portents for Douglas and for the Union, portents as ominous as Southern jeers that there was not a dime's worth of difference between the Republican and the Democrat. Clearly, something important had happened at Freeport.

Or had it? In the century that followed the debate, and beyond, a second Freeport debate ran intermittently. It continues today. The participants have not argued over slavery in the territories; that question Lincoln and the Republicans (and the Union Army) settled within the decade after an "annihilated" Douglas "crawled off" to meet with those "aristocratic Democrats" at the Brewster House.

The modern-day debate concerns what did and did not happen at Freeport. One side of the debate was summarized in a pamphlet by an early twentieth-century local historian: "Freeport has taken its place among the hallowed spots where occurred a great event that raised aloft the banner of freedom. Time and her historians have placed this Illinois city beside Plymouth Rock, along with Independence Hall in Philadelphia, and the Washington Chapel at Valley Forge." If that sounds a little rich, one needs to understand more fully the reasoning of those who believe that "The Fate of the Nation Was Decided at Freeport." 33

The reasoning goes like this. Lincoln cleverly and against the advice of his allies sprang the Freeport question on Douglas. Ever the wily cross examiner, Lincoln would force Douglas to alienate one of two constituencies. By answering in full support of the *Dred Scott* ruling, Douglas would please Southern voters, and this would pave his way to the presidency in 1860; he might also win back some of the alienated Buchaneers in his home state. But by doing so, he might anger home state Democrats who had rallied to his side in support of the great principle of popular sovereignty. If he instead asserted that principle over *Dred Scott*, then he would surely strengthen his chances of re-election to the Senate, but he would kill his own chances of winning Southern votes in 1860. Various Lincoln intimates have claimed that Lincoln sagely confided his strategy, "I am after bigger game. . .The battle of 1860 is worth a hundred of this." 34

And so the story goes: smart, slick Stephen A. Douglas walked right into the trap. In the rematch in 1860, Lincoln bested the Little Giant, who had been victimized by a Southern walk-out from the Democratic convention over a) the refusal of Northern Democrats to include a fugitive slave clause for the territories, a direct response to Douglas' "Freeport Doctrine," and b) their detestation of Douglas. When he visited Freeport in 1903, President Theodore Roosevelt, himself a historian of some distinction, bellowed, "Here was sounded the keynote of a struggle, which after convulsing the nation, made it united and free." 35

Told this way, Lincoln's second Freeport question and Douglas's Freeport Doctrine were critical to the division of the Democratic Party, to Lincoln's 1860 election, to the outbreak of the Civil War, to emancipation, and to the eventual reunification of the nation.

But beginning near the centennial of the debates and of the war that followed, professional historians did what they do best. Which is to say, they scrutinized this line of reasoning. And you can guess what happened. They noted that Lincoln advisors Norman Judd, Ebenzer Peck, and Joseph Medill had written to the candidate on August 27, urging him to use the first three questions. They found no documentation for Lincoln's sly "I am after bigger game" remark. (It first appeared in an 1860 campaign biography.) They noted that Douglas had been asked the question before, both in Washington and in Illinois, and had given in effect the exact same answer that he gave in Freeport. So had a number of other members of Congress, including some prominent Southerners, such as Speaker of the House James L. Orr and none other than Jefferson Davis of Mississippi (although Southerners had not spoken of enacting "unfriendly legislation." Their emphasis had been on the potential impact of the failure of territorial legislatures to enact "friendly legislation.") Davis, in fact, made substantially the same point in a speech at Portland, Maine only weeks after Douglas's Freeport appearance. And how would losing a race for the Senate offer a springboard to the highest office in the land? Wouldn't the Illinois *winner* be better positioned to claim the presidency?

Furthermore, Douglas had already sustained horrendous damage in the South earlier in 1858 by blocking Kansas' admission as a slave state under the Lecompton Constitution; the wounds were already fatal. So, career politician that he was, Douglas spoke to his base, for "any attempt to crawl back into the good graces of the slaveholders and the Buchanan administration would invite almost certain defeat" in Illinois, where a moderately free-soil (but anti-abolitionist) position would sway voters in those central counties to elect Democrats to the state legislature, where the vote would take place. 36

But Democratic papers such as the Washington *Union* and the New York *Herald* gave Douglas's comments on unfriendly legislation the same sort of pasting as had the Louisville *Journal*. The New York paper cried, "Is this the feast to which the author of the Nebraska bill has invited the South?" 37

And most of Douglas's slave state Senate colleagues picked up on the Illinoisan's new infatuation with the doctrine of "unfriendly legislation." And they made him pay when the Senate returned to session after the November elections. In December, the Southern-dominated Democratic caucus stripped him of the chairmanship of his beloved Committee on Territories. This was big; at a time when almost half of the nation's land mass was not yet organized into states of the Union, Territories was the most prominent of Senate committees. On the basis of his Freeport remarks, the caucus considered Douglas no longer a Democrat in the truest sense of the word. This must have stung the Little Giant badly given his devotion to the gospel according to Andrew Jackson. (Never mind that Douglas's position was eminently Democratic, for it sought to ensure local self-government while promoting westward expansion and migration.) James Henry Hammond of South Carolina reported that Southern senators and Buchananite northerners were "keen for his blood," and they attacked again in the winter of 1859. Davis and his Mississippi colleague Albert Gallatin Brown ganged up on Douglas in what Douglas's biographer calls a "running debate," in which Douglas repeatedly had to defend popular sovereignty. Echoing the New York *Herald*, and recalling the Nebraska bill, Virginia's James M. Mason shrieked across the Senate floor at Douglas, "You promised us bread, and you have given us a stone; you promised us fish and you have given a serpent; we thought you had given us a substantial right; and you have given us the most evanescent shadow and delusion." 38

Certainly Douglas had waded into these waters before, and Lincoln knew it; lawyers ask questions to which they already know the answers. What made the Freeport question so important historically was neither Lincoln's slyness, nor Douglas's professed astonishment, nor his stunning response; all of those were truly "non-events." Everyone who knew politics knew that Douglas wanted the people of the territories to decide for themselves on slavery in their homelands; everyone. Even Jefferson Davis and the aggrieved gentleman from Virginia, Mr. Mason.

What made the Freeport Doctrine political dynamite was its setting. If in 1976 Gerald Ford had opined that Poland was not under Communist domination somewhere other than a nationally-televised debate with Jimmy Carter, it would perhaps not have had the impact on voters that it did. Those voters doubted Ford's smarts, even while trusting his decency. In 1980 Ronald Reagan may have asked Americans hundreds of times, "Are you better off today than you were four years ago?" But when he raised it in a one-on-one debate with that same Jimmy Carter, it stuck. When in a 1988 debate with George H.W. Bush Michael Dukakis responded to a question on how he would react to the rape and murder of his wife with a bloodless answer that relied entirely on statistics relating to his state's falling rate of violent crime, it confirmed voters' unease with his technocratic lack of passion. Bill Clinton promising a young African-American woman that "I feel your pain," (while Bush checked his watch) . . . had Clinton—Clinton?—never used such a line before?

Southerners had seen Douglas as slick ever since the Lecompton fight. To a great degree, the Freeport Doctrine's importance lay in the confirmation of that perception. Douglas may have said nothing new at Freeport; but he had never before said what he said in the greatest fight of his political career, in a race that everyone knew he dearly needed to win, with a large press contingent following him closely. When—on the stump, in front of as national an audience as one could have in those pre-television days--he offered territorial settlers a back-door approach to making their territories free . . . .He was Ford, he was Reagan, he was Dukakis, he was Clinton in the perceptions of all who cared to read what he said.

And fire-eating Southern politicians did care. At Charleston, South Carolina in 1860, they broke the Democratic convention and the party when their demand for a federal fugitive slave code for the territories— "friendly legislation" in their mind--failed to garner support from the Douglas wing of the party, Northerners who had in the Little Giant's 1858 race seen the depth of free state opposition to such protections for territorial slavery. In doing so, men like Jefferson Davis attempted to head off the enactment of the sort of territorial "personal liberty laws" that Douglas had so helpfully suggested territories consider, and that had since 1850 driven Southerners to distraction when enacted by states such as Massachusetts. And they delivered the presidency to the Republicans.

Chapter Three: "Why Didn't You Shoot Him?"

"...And Not One to the Interests of the White Man"

Buoyed by a stronger performance in Freeport, Lincoln left that Republican bastion and set his face for Egypt and the appointment with Douglas in Jonesboro. Thus far he had enjoyed home field advantage; he would not be so fortunate in the rugged hill country of Union County, country green and undeveloped and wedged between the Mississippi and the Ohio. He had seen a hostile crowd unhinge his rival under the slug-gray late summer skies of Stephenson County, but in Jonesboro *he* would face the hostility of Southern migrants, and he had to make sure that he did not fluster as easily as had his more famous rival. (Although Douglas would himself receive a less enthusiastic reception in Egypt than he had predicted in Ottawa. Many southern Illinois Democrats clung loyally to the Buchanan administration and its preferred candidate, Judge Sidney Breese. They craved a Douglas defeat. A handful of prominent northern Illinois Democrats, such as the powerful Chicago postmaster, Isaac Cook, had also jumped Douglas's ship. Douglas had once used his influence to replace Cook as Chicago's postmaster. After the Little Giant ran afoul of Buchanan, the President pointedly returned Cook to office.) 1

Making the best of a bad situation, Lincoln used the weeks between Freeport and Jonesboro to work his way through the critical central regions of the state, testing themes that he hoped would win over onetime Whigs, free-soil Democrats, and nativists. He also logged many miles over the roads and rail lines of central and southern Illinois.

On August 30, three days after the triumph at Freeport, he appeared at Tremont, southeast of Peoria in Tazewell County. The next day he headed south to Carlinville, southwest of Springfield in Macoupin County. Two days later he swung back north and spoke at Clinton, in DeWitt County, north of Decatur and south of Bloomington. (In Clinton he may or may not have coined the phrase, "You can fool some of the people some of the time. . ." Lincoln scholar Thomas Schwartz doubts it.) Then further north to Bloomington itself, on September 4. On the morning of the seventh he spoke in Tolno and Mattoon in Coles County. Later that day, Lincoln visited Paris. (The one near the Embarrass River, not the Seine.) He reversed field again, crossing the state to give a major speech in Edwardsville, east of St. Louis, on the 11th, and then traveled back northeast to Greenville, in Bond County, for a speech on September 13, two days before his showdown with Douglas in Jonesboro. 2

Nor was Douglas idle. Having left the unfriendly north, the Little Giant set out on an equally strenuous tour, traveling mostly in a private car bequeathed by a former US Army officer, the chief engineer of the great Illinois Central Railroad, George McClellan, a Democrat. Douglas's campaign train had that portable cannon mounted on one car, and the gun crew could announce the Senator's arrival well before the crowds—many of whom had never laid eyes on the Washington insider who represented them—could see him. 3

Republican newspapers delighted in mocking Douglas's public appearances. The correspondent for Galena's *Weekly North-Western Gazette* wrote of a question-and-answer session in Pontiac that Douglas "constantly dodges and seeks to evade an honest avowal of his opinions, by crying out 'Nigger!' or 'averring that a man is a fool to ask him a question he is afraid to answer.'" The *Gazette's* reporter asked Douglas, "If a person holds a slave in a Territory by virtue of the Constitution of the United States, in which there are no 'police regulations' enforcing his right to hold such property, and that slave goes into a Free State, can he be recovered as a Fugitive Slave, under the provisions of the fugitive slave law?"

When we put this question to him, he looked at us as though he would take perfect delight in eating us up, or would derive exquisite pleasure in knocking the daylights out of us. Approaching us, with upraised hand and flashing eye, shaking his shaggy locks, and fairly trembling with rage, he answered: "Yes, sir, he can be captured under the Fugitive Slave

Law!" He then commenced a volley of billingsgate which would make a fishmonger blush, calling us an Abolitionist; that we were in the habit of going round lecturing in church basements, making abolition harangues, after the fashion of Lovejoy and other pincushion lecturers.

"The little giant is doomed," announced the *Gazette,* and "the apprehension of this fact, we presume, causes him to use the passionate and insulting language for which he has become so noted in the present canvass." 4

For his part, Lincoln tended to drive home five recurring points in the series of speeches prior to Jonesboro. He claimed to be an heir of Henry Clay. He attacked Douglas's crabbed reading of "all men are created equal," (since Douglas had contended that all that famous phrase meant was that the American colonists had as much right to self-government in the 1770s as did the people of Britain.) He repeated Douglas's role in the reopening of the slavery agitation. He reiterated his own denial of any plans to introduce social or political equality between the white and black races. And he attempted to claim kinship with the Founding Fathers who had foreseen the "ultimate extinction" of slavery.

He also used the word "nigger" with greater frequency.

Lincoln sought to deflate Douglas's allegations of abolitionism, and to inoculate himself against charges that he was a philosophical kinsman of Giddings, Lovejoy, Salmon Chase of Ohio, or of "Fred" Douglass. Lincoln labored to lay to rest any suggestion that he was soft on the Negro Question. His opposition to territorial slavery, he vowed, flowed from his concern for white working folk. At Carlinville, he all but led off by asking the rhetorical question, "why this fuss about niggers?" Minutes later, noting erroneously that the Taney Court had made blacks "property anywhere in the light that horses are property," he admonished the crowd not to vote for Democratic candidates. "Sustain these men and Negro equality will be abundant, as every white laborer will have occasion to regret when he is elbowed from his plow or his anvil by slave niggers." Here, stunningly, Lincoln spoke out against equal opportunity for blacks and whites in the job market, blaming Roger B. Taney of all people for promoting this radical doctrine. 5

He drove on, "where is the justness of extending the institution to compete with white labor and thus to degrade it? Is it not rather our duty to make labor more respectable by preventing all black competition, especially in the territories?" Lincoln quoted his Peoria speech for neither the first nor the last time in the 1858 campaign, (". . .What next? Free them, and make them politically and socially, our equals? My own feelings would not admit of this; and if mine would, we well know that those of the great mass of white people will not . . .We can not, then, make them our equals . . .") The Republican candidate then wrapped up on a particularly dismaying note to 21st century readers. The Senator "pretends to be horrified at amalgamation, yet had he not opened the way for slavery in Kansas, could there have been any amalgamation there? If you keep the two races separate is there any danger of amalgamation? Is not slavery the great source of it?" Douglas had said "he does not care whether they vote slavery up or down in Kansas," so who, asked Lincoln, "is the most favorable to amalgamation, he who would raise his finger to keep it out, or I who would give my vote and use my lawful means to prevent its extension . . ." 6

Lincoln liked this line of argument so much that he used it again. In Clinton, he denied Douglas's charges that Republicans wanted whites and blacks to intermarry, and denied that his party wanted to "elevate black men to office and associate with them in terms of perfect equality." After yet again quoting the Peoria extract, Lincoln crowed, "In the slave States there were, in 1850, three hundred and forty-eight thousand mulattoes—all of home production; and in the free states there were no less than sixty thousand mulattoes—and a large number of them were imported from the South." 7

. . . Imported to places such as central and southern Illinois, areas where no white politician desperate for the votes of white workingmen could go wrong by denouncing "race mixing" as beyond the pale. By treating miscegenation as a subject for knowing laughter, and by alluding to "home production" of mulattoes, Lincoln could also subtly play on class tensions, as all knew that the Southern master class was the main source of that home production.

Lincoln continued along these politically shrewd but morally questionable lines, playing on white anxiety over the blackening of the western plains. In Paris he attacked Douglas' claim to have originated popular sovereignty. What *was* popular sovereignty, anyway? "Was it the right of emigrants in Kansas and Nebraska to govern themselves and a gang of niggers, too, if he [sic] wanted them?" Charging that Douglas had claimed ownership of an idea first broached by Senator Lewis Cass, Lincoln argued that, "it never occurred to Gen. Cass to call his discovery by the old name of 'Popular Sovereignty.' He had not the *impudence* to say that the *right of the people to govern niggers* was the *right of the people to govern themselves.* His [Cass's] notion of the fitness of things were not moulded [sic] to the brazen degree of calling the right to put a hundred niggers through under the lash in Nebraska, *'a sacred right of self-government.'* . . . [Douglas] discovered the right of the white men to breed and flog niggers in Nebraska was POPU-LAR SOVEREIGNTY!" 8

Lincoln went further in Bloomington, suggesting that whites such as the people of Illinois had much to fear from the spread of slavery. Reviving the charge that Douglas was "preparing the public mind" for the "next" Dred Scott decision, Lincoln asked his audience to ponder what would happen next: "When the public mind *is* prepared for it, the decision will come." Having "stricken down the principles of the Declaration of Independence, and thereby consigned the negro to hopeless and eternal bondage, are you *quite* sure that the demon will not turn around and rend you? Will not the [white] people be ready to go down beneath the tread of any tyrant who may wish to rule them?" 9

Assuring crowds that he had voted for Clay, Harrison, Clay again, Taylor, and Winfield Scott, ridiculing Douglas for his reading of the Declaration and his role in restarting sectional tension, Lincoln had in his swing south appealed to Whiggish central Illinoisans to do the *right* thing (to block slavery's expansion by voting Republican) for what now look like the *wrong* reasons: to deter interracial sexual relations, to ward off economic competition by blacks (although the slaveholders would be the true sources of that competition), and to protect *their own* claims to equality. As regarded the last of these, Lincoln asserted that in some undefined way the equality of blacks, an equality that would be neither social nor political, would be a means to an end, with the end being more secure freedom for *whites*. Not Lincoln at his best.

Still, as he neared the face-off in Jonesboro, Lincoln said some things which suggest that the journey to Union County had its redeeming moments. In Bloomington, after the obligatory Peoria passage—he did love that speech!— he turned on Douglas's claim to serve as the standard bearer for Henry Clay's principles. The Bloomington *Pantagraph* reported Lincoln's assertion that, "Clay always denounced slavery as unjust." But incredibly, Douglas had never once in public indicated whether he thought slavery right or wrong. Douglas was thus a far cry from Henry Clay, and a bad bet for the people of Bloomington. 10

And, it seemed, for the voters of Edwardsville, a southern Illinois town not far from a region of the state notorious for its support of the fugitive slave laws. There, Lincoln drew a strong contrast between the Republicans and Democrats: "the former consider slavery a moral, social, and political wrong, while the latter *do not* consider it, either a moral, social, or political wrong." Lincoln would not charge that the Democrats considered slavery to be right, but each measure of the Democrats "has corresponded with this notion of utter indifference whether slavery or freedom shall outrun the race of empire across the Pacific—every measure, I say, up to the Dred Scott decision, where, it seems to me, the idea is boldly suggested that slavery is *better* than freedom."

Lincoln wound up with a passionate appeal to the Edwardsville voters' compassion and to their concern for their own cherished liberties, reviewing the Democratic-sponsored measures taken to further cement slavery into the life of the nation:

> Now, when by all these means you have succeeded in dehumanizing the negro; when you have put him down, and made it forever impossible for him to be but as the beasts of the field; when you have extinguished his soul, and placed him where the ray of hope is blown out in darkness like that which broods over the spirit of the damned; are you quite sure that the demon which you have roused *will not turn and rend you?* What constitutes the bulwark of our own liberty and independence? It is not our frowning battlements, our bristling sea coasts, the guns of our war steamers, or the strength of our gallant and disciplined army. These are not our reliance against a resumption of tyranny in our fair land. All of them may be turned against our liberties, without making us stronger or

weaker for the struggle. Our reliance is in the *love of liberty* which God has planted in our bosoms. Our defense is in the preservation of the spirit which prizes liberty as the heritage of all men, in all lands, every where.

Lincoln was hitting his stride, advancing and embellishing themes that he'd introduced in Bloomington and other venues.

Destroy this spirit [he continued], and you have planted the seeds of despotism around your own doors. Familiarize yourself with the chains of bondage, and you are preparing your own limbs to wear them. Accustomed to trample on the rights of those around you, you have lost the genius of your own independence, and become the fit subjects of the first cunning tyrant who arises. 11

He looked over the Egyptians arrayed before him, towering over them from the speakers' platform.

"And let me tell you," he shouted, "all these things are prepared for you with the logic of history, if the elections shall promise that the next Dred Scott decision and all future Dred Scott decisions will be quietly acquiesced in by the people."

"Loud applause," reported the Alton *Weekly Courier*. 12

After a speech in Greenville two days later, Lincoln and his tail of reporters and supporters would descend, dusty and tired, on Jonesboro. Lincoln spent the night of September 14 in nearby Anna (a newly-incorporated town a mile east along the north-south railroad line, already beginning to pass backwater Jonesboro in prominence.) He stayed at the home of David Layman Phillips, the Republican facing the unenviable task of running for Congress in the Ninth District. The ink-stained wretches spent a restless night in Jonesboro's one hotel. One complained of a "day of semi-starvation and the night with half-a-dozen roommates" at the Union Hotel. 13

Douglas and his wife Adele arrived the next day, having taken the steamboat to Cairo, where John Logan and George McClellan headed the welcoming committee. (McClellan supported Douglas throughout this campaign, and spent time with the Senator frequently. Douglas's drinking astonished him.) The party then road the rails north. Lincoln, returned from a morning carriage ride west with Phillips, his son, and a local doctor, could hear the cannon thundering from the south, bearing Douglas and a trainload of loyalists. 14

By 2:00 p.m., Douglas and Lincoln stood on the speakers' platform in a grove at the Jonesboro fairgrounds before a paltry 1,200 to 1,500 spectators. Republican newspapers, which had already needled the people of Egypt as backward, would jeer that the locals arrived in "old oxcarts that looked 'as though they were ready to fall in pieces.'" Attendance also suffered from the fact that the debate was held on a Wednesday, and at the same time as the state fair in nearby Centralia. 15

The *Tribune* reported that "the brass cannon was subdued with difficulty," and Douglas rose. Quickly, the senator moved to a new theme, specially tailored to his Egypt audience. Playing on a time-honored theme of demagogic white politicians, one that even Lincoln had recently used, Douglas told the crowd that gains for blacks would come at the expense of whites. By implication, the whites who would suffer would not be the big men; it would be the small farmers driving the broken-down oxcarts who would feel the pinch. Douglas spat out the news of a Republican convention in New York which adopted a platform "every plank of which was black as night, each one relating to the nigger and not one to the interests of the white man." Later in his opening, Douglas needled New York and Maine for allowing free blacks to vote; Maine even allowed blacks to "hold office in equality with the white men." Proclaiming his trustworthiness on this issue, Douglas shared this uplifting nugget, to laughter and cheers: "I had occasion to say in a discussion with the Senator from Maine last session, that if they thought the white men within the limits of their State were no better than Negroes, I would not quarrel with them, but they must not come to Illinois and say that my white constituents were no better than Negroes." Having trotted his foe down to Egypt, Douglas would try to engage Lincoln in a contest to see who could best portray himself as a defender of the white man's status.

Otherwise, Douglas said many of the same things that he had said in the north. He again noted the now dubious "Springfield" platform, gambling that his audience didn't care that he had erroneously placed Lincoln at its drafting. He chided Republicans for changing their views as they moved South ("Republicans or Abolitionists at the North . . . Anti-Nebraska men when they got down about Springfield, and down here they talk about the impolicy and inexpediency of the repeal of the Missouri Compromise . . .") He trotted out his favorite bogeyman to raise hackles in Union County. In northern Illinois, "you find Fred. Douglass, the negro, following Gen. [Lewis] Cass, and attempting to speak in behalf of Mr. Lincoln and Trumbull and abolitionism against that illustrious Senator." Douglas also noted Fred's scandalous Freeport carriage ride, and elements of the crowd shouted "shame" as he reached his line about the white husband "having the honor to drive the coach to convey the negro."

It wasn't easy defending the rights of embattled white men, either, not when your enemies had ganged up on you. By the time he'd gotten to Springfield, called Douglas, "I was brought into discussion on the one side against Mr. Lincoln, Lovejoy, Trumbull, Sidney Breese,"—the *Times* reported laughter at the Danite's name amid the Republicans—"and Father Giddings, the high priest of Abolitionism and [Ohio's Salmon P.] Chase came before I left."

Someone, no doubt a descendant of the rough-hewn earliest settlers of Egypt, barked out, "Why didn't you shoot him?"

Douglas cheerfully answered, "Why I had to take a running shot at them, single handed against the crowd, and as they were so big a drove, white, black, and mixed, I had to take a shot gun and fire at the crowd instead of taking them single handed with the rifle." The crowd laughed and cheered Douglas's fantasy of gunning down his "drove" of tormentors. Not exactly Douglas at his most statesmanlike. (And who was the "mixed" one? Lincoln the race mixer?)

Douglas then covered yet again the elevation of Trumbull over Lincoln to the Senate in 1855, noting in passing that "Lovejoy, the high priest of Abolitionism [can you have *two* high priests?] brought in resolutions defining the Abolition creed," and required all Republican delegates to pledge themselves to these resolutions. Although Lincoln thought he had an agreement with Trumbull, "Trumbull violated the bargain, and played a Yankee trick on Lincoln the very first time they came to a division of the spoils." At this last line, reported the pro-Douglas *Times,* Lincoln sat "greatly agitated, his face in his hands."

As Douglas narrated Lincoln's humiliation, which, the Senator explained, could only be assuaged by assuring him the 1858 nomination, the *Times* interjected (amid reports of a cheering, laughing crowd) "Lincoln looking very miserable . . ."; "Lincoln looking as if he had not a friend on earth, although Herr [Herman] Kreisman whispered 'never mind' in his ear." At another juncture the *Times* reported "A groan from Lincoln and great laughter."

Douglas launched familiar attacks on the house divided doctrine, on Lincoln's criticism of the Supreme Court, and on the Republican's use of "all men are created equal." Why can we not exist half-slave, half-free, he called? Under that arrangement, "we have increased from four millions to thirty millions of people. We have extended our territory from the Mississippi to the Pacific Ocean. We have acquired Texas and the Floridas . . ." Douglas reached a little beyond reality when he argued that the nation had grown "in naval and military power beyond any example on earth till we have become the terror and admiration of the civilized world," all under a Constitution denounced by Lincoln as "a violation of the law of God." Minutes later he proclaimed that the terror of the civilized world should advance its interests by acquiring Cuba. When—not if—we took that island (with its slave-based sugar cane economy) we should "leave the people of Cuba to decide the question of slavery for themselves without the interference of the federal government." One suspects that "the people of Cuba" to whom the Senator alluded would be white migrants who spoke English with Gulf Coast drawls.

Earlier Douglas had sounded a favorite theme that seemed to settle the question. This government was made "on the white basis," of, by, and for white men "and their posterity." The signers of the Declaration knew what they meant by "all men are created equal," even in the Republicans did not. The Fathers "had no reference either to the negro or to the savage Indian or the Feejee, or the Malay, or any other inferior or degraded race when they spoke of the equality of men." (Douglas allowed that this did not mean that blacks *had* to be slaves, but he followed at length on the idiocy of northeastern states allowing blacks to vote and hold office.)

The *Times* reported "three hearty cheers for Douglas." The *Tribune*, for its part, preferred to close its transcript of the Little Giant's opening remarks by mocking Douglas's artillery and his personal secretary. As Douglas spoke, "the brass cannon was fired at intervals; and a young person on the stand with weak legs and fiery mustaches, who accompanies Mr. D as a letter writer, shot in such expressions such as 'Hit him again' 'Bully for you&c.'"

"He Must Have Been Out of His Mind"

Just after 3:00, Lincoln rose. The *Times* sneered that "one of the numerous peddlers who haunt these meetings, mounted a seat and cried out in a feeble voice for Lincoln, whereupon some five persons in the crowd halloed."

At least Jonesboro had seating. Maybe. Local traditions suggest that the only chairs were on the rough-hewn speakers' platform, anchored on one side to a large tree. Whatever the case, the *Tribune* saw Lincoln's reception differently: "Mr. Lincoln was then introduced by D.L. Phillips, Esq., and was greeted with three cheers, and then three more." 16

He looked out over the small, unfriendly crowd. Union County local historians and long-dead eyewitnesses have contended that a pack of fiddlers started playing as soon as Lincoln began speaking, and that Douglas had to stand up and ask them to stop. Somewhere out there was the good citizen who had shouted that Douglas should have shot Salmon P. Chase, Lyman Trumbull, Lincoln, and various high priests of abolitionism. 17

"I hope you won't make fun of the few friends I have here," said Lincoln. "That is all I ask."

This set the tone for many of Lincoln's remarks in Jonesboro. He contended, "There are very many principles that Judge Douglas has stated that I most cordially approve, and there need be no controversy over them." These included the right of states (though by implication not the territories) to do as they wished on slavery. Again and again he would tred softly in this hotbed of Democratic white supremacy, having gone to school on Douglas's dismaying dust-up with the crowds in Freeport.

Nonetheless, knowing that his remarks would be reported beyond Egypt, he needed to distinguish himself from his foe, and he needed to give the lie to Douglas's repeated charge of pandering for votes. So he quickly went to "the exact difference between us." Douglas had "changed the policy from the way in which our fathers originally placed it." The Fathers had intended to preside over slavery's exclusion from the territories, allowing it to gradually whither away; but "Judge Douglas and his friends have changed that policy, and placed it where it shall spread until it becomes alike lawful in all states, old as well as new, North as well as South." In this, charged Lincoln, Douglas could count as his "friend" the vicious Congressman Preston "Bully" Brooks, who in 1856 had responded to a biting abolitionist speech by Senator Charles Sumner of Massachusetts by marching onto the Senate floor and pounding Sumner about the head and shoulders with a gutta-perch cane. Sumner had collapsed unconscious in a pool of own blood, Massachusetts had left the Senator's seat unfilled in silent rebuke to the "slave power," and Brooks, recalled Lincoln, "was complimented by dinners and silver pitchers, I believe, and gold-headed canes" throughout an adoring South. 18

Gingerly, Lincoln took on Douglas's reconstruction of the great Trumbull/ Lincoln falling out of 1855. "I don't want any harsh terms indulged in here, at all, but I know not how to deal with that persistent telling of a story, when I do know that it is not true. I don't know how to meet that sort of an argument," said Lincoln. "I don't want to have a fight," continued Lincoln, sounding for all the world like the biggest, but nicest kid on the schoolyard menaced by a smaller, tougher bully.

And then he turned: ". . . I know of no way of working an argument upon it into a corn cob and stopping his mouth with it." The *Trib* reported laughter and applause at the image of the bombastic Douglas silenced by a corn cob. Lincoln added that Douglas' account of the supposed split depended heavily on a speech from a long-time Lincoln associate, James Matheny. "I hope the Judge will not be angry if I have not the highest confidence in documents that he produces since he produced the Springfield resolutions." Although many of those in the Jonesboro audience may have missed the reference, Lincoln was speaking to a broader reading public.

Defending his House Divided doctrine yet again from Douglas' charge that the Republican wished to introduce uniformity among all the states on all things, Lincoln assured the audience that he had no such intent as regarded the various state laws and customs regarding agricultural and industrial production. These local ways of life and the laws that govern them "don't make a house divided against itself. They are the props of the Union; they sustain and really hold up the house." But slavery was different: "have we not had quarrels and difficulties about it in all time," asked Lincoln, "and when is it expected that we are to cease to have quarrels and difficulties about it?"

As that gloomy question hung in the humid Egyptian air, Lincoln leveled with his audience.

"Now, I want to talk to this intelligent people—very few of whom I expect to be my political friends—I want to ask them if this agitation will cease with all the cause of the agitation still existing." Here, in deep southern Illinois, in front of a hostile crowd, in a region that seems in retrospect to have been at least as Jim Crow as any of the post-Civil War upper South states, Lincoln went right up to the brink of, of . . .abolitionism.

But then a more ambiguous, equivocal follow-up: "Do you expect that the Almighty will change the constitutions of men, or that the nature of men will be so changed that that same cause will cease to agitate them? Will Judge Douglas be able to persuade men to accept these views? Will Judge Douglas be able to persuade all these men so that the cause will cease to agitate?"

These three sentences lacked clarity, just as to us they lack moral courage. Lincoln's next sentence after his rhetorical question on whether the agitation would cease without the cause of the agitation ceasing looked at first glance like a call for the eventual end of slavery (the "cause of the agitation.") But that was not what Lincoln was thinking. Instead, he seems to have seen the "cause of the agitation" as having been the negation of the Fathers' providing for the "ultimate extinction" of the peculiar institution. In other words, as long as we continued to bar slavery from territories (such as the old Northwest, in the ordinance of 1787), the house would not divide.

But did the fathers provide for the ultimate extinction? They had barred slavery north of the Ohio River, but Lincoln was speechifying in a region which had thumbed its nose at the framers through its embrace of "registered servant" laws, laws that protected a form of slavery. And the founders had placed no restrictions on slavery in 1787 when organizing the oft-forgotten Southwest territory, from which the slave states Kentucky and Tennessee (and eventual super slave states Alabama, Mississippi, and Louisiana) would be carved. They included a fugitive slave clause in the Constitution, and later enacted enabling legislation, thus protecting the peculiar institution. They permitted the Atlantic slave trade to continue until the year before Lincoln's own birth, and in debates in 1807 they body-slammed an attempt to curtail the domestic auction block. Henry Clay, in Lincoln's mind the greatest "son" of the Founding generation, had pushed through legislation in 1820 opening further southwestern lands to slavery and welcoming in a new slave state across the Mississippi from Egypt. Clay had also supported Douglas and Cass in implementing "popular sovereignty" in the newly-drawn Utah and New Mexico territories in 1850.

The problem with Lincoln's rhetorical question to "this intelligent audience" is that the Founders and their most august successors had not really put slavery in the course of ultimate extinction; at best they had done a half-hearted job of it at the national level. And perhaps for good reason. For to dare South Carolina and Georgia and the Daniel Boone types who populated the trans-Appalachian Southwest to peel themselves off from the promised Union would have been even more devastating to subsequent American history than the terrible consequences of keeping slavery intact until the 1860s. As multiple nations arose, divided, unified, sought new *lebensraum*, the continent might have become just another Europe or Asia with frequent, bloody, recurring border wars in which black and white casualties might have approached or exceeded those of other continents.

But make no mistake about it: at Jonesboro and throughout the campaign Lincoln was endorsing an only slightly less timid form of appeasement of the slaveholding South. No real action taken against slavery, but the return to a modest policy of containment. If not identical to the fathers' policy that relied on rivers and latitude lines to demarcate the line of freedom, at best a new, improved version of it. When would Mississippi have freed its slaves under Lincoln's House Divided doctrine?

Lincoln then spent a substantial amount of time turning the tables on Douglas, citing examples of Democrats—Douglas Democrats—who had endorsed views on slavery close to Lincoln's own, and at variance with Douglas' position. Just as Douglas had attempted to tar Lincoln with abolitionism by association at Ottawa and Freeport, now Lincoln would carry water for the Danites by suggesting that Douglas—Douglas!—was himself a fellow traveler. Citing the example of Thompson Campbell, an 1850 Democratic candidate for Congress in the Galena district, Lincoln noted that Campbell had voiced his opposition to the admission of any new slave states, had supported the repeal of the tough new fugitive slave act, had called for the election of an aggressively pro-Northern House Speaker, and had backed federal regulation of the interstate slave trade, which Campbell characterized as "'this most inhuman and iniquitous traffic.'"

From his seat, Douglas cut in, "Please to give the date of that letter."

Lincoln replied, "The time he ran was in 1850. I have not got it on the paper, but my understanding—indeed I am quite confident of it that it was in 1850—some time in 1850, Mr. Campbell was elected to Congress" over Martin P. Sweet. When Campbell failed in his bid for re-election, continued Lincoln, shifting his remarks away from Douglas and back to the crowd, "his very good friend, Judge Douglas, got him a very high office from President Pierce, and sent him to California." Enjoying the fruits of his foray into opposition research, Lincoln crowed, "Now, is that not so? I think that is so!" And better yet, "Judge Douglas and myself, on the 22nd of last month met at Freeport, and here was the same man, Tom Campbell, spoken of, as come back all the way from California to help Judge Douglas, and there was Martin P. Sweet 'sneaking about'. . . ."

Lincoln caught himself; he turned to the reporters and said, "I take back that ugly word. . .you must not put that in."

Then he finished the sentence. Martin P. Sweet was in Freeport ". . .doing all he could to help me along." (The *Tribune* reported it as, ". . .to help poor me get elected.")

Lincoln did not stop with Campbell; there was the Democratic Convention held in Joliet in 1850, which had nominated Dr. R.S. Molony. The convention had resolved, "That we are uncompromisingly opposed to the extension of slavery." Lincoln had seen handbills in Freeport, he said, announcing that Molony would be speaking in support of Douglas.

Lincoln reeled off the list of Cook County delegates to the Joliet Convention: "E.B. Williams, Charles McDonnell, Arno Voss, Thomas Hayne, Isaac Cook, F. C. Sherman—" Lincoln halted, taking a second look at the list, noting the most prominent northern Illinois Danite's presence at the convention.

"I reckon we ought to except Ike Cook."

The *Tribune* reported laughter at Lincoln's barb.

". . . John Hise, William Reddick. . ." The *Tribune* reported another Lincoln gag. "William Reddick! Another one of Judge Douglas' friends that stood on the stand with him at Ottawa, at the time the Judge says my knees trembled so that I had to be carried away!" As the audience laughed, Lincoln closed his whimsical attack: "The names are all here."

Lincoln kept going, noting similar Democratic resolutions from Naperville, and he was about to introduce Democratic resolutions from Douglas's native Vermont when someone called, "Your time is half over!"

The *Times*—but not the *Trib*--reported that Lincoln gasped, "*I did not know I was wasting time in that way.*"

He probably had not wasted time, even if he had horsed around a lot. He *had* taken a calculated risk. The whole point of the exercise was to make Douglas look like a free-soiler. That would serve Lincoln's purposes in Egypt, where he knew his own cause was lost, but where a strong Danite vote for the more reliably white supremacist Democrat, Sidney Breese, might cost the Little Giant needed support in a close race. On the other hand, in the all-important central regions, making Douglas look like an opponent of slavery's expansion might strengthen the incumbent's support, costing Lincoln dearly. Lincoln gambled that a strong repudiation of Douglas in southern Illinois would negate any gains that Douglas might make in the central districts.

Lincoln then teased Douglas for flip-flopping on whether he had or had not said that the question of territorial slavery was a question for the Supreme Court to decide. Lincoln noticed his opponent's reaction.

"He shakes his head! Now I want to appeal to these people, did he not say it was a question for the Supreme Court to decide? Has not the Court decided the question? Now does he not say that it is a question for the people? Does he not shift his ground?"

The Jonesboro audience had been much less disruptive than the northern audiences, and Lincoln, who had started by begging the crowd not to torment his few friends, seemed to have gained confidence. He put a "fifth" question to Douglas, a menacing one, too, for Douglas' prospects in 1860: Lincoln asked for Douglas' position on a congressional fugitive slave code for the territories, a question that Douglas asked Lincoln to repeat.

He seemed to be enjoying himself immensely by now. So much so, that he took up his notebook and quoted at length an article on the debates from the September 9th issue of the Mobile *Republican*. Lincoln read Douglas' comments to that paper:

'You know at Ottawa, I read this platform, and asked him if he concurred in each and all of the principles set forth in it. He would not answer the questions. At last I said frankly, I wish you to answer them, because when I get them up here where the color of your principles is a little darker than in Egypt, I intend to trot you down to Jonesboro. The very notice that I was going to take him down to Egypt made him tremble in the knees so that he had to be carried from the platform. He laid up seven days, and in the meantime held a consultation with his political physicians, they had Lovejoy and Farnsworth and all the leaders of the Abolition party, they consulted over it, and at last Lincoln came to the conclusion that he would answer, so he came up to Freeport last Friday . . .'

"Well," shouted Lincoln, studying the crowd and perhaps laying the clipping aside. The crowd waited for an outraged rejoinder; certainly Douglas, were the roles reversed, would spit gall at such a slanderous account. Men had fought duels over such comments; even Lincoln had once been headed for such a duel, with James Shields over near Alton, until cooler heads had ended it.

"I know that sickness furnishes a subject for philosophical concentration," he continued and the crowd laughed, according to the *Trib.* ". . . and I have been treating it that way, and. . ."

And? And?

Lincoln announced, "I have really come to the conclusion (for I can reconcile it no other way) that the Judge is crazy."

More laughter.

"If he was in his right mind, I cannot conceive how he could have risked disgusting the five thousand of his own friends" at Ottawa, who knew that no such thing happened.

A voice, Douglas's voice, called out, "Did they not carry you?"

"Yes sir!! Now this shows the character of this man Douglas. He smiles now, and says, 'Did they not carry you?' You have said I had to be carried. He sought to teach the country that I was broken down—that I could not get away; and now he seeks to dodge it. Why did you not tell the truth?"

To "great laughter and cheers," Douglas answered, "I did."

Ignoring the Giant's response, Lincoln moved on to the charge that he had been "laid up for seven days," and restated his revolutionary new thesis: "I say there is no charitable way in the world but to say he is crazy."

And, when Douglas inferred that "I would not come to Egypt if he did not make me—that I would not come to Egypt at all, unless he, giant-like, forced me," the crowd laughed, ". . .Judge Douglas, when he made that statement, must have been crazy—he must have been out of his mind, else he would have known that promises, and windy promises of his power to annihilate Lincoln would not be sustained at all."

Had some part of Lincoln feared real trouble in Union County? If so, the trouble had not arisen; and Lincoln was already celebrating his survival in this hostile territory. "Now, how much do I look like being carried from here? Now, let the Judge come back on me in his half hour, and I want you, if I can't get away from here to let me sit here and rot, unless I am able to carry him to the tavern," a neat bank shot at Douglas's drinking habits. (Perhaps fearing the loss of the temperance vote, the *Trib* changed "tavern" to "hotel.")

Lincoln wrapped up with an appeal to the people of Egypt. "What did the Judge think about trotting me here to Egypt and scaring me to death? Did he suppose that he would be able to make his friends turn on me and hurt me?" Invoking his own Southern origins, Lincoln contrasted himself with the Vermont-born Democrat: "I know this class of people better than he does. I was raised among this class of people, I am part of this class of people. The Judge was raised farther North. He perhaps had some horrid notion about what they might be indeed to do to him."

Before ending, Lincoln returned to Douglas's boasted superiority in debate. "I don't want to call him a liar, yet, if I come square up to the truth, I do not know what else it is. I do not want to do any fighting," shouted Lincoln. Then he added, cryptically, "I want to reserve my fighting for a proper occasion."

With ten minutes still to go, Lincoln was through for the afternoon. "I suppose my time is really out, and if it is not, I will give up" he shouted.

". . . and let the Judge set my knees to trembling."

He sat.

"To Slander the Grave of His Father"

Douglas had trotted Lincoln down to Egypt, and the annihilation had not thus far taken place, at least not by 4:30 p.m. Instead, Lincoln's cracker barrel wit and some well-done opposition research had left the challenger standing and the audience chuckling.

What now? Douglas had only thirty minutes in which to win this debate. Douglasites in the crowd cheered and applauded as the great man rose, only to hear him fall back on a familiar line.

"I am very grateful to you for the enthusiasm you exhibit but I will say to you in all frankness that your silence during my half-hour will be more agreeable than your applause, for so much would your applause deprive me of the time to reply."

"All right," called voices from the audience, "Go ahead, we won't interrupt."

Douglas must have consciously or unconsciously decided during Lincoln's comedic final minutes not to try to enter a contest for laughs. The senator was not by nature as funny as Lincoln, so this probably made sense. And he would never again in the four remaining debates appear before as Democratic a gathering as this one. He had to hit hard. He had to save the day by making the most of this last half hour before the debates headed back north. Unfortunately, Douglas went priggish.

He vowed "to make a serious comment upon the serious complaint of his about my speech at Joliet." Confessing that he had said then "in a playful manner" that Lincoln had trembled and had had to be carried off, and that it had taken a week to work up replies to Douglas's Ottawa questions, Douglas then swerved back, reworking the fantastic charge: "That he didn't walk off the stand he won't deny; that when the crowd went away with me, a few persons took him on their shoulders and led him down." The *Times* reported laughter at this. "And," bellowed Douglas, "whenever I degrade my friends or myself by allowing them to carry me on their backs through the public streets when I am able to walk, I will be willing to be deemed crazy."

According to the *Times*, this went down well with the crowd, as people called "all right," while--having seemingly left his prominent spot at the front of the debate platform--Lincoln lurked, "chewing his nails in rage in a back corner." If Lincoln was doing this, his mood had swung rapidly, from being the life of the party to being beside himself with rage.

Brushing aside the revelations on Campbell's and Molony's anti-slavery statements, Douglas went back on the offensive. It was Lincoln whose supporters were the real abolitionists. "Farnsworth, who is the candidate of his party in the Chicago district, made a speech in the last session of Congress, in which he appealed to God to palsy his right arm if he ever voted for another slave state, whether people wanted it or not. There is Lovejoy, too, making speeches all over the country for Lincoln, and declaring against the admission of any more slave States," and Washburne in Galena, and in fact "every man running for Congress in the Northern Districts takes that Abolition platform as his guide. . ." Since Republicans were saying no such things in the central and southern regions, "his party represents the extraordinary spectacle of a house divided against itself, and consequently it cannot stand."

The *Times* reported a "hurra" on that last line; but Douglas's better-informed supporters knew that the Democratic house faced the real "division." The division that Douglas attributed to favorite targets such as Farnsworth, Lovejoy, and Washburne (what, no high priests? No Fred Douglass?)—were child's play compared to the severe rift within the Democratic ranks embodied by Sidney Breese, Isaac Cook, and Dr. Charles Lieb, and by segments of the sparse crowd arrayed before him.

Douglas then turned on Lincoln's claim to Egyptian pedigree. Mischaracterizing the Lincoln family's status—they owned no slaves, and Thomas Lincoln probably left Kentucky and migrated to the free states to flee competition from slaveholding farmers and planters—Douglas scolded his opponent. "I don't know that a native of Kentucky who was raised among slaves, and whose father and mother were nursed by slaves, is any more excusable when he comes to Illinois and turns Abolitionist, to slander the grave of his father and the institutions under which he was born and where his father and mother lived."

Desperation seems to have set in. Douglas was wildly guessing that Lincoln's family had held slaves, and that his parents had been born into slaveholding families. But none of the Lincolns had owned slaves. Douglas chastised Lincoln for disloyally becoming an 'Abolitionist," after having migrated to Illinois from a slave state.

Douglas was fortunate that he advanced this argument at the debate's tail end. Had Lincoln gotten another shot at his foe, he might have turned the tables on the Little Giant. What was less honorable, Lincoln might have asked, to be born in a slave state and to later become an opponent of slavery, or to be born in a free state, and become a manager of a Mississippi plantation employing hundreds of slaves? Republicans made very little of this issue throughout the campaign until its last week, and it might not have scored Lincoln many points in Egypt. But Douglas had certainly opened himself to the question, and it is hard to imagine modern-day campaign operatives allowing Lincoln *not* to make that a sixth question for the Little Giant.

Still, Douglas could not leave his Jonesboro audience with the impression that Lincoln had created, that Douglas was what we would later call a carpetbagger, and from abolitionist New England to boot. So, after paying cursory tribute to his native Vermont, he recalled his trip to Middlebury College to receive an honorary doctorate of law. The same degree, he told the crowd, that Harvard had once bestowed upon Andrew Jackson. Making one last "plain folks" stab at the audience's loyalties, Douglas recalled, "When they had given me my degree, they read it in Latin, and I give you my honor that I understood just as much of it in Latin as Old Hickory did."

The crowd laughed.

Douglas recalled the speech he delivered, and his migration to Illinois. As the Senator's heart swelled "with gratitude and emotions as I looked out upon the mountains and valleys, I told my friends that Vermont was the most glorious spot on the face of the earth for a man to be born in, provided he migrates when he is very young."

The crowd erupted in laughter at the one-liner. (Douglas also deserved credit for using the word "spot" without making a wise crack about the Mexican War.)

He continued, "I came here when I was a boy," and soon "my mind was liberalized and my opinions enlarged as I got on those wide and expansive prairies, where only the heavens bound your vision, instead of having them bounded by the narrow little valley where I was born. . ."

Douglas concluded by reinforcing his commitment to the Freeport doctrine, and urging his audience to "sustain the Constitution as our fathers made it, maintain the rights of the States" and "sustain the constitutional authorities as they exist." By doing this, he promised, "we will have peace and harmony between the different States and sections of this glorious Union." To "applause" or to "prolonged cheering" (depending upon which Chicago paper you read) the Senator ended the showdown in Egypt.

Just in case three hours of oratory was not enough for the Jonesboro audience, For-God's-Sake Linder "being loudly called for" followed up after the debate's close with a short speech for Douglas. A popular local Danite, John Dougherty, followed Linder. In the words of one Republican paper, Dougherty "made a stirring Buchanan speech, denouncing Douglas in the strongest possible terms." 19

"The Most Ludicrous Failure"

Relieved that he had survived his journey to Egypt, Lincoln headed north for the state fair at Centralia, arriving there on the 16th. His redoubled determination caused him to write three letters from the local office of the Illinois Central. Each stemmed from the Jonesboro debate, and all showed Lincoln eagerly angling for political advantage, looking ahead to the next debates and to the election, now less than two months away.

One went to Elihu Washburne up in Galena. Noting that Douglas, "yesterday at Jonesborough [sic]" had alleged that Washburne had broadly proclaimed his opposition to the admission of any new slave states, Lincoln had two requests of the Congressman: "If his allegation be true, burn this without answering it. If it be untrue, write me such a letter as I may make public with which to contradict him." No return letter exists; Washburne's copy may well have gone into the fireplace. 20

To M. P. Sweet, whom he'd clumsily characterized as "sneaking about" in Freeport, he apologized:

... As my attention was divided, half lingering upon that [the Campbell] case, and half advancing to the next one, I mentioned your name, as Campbell's in a confused sentence, which, when I heard it, struck me as having something disparaging to you in it. I instantly corrected it, and asked the reporters to suppress it; but my fear now is that those villainous reporters Douglas has with him will try to make something out of it. I do not myself exactly remember what it was, so little connection had it with any distinct thought in my my [sic] mind, and I really hope no more may be heard of it; but if there should, I write this to assure you that nothing can be further from me than to *feel,* much less intentionally *say* anything disrespectful to you. 21

Lincoln added, "I sincerely hope you may hear nothing of it except what I have written." How much of this was political calculation and how much was sincere mortification over having disparaged a friend in public one cannot know. Lincoln needed the enthusiastic support of men such as Sweet to stand a chance at getting out a large vote in the northern districts; alienating him could harm Lincoln in a close race. At the same time, Lincoln's aversion to inflicting pain on others--Douglas excepted--lends the letter of apology a sincere tone. Lincoln resembled so many of us, who having said something that might get back to someone with hurtful consequences, fess up and express regrets, hoping for the best. 22

To Edwardsville's Joseph Gillespie, Lincoln wrote of news reports of the failure of Republicans and Know-Nothings in New York to join as one in that state's upcoming elections. Lincoln foresaw trouble, and hoped to head it off: "This fact may be seized upon to prevent a union in Madison Co., and I am more than ever anxious that you should be at home Saturday to do what you can. Please do not fail to go." Lincoln's entreaties to Gillespie reveal the elaborate scaffolding that the Republicans erected to displace Douglas, and their shamelessness: Gillespie was to work in Madison County to bring together the anti-immigrant "Americans" and Lincoln's own Republicans. Meanwhile, the Republicans worked mightily to win the support of German voters by wooing their great leader Gustave Koerner. (The Irish weren't worth the effort.) In a campaign in which Billy Herndon went so far as to travel to Boston to romance William Lloyd Garrison and Theodore Parker, the Republicans also provided clandestine support for candidates loyal to James Buchanan, the president who had applauded the *Dred Scott* ruling and who had tried to ram Kansas into the Union as a slave state. Defeating the Little Giant meant playing both sides of more than one street. 23

Lincoln allowed himself some modest boasting, reporting that the Jonesboro debate "was not large; but in other matters altogether respectable. I will venture to say that our friends were a little better satisfied with the result than our adversaries." He closed: "Be sure to go home to the meeting on Saturday." 24

The mere fact that Lincoln had not been vanquished in Egypt drew a telling reaction from the Republican newspapers. They did not so much laud Lincoln's performance as mock Douglas, beginning with his arrival in Anna the morning of the debate. Springfield's *Illinois State Journal* jeered, "When the train arrived at the [station] his cannon . . .fired his own salute, an [sic] a crowd of about a hundred persons rushed to the cars. He stepped forth, waved his hand, and nobody appearing to take any notice of him—(they are a *very* cool set of people down here, notwithstanding the hot weather they are having)—he went to a carriage prepared for him and left." The *Journal's* correspondent added, "There was no cheering—no anything." The paper then described three boys with Douglas banners and two brawny men with American flags attempting to organize a Douglas parade, "expecting 'the people' to follow them in procession behind Douglas' carriage—But 'the people' didn't!" The party of five marched up the street alone, "presenting a spectacle that excited the laughter and ridicule of 'the people'." The *Journal* concluded that "Douglas' reception here was the most ludicrous failure that we have ever witnessed in a political campaign." But the *Journal's* man should not have been surprised, for, he reported that on the train from Cairo, even though "the cannon was fired at every station, *not a solitary cheer was given,* nor any sign of enthusiasm manifested" for the Little Giant. The paper guessed that Buchanan Democrats predominated in Egypt, and then indulged in some wishful thinking: perhaps Egypt was "becoming Republicanized, or as the Douglasite libelers would say, '*Abolitionized!*' Jonesboro' itself, the very center of 'Egypt,' is a Republican town!" 25

Maybe so, but in the November elections, Republicans were thin on the ground. John A. Logan, the Democratic Mexican War veteran and erstwhile slave hunter, eeked out a victory in Union County in his bid for Congress by 819 to 65 over poor D.L. Phillips, Lincoln's host and Logan's Republican challenger. The Republican candidate for State Treasurer had even less success in Union County; *he* got 61 votes while the Douglas Democrat pulled 584 to the Danite's 462. Lincoln had survived his trip to Egypt, but he hadn't abolitionized many of the voters. Of course, he had not set out to do any such thing. 26

CHAPTER FOUR: "I WILL STAND BY THE LAW OF THIS STATE"

"I Can Just Leave Her Alone"

Three days after breaking the news in Jonesboro that his opponent was crazy, Lincoln took on Douglas on friendlier soil, in the rich farmlands of Coles County near the Indiana line. At nineteen, Lincoln and his family had entered Illinois from the Hoosier state. The family eventually set down roots at Goosenest Prairie, only eight miles from Charleston, the county seat. His stepmother Sarah Bush Lincoln still lived in the area, as did his boyhood chum (and kinsman) Dennis Hanks. Although he long ago had struck out on his own across state, first in New Salem and later in Springfield, Coles County must have felt something like home to the Republican. Politically the region was a toss-up. 1

Charleston saw the debate as an opportunity to showcase itself, and after the tepid response of the Union County crowd, the women, men, and children of eastern Illinois injected new life into the debates. Trains carried large contingents from as far away as Terre Haute, Indiana, and rollicking processions escorted both men to the county fairgrounds from nearby Mattoon, just to Charleston's west. Lincoln took the south road, Douglas the north. This time, no one could scoff at either man's entrance: the Douglas parade featured marching bands and 32 young women on horseback, each carrying a 32-star American flag flying from hickory or ash flagpoles in honor of Andrew Jackson and Henry Clay ("Old Hickory" and Clay's mansion, "Ashland.") Each rider represented one of the states of the Union. 2

Someone on one side or the other must have let spill the 32 states approach, for the Lincoln procession featured a "basket of flowers float," a large, double-decked wagon "draped in white silk and muslin" and trimmed in cedar with—guess what?--thirty-two young women inside. They wore white dresses and white hats, and red, white, and blue sashes, each bosom bearing the name of a state. A Goddess of Liberty stood at each end of this "ship of state." One banner read: "WESTWARD THE STAR OF EMPIRE TAKES ITS WAY/THE GIRLS LINK-ON TO LINCOLN/ THEIR MOTHERS WERE FOR CLAY." Behind the Republican float rode a lone female, Eliza Marshall, on a white horse bedecked with a banner that said "KANSAS" down one flank, and "I WILL BE FREE" on the other. Cracked Horace White, Robert Hitt's partner from the Chicago *Tribune*: "As she was good looking, we thought she would not remain free always." Another Republican journalist wrote that the "large and commodious Republican car" carried "thirty-two handsome young ladies." As for the Democratic procession, it could only muster a car "laden with sweet looking little misses, forming a handsome little group, which would have been much admired had they not been brought into contrast with the magnificent car load of charming young ladies, just ripened into womanhood." This admirer of feminine pulchritude "couldn't help sympathizing with the sweet little innocents, who were doomed to a seat in the Douglas car, and driven into competition with that splendid array of ripe beauty, in the Republican car." 3

The roads from Mattoon were of course dirt, and one imagines that those Republican beauties in white, the bandsmen, the local politicians, and the cheering crowds—as well as the two great men--would all have been coated in dust as they came into town. There, banners celebrated "ABE'S ENTRANCE INTO CHARLESTON THIRTY YEARS AGO," and "LINCOLN WORRYING DOUGLAS AT FREEPORT." The former showed a young Lincoln driving a team of oxen. The latter included an illustration of the challenger bashing Douglas to the ground; supposedly, when Douglas first saw it, he vowed to leave the procession were it not removed. (When the banner was brought up close to the speakers' platform at the county fairgrounds, Douglas insisted it be hauled down.) Another banner read "OLD EDGAR FOR THE 'TALL SUCKER,'" which doesn't seem like much of a compliment unless you know that Illinois was known as the "Sucker State," after the fish that swam its waters. Edgar County Democrats bore their own message: "EDGAR COUNTY 500 MAJORITY FOR THE LITTLE GIANT." 4

Local lore has enthusiastic Democrats lifting Douglas' carriage up off the ground, with the Senator and Adele inside, and hoisting it up and down as some yahoo called, "Three cheers for Douglas!" Someone persuaded the fellows to put it down; another local legend has Lincoln noticing his stepmother in the crowd by the roadside, stopping his carriage, and climbing out to give Sarah Bush Lincoln a hug and a kiss. One Douglas banner read, "THIS GOVERNMENT WAS MADE FOR WHITE MEN—DOUGLAS FOR LIFE." Another Douglas sign announced "NEGRO EQUALITY," and featured an illustration of Lincoln and a black woman. One Republican account of the debate sneered at a similar "slow-witted Douglasite" poster, showing a white man, a black woman, and mulatto child. The writer jeered that it "must be a picture" of Colonel Richard M. Johnson, the former Democratic vice president, who had scandalized white society by siring children by a black mistress. (Later, when the "Negro Equality" banner came close to the platform, Joseph Dole and Edward True jumped down into the crowd and destroyed the sign, nearly igniting a ruckus. Lincoln and Douglas joined in quieting the crowd.) Race would loom large in the minds of Charleston voters. In a July letter, Eliza Marshall's father, the county Republican leader Thomas A. Marshall had written to Lincoln, coaching him on how to handle all such queries: "That as for Negro equality in the sense in which the expression is used you neither beleive in it or desire it. You desire no temptations to negroes to come among us, and therefore you do not propose to confer upon them any further social or political rights than they are now entitled to." Lincoln would score few points with Coles' County's erstwhile Whig voters, many of whom shared his Southern roots, by repeating his Chicago plea that we stop quibbling about this race and that race. He would need instead to make a distinction between free-soil principles and the amalgamationist ideology with which Douglas had all along tarred him. 5

At about 1 o'clock, a "large mass of people began to move from the streets to the Fair Ground, about a mile west." By 2:45 on this Saturday afternoon 12 to 15,000 people crowded the ground. Thomas A. Marshall stepped forward from the 60 very important persons seated on the platform to introduce Lincoln. Lew Wallace (destined as a Union general to get his command lost at the Battle of Shiloh, and then to go on to write *Ben Hur*) attended as a Douglas supporter. He did not qualify for special seating. Standing near the back of the crowd, Wallace thought the distant platform "An island barely visible in the restless sea so great was the gathering." Wallace must have edged up closer, for he would later write that on that day he changed his allegiance to Lincoln, in part because he saw "a whole world of kindness" in the Republican's eyes. 6

Lincoln rose and, according to the *Tribune*, was "greeted with vociferous applause." No fiddlers, no straggly peddlers this time. Instead, cock-a-hoop from a spirited, encouraging performance in Jonesboro, he looked out over a fairly friendly crowd. He had to have realized that this represented one of his most important joint appearances with the incumbent. Coles County was the sort of central Illinois, agrarian, one-time Whig bastion that he needed to win. He must perform well, for this county was a toss-up. 7

And he then delivered what was probably the worst five minutes of political rhetoric in his life, and over the hour allotted him, surely his worst performance in the Lincoln-Douglas debates.

After taking a page from his adversary's book—"it is very important that as profound silence be observed as is possible"—Lincoln began a "little story," the kind of amusing yarn that he loved to rely upon to make a point to political associates his whole life.

"While I was at the hotel to-day, an elderly gentleman called upon me to know whether I was really in favor of producing a perfect equality between the negroes and the white people."

The crowd exploded in laughter.

As he let the guffaws die out, Lincoln continued, calling:

"While I had not proposed to say much about that subject, as that question was asked me, I thought I would occupy, perhaps, five minutes in saying something in regard to it."

It seemed a question that might deserve more than five minutes, but Lincoln had other urgent issues to attend to in his opening remarks. So:

"I will say then," he shouted, "that I am not nor ever have been in favor of bringing about in any way the social and political equality of the white and black races . . ."

The crowd applauded.

". . . that I am not, nor ever have been in favor of making voters of the negroes, or jurors, or qualifying them to hold office, or having them marry with white people."

He declared, "I will say in addition, that there is a physical difference between the white and black races, which I suppose, will forever forbid the two races living together upon terms of social and political equality, and inasmuch, as they cannot so live, that while they remain together, there must be the position of superior and inferior, that I as much as any man am in favor of the superior position being assigned to the white man."

But there was more. "I do not perceive that because I do not court a negro woman for my wife, that I must necessarily want her for a slave." The crowd cheered and laughed, noted Hitt.

Picking up on the laughter, Lincoln continued:

. . . My understanding is that I can just leave her alone. I am now in my fiftieth year, and certainly never have had a black woman either for a slave or wife, so that it seems to me that it is quite possible for us to get along without making either slaves or wives of negroes.

I will add that I have never seen, to my knowledge, a man, woman, or child that was in favor of producing a perfect equality, socially and politically, between the negro and white people . . .

Lincoln may not have met Frederick Douglass or William Lloyd Garrison, but these men were among the well-known Americans who did profess to believe in racial equality, so these words rang false. He then moved toward the punch line of his discussion of race:

"I recollect of but one distinguished instance that I have heard of a great deal so as to be entirely confident of it," he began, and as you read the transcript you can almost feel elements of the crowd grinning in anticipation of mischief to be done, "and that is the case of my old friend Douglas' old friend, Col. Richard M. Johnson."

The crowd laughed—derisively, one suspects--and according to the *Times*, people cheered, "Hurrah for Lincoln" and others answered back "hurrah for Douglas."

As the laughs again faded, Lincoln kept going.

"I will add to the few remarks that I have made," he said, reminding his audience, "I am not going to enter at large upon this subject," that he had "never had the least apprehension that I or my friends would marry negroes if there was no law to keep them from it."

Hitt reported laughter on that line.

But, shouted Lincoln, "as my friend Douglas and his friends seem to be under great apprehension that they may be if there was no law to keep them from it"—the hilarity built—"I give him the most solemn pledge that I will stand by the law of this State that forbids the marriage of white folks with negroes."

Continued laughter and applause, according to the *Tribune*.

But Lincoln was not done. "I don't understand," he called, "that there is any place where any alteration of the relation—the social and political relation of the negro and the white man would be changed except in the state legislature and [not] in the Congress of the United States," and as "I do not really apprehend the approach of any such thing myself, but as Judge Douglas does seem in constant horror of some such thing I do recommend that the Judge be kept at home, and be placed in the next legislature to vote it off."

The *Tribune* reported "uproarious laughter and applause"; the *Times*, cries of "'hurrah for Lincoln' and 'hurrah for Douglas.'"

Hitt also reported that Lincoln punctuated his remarks triumphantly, with, "I do not propose dwelling any longer at this time on this subject."

Lincoln then spent a scintillating 55 minutes defending Lyman Trumbull against Douglas's charge that the Republican senator had forged evidence in an attack speech against Douglas in 1856. Lincoln tapped heavily into a recent speech given by Trumbull in that senator's hometown, Alton. As at Ottawa, Lincoln used substantial blocks of time to read back segments of an earlier speech; and in this case an earlier speech by another politician. The Trumbull digression appears one of Lincoln's least effective segments in all of the debates, so much so that when he came back on ninety minutes later he confessed that he may have lost the crowd. 8

Lincoln sat down, finally. In some ways he had said nothing new on racial equality. In fact, as early as June 26, 1857 in a Springfield speech on the *Dred Scott* ruling, he had said, "There is a natural disgust in the minds of nearly all white people, to the idea of an indiscriminate amalgamation of the white and black races," and that Douglas wrongly claimed this disgust all for himself. Denying that Republicans wanted "to vote, eat, and sleep, and marry with negroes," he foreshadowed his Charleston performance. But in Springfield Lincoln had also defended that hypothetical black woman. In her God-given right "to eat the bread she earns with her own hands without asking leave of anyone else, she is my equal and the equal of all others." In August of 1858 he had returned to this theme in Ottawa, denying the social and political equality of the races but defending equality of economic opportunity for blacks. At Charleston, however, Lincoln left unspoken his earlier defense of the natural economic rights of African Americans, a telling omission. 9

Lincoln's Charleston remarks were partly the product of political calculation. All along, trusted advisors such as David Davis and Thomas Marshall had warned him to openly renounce racial equality. But these views were also of a piece with his commitment to the American Dream. To Lincoln the right to the fruits of one's own labor trumped the right to vote or serve on juries. In 1858, Lincoln would join the white supremacists on the latter—it's not unfair to say that he *was* a white supremacist on political and social equality—but he would not give an inch on the former. When it came to the right to improve one's own economic standing, Lincoln was no bigot. 10

Still, it wasn't what Lincoln had said (or had not said) in Charleston that disappoints so much as the way he said it. He treated the issue of racial equality as a big joke, the rhetorical equivalent of a round of locker room towel snapping. In a sort of race to the moral bottom he had tried to turn the tables on Democrats who labeled him a miscegentationist. Although Lincoln's hour may have played better to east central Illinois voters than it does to modern readers, it is hard to imagine exactly how . . . other than by acting like one of the boys on racial issues.

"I Thought I Was Running Against Abraham Lincoln"

Seeing opportunity in Lincoln's dreadful opening, the Little Giant attacked. Usually in debates such as these, the opening speaker lays out the questions that he hopes the debate will answer, said Douglas. "Let me ask you," he continued, "what questions of public policy has Mr. Lincoln discussed before you touching the welfare of the States or the welfare of the Union." The phonographers reported "great applause" and cries of "None, none!"

"Allow me to remind you that silence is the best compliment, for I need my whole time, and your cheers only occupy it."

Douglas bore in. He professed amazement that his opponent would spend so much of his time reading from Trumbull's Alton speech. He reiterated: "Why, I ask, didn't Mr. Lincoln make a speech of his own . . . ?"

And just in case anyone had missed his point, "I had supposed that Mr. Lincoln was capable of making a public speech on his own account, or else I should not have accepted his banter from him for a joint discussion, if I had supposed the whole time was to be occupied in reading Trumbull's speech instead of his own." Having made the point three times—he liked to make certain points three times before letting them go—Douglas heard applause, according to the *Times*. And then, a voice:

"Why don't you reply to the charge?"

Douglas's response was more temperate than it had been in Freeport.

"Now, sir, don't you trouble yourself, gentlemen; I am going to make a speech in my own way, and I trust that as Democrats listened patiently to Mr. Lincoln, that his friends will not interrupt me while I am speaking."

Douglas then took a few swipes at Trumbull, a former Democrat turned Republican, a colleague for whom Douglas had little respect or affection. He noted that a recent Trumbull speech was full of "assaults on my public character" that were "entirely without provocation." He reported that in Alton, his Senate colleague had vowed to "'cram the truth down any honest man's throat'" on Douglas's conspiracy to force a slave-state constitution on Kansas. Trumbull had also vowed to "'cram the lie down the throat" of any man who denied Douglas's role, "'till he shall cry enough!'"

"Here," fumed Douglas, "is the polite language of Senator Trumbull applied to his colleague when I was a hundred miles off."

"That's like him," called a voice, according to Henry Binmore of the *Times*.

"Why didn't he apply it in the Senate and cram the lie down my throat?" asked the Senator. When he'd been engaged in a "hand to hand fight" with Pennsylvania's Senator Bigler over the Kansas constitution, Trumbull had stayed out of it. "Why didn't he then rise and make the charge and say that he could cram the lie down my throat?" Trumbull only raised the Kansas conspiracy charges when "I was driving Mr. Lincoln to the wall until white men would not tolerate his rank abolitionism," a transparent attempt by Trumbull to salvage Lincoln's foundering candidacy.

Sensing that he'd worked the Trumbull point satisfactorily, Douglas rounded off:

"Are you going to elect Trumbull's colleague on an issue between Trumbull and me?"

Binmore reported laughter and cries of, "No, no!"

"I thought I was running against Abraham Lincoln. . ."

The audience laughed.

"I thought Mr. Lincoln intended to be my opponent. I thought Mr. Lincoln was discussing the public questions of the day with me;

I thought he challenged me to such a discussion, and it turns out that he is going to ride into office on Trumbull's back and Trumbull is going to carry him by falsehood into office."

"Cheers," reported the *Times*.

Having entertained the crowd by mocking Lincoln's turgid hour, Douglas changed tone. He now became the wounded fighter who had tried to take the high road.

When the campaign began on that hotel balcony in Chicago, with Lincoln by invitation seated nearby, Douglas had referred to his opponent "in terms of kindness and respect as an old friend," as a person of "respectable character, of good standing, and of unblemished reputation. . .I had nothing to say against him." And the Senator had repeated these remarks many times, "until he became the endorser for these and other slanders against me." Douglas lamented that "If there is anything personally disagreeable, unkind, or disrespectful in these personalities, the sole responsibility is on Mr. Lincoln, Trumbull, and their backers." He continued, "you see that the object is clearly to conduct the campaign on personal matters, hunting me down, and making charge after charge," but, shouted Douglas, "I am willing to offer my whole public life and my whole private life to the inspection of any man, or of all men, who desire to investigate it." This from a man who had spent "twenty-five years among you and nearly the whole time a public man, exposed, perhaps to more assaults and abuse than any man living of my age, or that ever did live."

It is impossible to know how these words went down with the crowd, but you have to credit Douglas as a trailblazer in American politics. 94 years before Richard Nixon's Checkers speech, Douglas resorted to the woe-is-me style, and his dodgy, take-a-look-at-my-public-and-private-life invitation foreshadowed countless scandal-ridden American pols.

Douglas then made the mistake of returning to the history of the two good old parties that had culminated in "the temporary excitement produced in this country by the introduction of the Nebraska bill." Phrased this way, some in the crowd might have shouted that the father of the Nebraska bill stood before them. Or that the "temporary excitement," which was really about murders and fraudulent votes and a violent attack on the Senate floor, came about largely because that same man had hoped to prove popular sovereignty's worth; to settle western territories peacefully and in orderly fashion; and to get the territorial slavery question off the floor of Congress all while furthering his own political prospects. He temporarily dodged that bullet, however, as no one had in the crowd the presence of mind to fire it. Perhaps Lincoln's deadly performance had taken the edge off the Republicans amassed before Douglas.

Douglas next played his own version of the race card, no doubt concerned that Lincoln had seemed altogether too white supremacist in his earlier minstrel turn. He noted that friends of Lincoln had tried to put "Fred. Douglass on the stand at a Democratic meeting, to reply to the illustrious Gen. Cass," and Binmore and Sheridan reported shouts of "Shame on them" from the Charleston throng.

But even worse, "They had that same Negro hunting me down," just as the Republicans "have a negro canvassing the principle counties of the North on behalf of Lincoln."

"Hit him again," the *Times* reported people shouting, "he's a disgrace to white people."

Why, Lincoln himself could verify that at Freeport, "there was a distinguished colored gentleman"—there was laughter at that line—"who made a speech that night and the night after a short distance from Freeport, in favor of Lincoln, and showing how much interest his colored brethren felt in the success of their brother, Abraham Lincoln." Douglas drew laughs with that last line, and the *Times* improved it, substituting "Abe" for Lincoln's full name in their transcript. Douglas added that he could read a speech given by "Fred." in Poughkeepsie, New York "in which he called upon all who were friends of negro equality and negro citizenship to rally as one man around Abraham Lincoln, as the chief embodiment of their principles."

Chief embodiment? Or chief mulatto? By mocking Lincoln as "their brother" Douglas went beyond merely saying that blacks were rooting for Lincoln. In 1848, 95% of Coles County voters had approved a provision to bar free blacks from Illinois. The incumbent had just watched his challenger make all sort of light of the notion of racial equality. The purpose pitch that he now threw Lincoln's way, in front of people who knew Lincoln's own family, raised questions about more than the Republican's sincerity as a white supremacist. It associated him with a taboo "tantamount to bestiality" in rural middle-nineteenth century central Illinois even while it established the Senator's reliability as a white supremacist. 11

Lincoln was not sincerely committed to white supremacy, implied Douglas, as evidenced by the Republicans' unwillingness to hold to one name and one set of principles in all regions of Illinois. They summoned to their ranks "Black Republicans" up north, "all men opposed to the Democracy" in Springfield, and the "Free Democracy" in Egypt. "When I used to practice law," called Douglas, "and the proof showed that a man charged with horse-stealing had gone by one name in Stephenson County, a second in Sangamon, and was arrested under a third down in Randolph, we thought the fact of changing names was pretty strong proof that he was guilty in the charge made against him."

Gaining pace, Douglas, asked why, if the "Black Republicans" believed in their principles, would they not hold to those principles north, south, east and west, "wherever the American flag waves over American soil?"

Someone yelled, "Don't call us Black Republicans."

"Why, sir, if you will go to Waukegan, fifteen miles north of Chicago, you will find a paper with Lincoln's name at the head, and you will find it said at the head of it, this paper is devoted to the cause of Black Republicanism." It was a much snappier response than had been Douglas's rantings at Freeport, and it drew applause, cheers, and calls to "hit him again."

Enjoying himself, Douglas returned to a favorite riff: "Their principles up there are jet black"—laughter, reported the *Times*—"when you get down into the centre they are a decent mulatto"—renewed laughter, wrote Binmore—"when you get down into lower Egypt they are almost white." Douglas let the laughter crest, before turning to Lincoln's opening speech.

"He said he was not in favor of the political or social equality of the negro, but he would not say up there that he was opposed to negro voting and negro citizenship." Lincoln had earlier "declared his utter opposition to the Dred Scott decision, and advanced as the reason that the Court decided it was not possible that a Negro should be a citizen under the Constitution of the United States." Douglas pressed deeper. If Lincoln opposed the decision on its denial of citizenship to blacks—a big "if" as Lincoln may have been even more opposed to the Court's denial to Congress of the power to bar slavery from territories—then the Republican *must* be in favor of citizenship for blacks.

In asserting that the Declaration of Independence and "divine law" made blacks equal to whites, Lincoln committed himself, said Douglas, to "negro citizenship." And, shouted Douglas, "when you grant negro citizenship, then you put them on an equality under the law."

The *Times* reported calls of "No negro equality for us" and "down with Lincoln" on that last line.

Douglas would leave no doubt in Charleston where he stood, just as he had left no doubt anywhere in Illinois:

> I say to you, gentlemen, in all frankness, that in my opinion a negro is not a citizen, cannot and ought not to be under the Constitution of the United States, I would not ever qualify my opinion, although the Supreme Court in the Dred Scott case say that a negro descended of African parents and imported into this country as a slave is not, cannot, and ought not to be a citizen. . .I declare that a negro ought not to be a citizen whether imported into the country or born here, whether his parents were slave or not. It don't depend upon the question where he was born, or where his parents were placed, but it depends upon the fact that the negro belongs to a race incapable of self-government, and for that reason ought not to be put on equality with the white man.

The "applause" or "Immense applause" that followed Douglas back to his seat said much about the political culture of the central counties where this election would be decided. Douglas had welcomed Lincoln onto the battleground of white supremacy, ground where the Little Giant, now triumphantly accepting congratulations from the Democrats on the platform, would not allow himself to be bested.

"Do We Have Any Peace on the Slavery Question?"

That did not mean that the Tall Sucker wouldn't give it one last try.

"Judge Douglas has said to you, I believe, that he has not been able to get from me an answer to the question as to whether I am in favor of negro citizenship. So far as I know, the Judge never asked me before. . . and he will have no occasion to ever ask again, for I tell him very frankly, I am not in favor of it. . ."

More applause, according to Hitt. And more laughter when Lincoln mockingly referred to "my disposition to produce perfect equality among the black and white races." The first five minutes of his opening speech had not been a mistake; Lincoln had said what he meant. Any quarrel Lincoln had with the black citizenship passages of the *Dred Scott* ruling did not stand on racial or moral grounds. Lincoln's objections stemmed from a Southern-flavored states' rights understanding of the Constitution. He shouted, "my opinion is, that the different States have the power to make a negro a citizen under the Constitution of the United States, if they choose. The Dred Scott decision decides that they have not."

And if the decision were reversed, what would he want his home state to do, having reacquired the power to grant blacks citizenship?

"If the State of Illinois had that power I should be against the exercise of it."

The *Tribune* reported "cries of 'Good, good,' and applause.

"That is all there is of that. That is the whole thing," concluded Lincoln.

Thankfully, he moved on. Douglas's attack on Lincoln's House Divided speech moved the Republican off his dispiriting stand-up routine on racial equality, off his weird digression on the Trumbull/Douglas feud, and back onto terra firma.

"Let me ask a few questions," raised by Douglas's Kansas-Nebraska Act.

As at Freeport, Lincoln the lawyer would now pose questions to which he and much of his audience already knew the answers. Douglas had already done his ninety minutes. The Charleston jury, Unionist and Whiggish (even if pretty white supremacist), would be left with Lincoln's questions, and without Douglas' answers.

Since Douglas's legislative workmanship became law, "Do we have any peace on the slavery question? Do we have any peace upon it?"[The *Trib*: 'No, no']

Lincoln cried, "When are we going to have any peace upon it if it is kept just as it is now? [The *Trib*: 'Never'] How are we going to have peace upon it?"

He answered his own question. "Why, to be sure, if we will just keep quiet and allow Judge Douglas and his friends to march on and plant slavery in all the states we shall have peace," jeered Lincoln. He reminded the crowd of the recurring clash over slavery in the west: the Missouri Crisis; the fight over Texas annexation; the Compromise of 1850; and finally Douglas's own Kansas-Nebraska Act, "when it was then settled forever," and "that forever turned out to be two years . . ."

Hitt reported laughter on that last line. Cheered on, according to the *Tribune*, by "immense applause" and "cries of 'Hit him again'," and "laughter and cheers," Lincoln shouted, "He tells us again that it is all over now. The people of Kansas have voted down the Lecompton constitution. How is it over?" Had Kansas entered the Union? Did her entry seem at all imminent?

Lincoln had come alive. He continued, "we can no more see where the end of slavery agitation is than we can see the end of the world itself . . .

If Kansas was swallowed up, and only a large hole was left in her place, it would not be settled . . ."

But how to settle it once and for all? Lincoln worked toward his own stock answer: ". . . to put it back on the basis that our fathers put it on," he said to cheers, according to Hitt, "restricting it to the old States and prohibiting it in the territories."

The *Times* did not report what Hitt and Horace White heard, "Tremendous and prolonged cheering," and "cries of 'That's the doctrine,' 'Good,' 'Good'. . ."

However the crowd responded Lincoln had advanced a dubious proposition. Fantasy it was to suggest that Preston Brooks and company would back off the territorial slavery question if Congress would only apply the Wilmot Proviso to all of the territories that Roger B. Taney and company had just thrown open to slavery.

Nonetheless, Lincoln had raised questions regarding Douglas's usefulness as a senator for Illinoisans who valued both the Union and the option of moving further west into "free-soil" territories, territories where they would not have to compete with slaveholders. If you cared about those two abstractions, you had two options. Lincoln had just supplied one.

"The other way is for us to surrender and let Judge Douglas and his friends plant slavery in all the States, and submit to it as one of the common matters of property among us, like horses and cattle."

(Another questionable statement, for Douglas would never support the re-introduction of slavery into the free states. It may have been demagoguery on Lincoln's part; but it was also the line of attack which had first drawn attention to his campaign months ago at the close of the Republican convention in Springfield.)

Nearing the end of this productive if fast-and-loose half-hour rejoinder, Lincoln then said something that boggles the mind of modern-day readers. He doubted, he called, that slavery could be ended in a day or in a year, nor could the institution "be brought to ultimate extinction in less then a hundred years, it would be carried on as best for the white and the black in God's own good time I have no doubt . . ."

Meaning that at the earliest America would abolish black slavery in time to make Dwight D. Eisenhower the Great Emancipator. And what did Lincoln mean by "carried on as best for the white and the black in God's own good time"? That it could be good for blacks to remain as slaves in at least some parts of the Union for the rest of their lives, and for their children to do so too, and for their grandchildren to spend at least some time in slavery? And that God might want it that way?

It is hard to know exactly what Lincoln meant by this, and to what extent the passage was his own true opinion versus a way to gain votes among a white supremacist audience that might fear a migration of freedmen into east central Illinois. Assuming that these were his own genuine feelings, one can only imagine that less than a decade later President Abraham Lincoln must have felt that he was in the middle of a revolution, a whirlpool, a cyclone as he signed the Emancipation Proclamation in 1863, and symbolically signed a copy of the 13th Amendment in 1865. On the fairgrounds in Charleston, in the midst of old friends and neighbors, Lincoln had predicted a proper and orderly end to slavery in the second half of the *twentieth* century; but five years later he himself would start the process in earnest. And a scant seven years after the Charleston debate Lincoln would lend the prestige of his office to killing the peculiar institution outright.

Douglas had been chivvying his challenger consistently, in Charleston no less than in the preceding debates, over Lincoln's Mexican War "Spot" resolutions, and suggesting that Lincoln had not supported appropriations to aid American forces. Lincoln decided to respond. The Judge "knows, in regard to that Mexican War" that Lincoln had in fact voted in favor of support for the war effort, even while opposing the war itself. Douglasite newspapers which had made similar charges "have been compelled to take it back and say that it was a lie."

But just in case the crowd didn't get the point, Lincoln would produce a surprise witness!

So saying, he turned to the assemblage of dignitaries and grabbed an old friend, the Douglas Democratic Congressman Orlando B. Ficklin, "by the left lapel of his coat," and, according to the *Times*, "literally dragged him to the front of the stand." (This was one of those times when Lincoln's size came in handy.)

The Republican then announced, "Now I do not dream to do anything with Mr. Ficklin more than to present him personally to your faces, and tell you that he knows it personally. He had a seat by my own when I was in Congress, and he knows that whenever there was an effort to approve the object of the war, I opposed it; I never denied that." Ficklin had not yet scrambled back to his seat, so Lincoln continued, "And he knows that whenever there was a call for supplies for the soldiers, I gave the same vote that he and Judge Douglas gave."

How would you like to have been Ficklin? Here you go to the debate, figuring that it's not exactly an off day, (no day is for a politician in a democracy) but it's a day where somebody else—two somebody elses—have to do the heavy lifting, speaking for ninety minutes each. All you have to do is show up, look like a respected leader, clap Douglas on the back after his speech, and be seen. And now this 6'4" friend of yours has clamped you in his powerful grip and put you on the spot. You've already been made to look silly, and now if you don't come up with the right answer to a question that you never dreamed you'd be answering in front of more than 12,000 people, the senior senator from your state, also a friend and one to whom you are pledged, will have your scalp. Why couldn't Lincoln have gone back over that Trumbull speech again?

Ficklin looked out over a crowd that must have been surprised to see him in a speaking role.

"I wish to say this," said the Congressman, "in reference to the matter."

What now?

"Mr. Lincoln and myself are just as good friends as Judge Douglas and myself. In reference to this Mexican war, my recollection is that on the Ashmun resolutions, in which it was declared unconstitutional, and commenced by the President of the United States, my friend Mr. Lincoln voted for the resolution."

It was a nimble response considering the shock that Ficklin must have felt. He had not answered Lincoln's question, but he had reminded the crowd that Lincoln had not supported a war won by the United States, a war that had brought the nation California and the southwest. Ficklin sat.

Lincoln allowed, "That is the truth." Then he returned to Douglas's repeated attempts to link the Republican to votes against the war effort itself, votes that Lincoln contended were always in favor of supporting our boys in uniform. "This is not the first time that he has said this thing," called Lincoln. Noting that "he did it in the opening speech in Ottawa," and that the charge was a decade old, he asked, now "isn't he a beauty to be whining about people making charges against him only two years old."

Which brought him back again to Trumbull. Even though Lincoln now admitted that in his opening, his comments on the two senators' feud "did not fix your attention," he made one last effort to get the Charleston crowd to see why they should care about Douglas's charge that Trumbull was using "forged evidence" in his attack on Douglas over the abortive Kansas constitution. To Lincoln, Douglas's part in that squabble said much about the way that Douglas fought when cornered, and by implication, much about the Senator's character.

"I take it that these people have some sense," he said of his audience, which had now crowded the fairgrounds for over three hours. It was nearing 6:00 p.m. And "I take it that he is playing the game of the fish, that he is playing the game of a little fish that has no means of defense but by throwing out a little black fluid so that its enemies cannot see it."

The *Tribune* reported "roars of laughter," and its transcription had Lincoln soaking in the laughter:

"Ain't the Judge playing the cuttlefish?"

Hitt wrote that the crowd called back, "Yes, yes," amid cheers.

After still *more* on Trumbull, Douglas, forged evidence, Alton, and the stillborn Kansas constitution, Lincoln sat, to cheers, according to the *Tribune*.

"The Prairies Are on Fire!"

The people of middle nineteenth century Illinois were an amazing bunch. Their appetite for politics and for political rhetoric seems superhuman. For after Lincoln closed, the Republicans marched to the courthouse lawn for a rally, with more speakers! And it wasn't just the Republicans who wanted more. Inside the courthouse, Democrats listened as For-God's-Sake Linder and Chicago's Richard Merrick followed up on Douglas's remarks. (Until some stealthy Republicans pulled one of the stock dirty tricks of ante-bellum politics, by extinguishing the lard and oxygen lamps, and plunging the meeting into darkness, and, in the words of one Republican, "driving the rabble. . .out in the yard with the Republicans.") There is no record of an ensuing fight; everyone may have been too tired to put up their dukes. 12

Whatever the case, days after the debate Chester Dewey applauded the Coles County citizens in the pages of the New York *Evening Post*. In an area "with one railroad and one special train, the turnout of the populace has ranked with the great meetings in the thickly settled northern portions of the State, intersected by railroads and steamboat routes, all pouring their special trains upon a common center." Dewey famously reported to readers that "the prairies are on fire!" Many *Post* readers may never have seen a prairie, but the message was clear: a little-known challenger stood to topple the greatest man in the dominant party in American politics, in front of passionate throngs of simple farmers. 13

In fact, Lincoln's performance had been uneven at best, and Douglas had performed with greater confidence. Nonetheless, the Republican *Weekly Belleville Advocate* wrote that *"Our first, last, and only choice for Senator,"* got so much the best of the debate" that Democrats "are ashamed of their idol." Passing up Lincoln's hour-long opening remarks (with good reason), the *Advocate* summarized Lincoln's half-hour closing for its readers, announcing predictably that it "finishes the little giant." Galena's *Weekly North-Western Gazette* also ignored the opening, publishing just the closing remarks, which it deemed "absolutely crushing. Every sentence tells; he piles up a pyramid of argument which Douglas cannot budge." Allowing that Douglas "was frequently applauded by his friends," the *Gazette's* man in Charleston surmised that "there appeared to be so much system in the thing, that we could not help thinking it was done in accordance with a programme long prepared for all such occasions in which Douglas figures." What was more annoying, during Lincoln's closing, "Douglas and some of his friends who were near us, continued talking nearly the whole time, so that it was impossible for us to hear much of what Mr. Lincoln was saying." (Then why had the *Gazette* termed those remarks "crushing?") The Republican paper huffed: "Great a demagogue as we knew him to be, from reading and hearing his speeches, we were not prepared for such an exhibition of ill manners in Judge Douglas." The *Gazette* called the applause that greeted Lincoln's closing so great that "nearly two-thirds were for him." (The *Gazette* got the right result, but overdid the margin; Coles County went Republican in the election, but Republican candidates for office only bested their Democratic opponents by about 300 votes out of roughly 3,400 cast. In the race for the state senate seat, Thomas Marshall defeated Linder.) 14

Meanwhile, the Democratic *Freeport Weekly Bulletin* chided Lincoln for his two-faced refusal to support "negro citizenship" at "Charlston," asking, "Now, will the Republicans condemn the Dred Scott decision after the above declaration from a man who is their *only* choice for United States Senator?. . . If he had uttered the same sentiments in this section it would have proven his sincerity more than it does after his abolitionism in the North." To its northern Illinois readers, the *Bulletin* jeered, "Dred Scott Decision Endorsed." So much for Lincoln's jet-black principles. 15

Despite Republican claims that Lincoln had vanquished the Little Giant, it was hard to see a debate victory for the challenger. Although he had regained his footing in his final half hour, his dismal opening hour had been his worst performance thus far, only approached by his interminable re-reading of the 1854 Peoria speech in round one at Ottawa. As much as Douglas had to be disappointed at the Jonesboro debate, Lincoln had to have left Coles County feeling unfulfilled. His decision to take up Trumbull's cause may have made sense in terms of repaying a key ally (and onetime Democrat) for his support, but it had little to do with selling himself to voters as a United States senator. For his part, Douglas had kept his cool on the one occasion when heckled, a skill he'd lacked at Freeport. He had taken advantage of Lincoln's ponderous performance, and he had driven home yet again the themes that would carry him through the campaign: white supremacy, Lincoln's shifting principles, the recklessness of the House Divided doctrine. Charleston's day in the sun had ended, and the Douglas and Lincoln show took a hiatus. The next debate, across state in Galesburg, would not take place until October 7.

Chapter Five: "A Monstrous Heresy"

"A General Melee Seemed Inevitable"

On September 23rd, one day after "a fine and altogether satisfactory" meeting at Danville, Lincoln wrote to Norman Judd that, "I believe we have got the gentleman, unless they overcome us by fraudulent voting" by Irish Douglas loyalists "imported" into the swing counties as railway workers. (Lincoln's solution? Counteract the Irish vote. Get German-speaking Republicans to places such as Vermillion County.) Meanwhile, the Illinois Central's president met with Judd and *Press and Tribune* editor John L. Scripps in Chicago, assuring them that the railroad would not interfere in the election. Four debates down and three to go, and Lincoln could see Washington, D.C. more clearly. Delicious it would be to go off to the Senate as the renowned slayer of the greatest man in the Democratic Party. 1

With a little more than one month to go in the race, the Republican had good reason to feel confident. Were one to score the first four rounds *a la* a boxing judge, Douglas might be called the winner at Ottawa, and Lincoln at Freeport. Simply because of his antagonist's inability to wound him in Egypt, you might give Jonesboro to Lincoln. Charleston had been an ugly performance to our modern eyes and ears, but Lincoln had rallied with a strong final half-hour's rejoinder. And remember: what counted was the capacity of Lincoln-pledged Republicans to get elected to the state legislature. Lincoln's Charleston debate comments may offend most of us today, but we weren't voting; to the white males of Coles County and vicinity, Lincoln's minstrel show in those first five minutes did not hurt at all (and may have helped.) Hadn't the crowd laughed, applauded, and cheered? Lincoln could come out of Charleston feeling as though he had fought Douglas to a draw. As of yet, the Little Giant had not finished his challenger, and every time that Lincoln held his own, Republican victory seemed more possible. Republicans seemed highly likely to carry the Ottawa and Freeport districts and in fact most of northern Illinois. And who knew what impact Sidney Breese, Ike Cook, the Washington *Union* and Dr. Charles Lieb might stir in Egypt? Increasingly, it seemed as though there were few areas the Douglas Democrats could consider safe.

Three weeks passed between Charleston and the showdown in Galesburg, a college town northwest of Coles County out near the Iowa line. Starting there, the debates would conclude with three tightly-spaced October encounters in the Mississippi Valley, all in towns with abolitionist pasts. This seemed to favor Lincoln.

Moreover, beginning at Galesburg, Lincoln would prove more willing, more committed to challenge the great man on moral grounds than ever before in these face-to-face confrontations. At Galesburg, for the first time in the debates, Lincoln found and sustained his moral voice, and he rode that music through to the series' end. Sometime after Charleston, the challenger took a giant step toward becoming Abraham Lincoln.

Both men raced from point to point during those three weeks, realizing that this election might go either way. The competition would actually intensify.

This caused heightened tension between the two campaigns, and it led to some rough and tumble just two days after the Charleston debate, in the town of Sullivan. Both men had scheduled appearances in that town on the same day. Douglasites contended that their man had announced the Sullivan appearance some six weeks earlier, and that Lincoln had returned to the obnoxious practice of appearing in Douglas' wake to "answer" his speeches. 2

Huddled with local Democrats Bushrod W. Henry, John Guin, Carn Knight, and John Y. Hill, Douglas received a visitor, George Lynn, Jr., bearing a pencil-written note in Lincoln's handwriting. Lincoln allowed that he had understood that the Senator had been scheduled to speak "before dinner" (read "lunch") and would be done with his speech by early afternoon. Hence he had announced that he would speak at Freeland's

Grove at 2:00 p.m. Having since heard that Douglas would instead speak at 1:00 pm., Lincoln proposed that if Douglas would announce Lincoln's change in plans, then Lincoln would postpone to 3:00. Douglas read the note, then scribbled a message accepting the terms. He handed it to Lynn, who carried it back to the challenger. 3

The Chicago *Times* reported that ninety minutes into Douglas's standard stump speech (references to Owen Lovejoy, Farnsworth, Trumbull, the Mexican War,) a blue-sashed Republican drove up to the rear of the crowd in a wagon and announced Lincoln's three o'clock appearance at Freeland's Grove, a few blocks away from the courthouse grounds where Douglas spoke. The interloper called for an escort of friends to lead the Republican to the grove. Democratic news accounts contended that the Republicans went out of their way to disrupt Douglas's speech, as a pro-Lincoln brass band imported from Indiana ("at unheard of expense") warmed up nearby with some tunes. And then, reported the *Times*, "the band marched on, followed by the few who were going to listen to the 'tall sucker'. . .the procession, if such it could be called, had faced in a direction opposite to the Abolitionist stand, with the evident intention of forcing a way through the Democratic meeting." And the *Times* correspondent reported, "Lincoln, as I am informed by a dozen men, was at this time in the procession . . ." 4

That was important; the Democrats would try hard to place Lincoln in the procession, for, according to the *Times,* "The blacks then advanced round the square" in front of the courthouse, where Douglas spoke, "taking all its sides, until they came to where the street was blocked by a portion of the Democratic crowd." As Republicans collided with Democrats, "A general melee seemed inevitable, but Mr. Douglas, leaving the stand, urged his audience to be patient." Still, reported the *Times*, "Blows were struck on both sides." The Indiana bandsmen, playing in a wagon, saw their vehicle "turned out of the road." The *Times* man smirked that the Hoosiers, "will probably return to Indiana with a lively remembrance of the agile manner in which they vacated their article." And then there was the Republican candidate himself, who "in his buggy, took the back track, went and laid by until three o'clock so as not to appear to have encouraged such a dastardly outrage by his presence." Republican buggies "wheeled about" in retreat, while the Republican "footmen" got out only with "great difficulty" at the hands of the Democrats. 5

Just in case anyone had missed it, Douglas immediately reviewed the dust-up. At 2:25, shouted Douglas, Lincoln "with his friends and a band of music, drove round the stand and came right up within forty feet of where I am now speaking. Driving in the midst of some of my friends, beating their drum so as to break up this meeting." Douglas called that the Republicans had "undertook to fight their way through." 6

A prominent Moultrie County Whig named Matthew Thornton called out, "Will any gentleman who saw Lincoln announce the fact?"

Someone sang out, "He was in, but turned around and went back."

Douglas shouted, "I do not know whether he was in the procession, but a gentleman at my side says that [he] was in the procession up to the time when a fight seemed likely to ensue, when he turned around and went in the other direction." 7

Potentially, this ranked up there with the rigid, sickly Lincoln being lugged off the stand at Ottawa as a virtual photo op for the Democrats. "[I]n violation of the written agreement which I hold in my hand," scolded Douglas, and seeing danger as a "preconcerted plan" to break up a Douglas meeting went bust, Lincoln fled the violence in his buggy. It was too good to pass up, especially since a respected old Whig had taken Douglas' side in this battleground county. 8

To make matters worse for Lincoln, neither Robert Hitt nor Horace White was on hand, and thus the Republican press would have trouble refuting the charge. So on September 26, the Chicago *Press and Tribune* ran an exclusive "special report" from an unnamed twelve-year resident of Moultrie County. Contending that the Democratic press had said nothing about Douglas's "hocus-pocus arrangement" at Sullivan, and suggesting that Douglas had intentionally moved back his starting time to deprive Lincoln of sufficient time to deliver his remarks, the *Tribune's* source said that one hour into Douglas's speech the Republican band headed for Freeland's Grove, and "the crowd began at once to disperse, and being more than half Lincoln men, the Little Giant began to beg not to leave them alone." Seeing that Douglas's "appeals to our charity had no perceptible effect," wrote the anonymous correspondent, "his friends thought they would adopt more potent measures." 9

And what sorts of friends did Douglas employ to restrain the crowd?

The first man who jumped into the street to stop the crowd is notorious in our community for two events. The first is that he tried his hand, a short time ago, at whipping his wife. In this he was successful—turning the poor woman into the street with her eyes discolored, and her person otherwise badly bruised. He afterwards bragged of the exploit. The other distinguished performance of this character was getting himself appointed a deputy officer to acquire the shelter of the law in shooting one of his neighbors, with whom he had had a fight in which he did not triumph as gloriously as when he fought his wife. This man and a few more of his political faith and social standing undertook to stop the crowd. The Lincoln boys knocked down three or four of them and the rest took to their heels." 10

The Quincy *Whig and Republican* ran a similar letter on October 11 forwarded to the paper by one J. G. Kearney. The letter contended that when the Republicans had approached the square, Douglas "gave orders to his friends to stop the procession and turn it back." So saying, "The Border Ruffians jumped over the fence, like a lot of bulldogs, yelling for their friends to come on. They threw rails in the spokes of the band wagon, clubbed and beat the horses most shamefully, and knocked the driver from his seat with a brick-bat, which struck him on the side of his head." Kearney wrote that by this time "we had all got *mad*, and the fight became general. It appeared as if all hell had been let loose." Six or seven combatants were "pretty badly hurt" on both sides, reported Kearney. The sides disengaged, and the Republicans marched to the grove. After which, reported the *Tribune's* source, Lincoln delivered his speech to a "much larger" crowd than had Douglas, a speech "infinitely superior in logic, manner, and morals." And although Democrats warned Republicans not to march around the town square that evening, "When speaking was over, we formed in procession, each man with a club in his hand—the Band playing Yankee Doodle. We marched all around town, and they never opened their mouths. . . We disbanded with three cheers for Lincoln forever." 11

But neither the *Tribune* nor the Quincy paper reported Lincoln's whereabouts during the incident; it did not put to rest the image of the lanky Republican flying from the brawl. And the *Times* did not let this go. Mixed in with some race-baiting it was simply too hard to pass up in the important central Illinois counties.

On the same day as the report by the anonymous Moultrie County Lincoln supporter ran in the Republican press, the *Times* reported on the two candidates' arrival at a fair in Urbana on the 23rd. There "Douglas spoke for two hours to one of the most attentive audiences" when Lincoln entered the fair ground at a far corner, "with a band of music, which he now carries with him (perhaps to show that he is not weak in the knees.)" Implying that Lincoln had learned his lesson in the clash at Sullivan, the *Times* wrote that the Republican "caused no disturbance or interruption whatever." But the sorry spectacle of "the pop-corn man, corn doctor, and other pedlars [sic]. . .Lincoln's most intimate friends" shouting their wares to scare up a crowd for Lincoln culminated in these lowlifes trying to sell their goods along with selling introductions "to their distinguished friend cheap as dirt." 12

And when Lincoln met a sword swallower, reported the *Times* correspondent, the Republican engaged in "interested conversation with him." Lincoln hefted the man's sword, announcing "his intention to hereafter carry a 'broad' sword always about his person, and to lop off the head of any man who should ever again, as at Sullivan, pitch the leader of his band out of a wagon, and invited the professor to accompany him and stand by him in the next trial of the kind." After the sword swallower promised to do just that, reported the *Times*, "they embraced and parted, not, however, before the professor had told Lincoln that he was his friend in principle, as he was partly of negro extraction himself . . ." 13

Himself? The implication was there for any central Illinois voter to take. Not only was Lincoln a coward, as the *Times* had earlier suggested; he was "partly of negro extraction," just like the sword swallower. Would Illinois be well represented on the floor of the United States Senate--where the great Henry Clay had once held forth--by a man who started and then ran from fights, a freak-show performer whose best friends sold popcorn and snake oil (the "corn doctors") and swallowed swords at county fairs, and who was himself a mulatto to boot?

Lincoln spent the weekend of September 25ᵗʰ at home in Springfield, seeing a wife and children whom he had not encountered for some time, and he left town at 7 a.m. on Monday morning after a Saturday night welcoming ceremony in which the Republican Clay Club serenaded him. (He also got hit up by one Henry Chew, an old acquaintance who needed money for furniture. Lincoln wrote a note pledging to pay $25 should Chew fail to make the necessary payments. In February of the next year, Lincoln had to pony up.) 14

On Monday, September 27, Lincoln arrived in Jacksonville at 11 a.m. and spoke in the afternoon. Then it was on to Winchester, where Lincoln was late. But he overtook his escort into town: "His horses were white with sweat and he and his friends were black with dust," reported the *Illinois State Journal*. After a speech and a barbecue, Lincoln wrote a poem in the autograph album of Rosa Hoggard, whose dad owned the hotel in which Lincoln stayed for parts of three days: 15

> You are young, and I am older
> > You are hopeful, I am not—
> Enjoy life, ere it grow colder—
> > Pluck the roses ere they rot.

> Teach your beau to heed the lay—
> > That sunshine soon is lost in shade—
> That *now's* as good as any day—
> > To take thee, Rosa, ere she fade. 16

Two days later, before leaving Winchester, he evened things up for Rosa's sister, Linnie:

> A sweet plaintive song did I hear,
> > And I fancied that she was the singer—
> May emotions as pure, as that song set a-stir
> > Be the worst that the future shall bring her. 17

So somehow, amid the rising intensity of the race, in amid the white-hot crucible of competition for the central counties, Lincoln was able to be something more than just a candidate for office; somehow he retained some vestiges of humanity in his dealings with people. Three days of relative rest in sleepy Winchester may have helped. That rest may not have been in the original campaign itinerary, but early in September, Jesse DuBois and Ozias M. Hatch had informed the candidate that the combination of the Morgan County Fair *and* a double hanging at Carrollton would require that Lincoln adjust his schedule. It looked as though "all Scott Co. will go to the hanging." Lincoln himself refrained from attending the execution. Instead, on the 29th he sat around examining back copies of the *Congressional Globe*, then delivered a speech in the evening. 18

Somewhere around October 1, Lincoln sat down, took pen in hand, and scratched an itch, dissecting the writings of pro-slavery theologians such as Reverend Frederick A. Ross, who had written and spoken on slavery's Christian propriety for the benighted black race. Lincoln wrote, "Suppose it is true, that the Negro is inferior to the white, in the gifts of nature; is it not the exact reverse justice that the white should, for that reason, take from the Negro, any part of the little that has been given him? '*Give* to him that is needy' is the Christian rule of charity, but 'Take from him that is needy' is the rule of slavery. . .But slavery is good for some people!!! As a *good* thing, slavery is strikingly peculiar, in this, that it is the only good thing which no man ever seeks the good of, *for himself*. . .Nonsense! Wolves devouring lambs, not because it is good for their own greedy maws, but because [it]is good for the lambs!!!" 19

As September ended, the itinerary intensified: October 1, Pittsfield; October 2, Naples; October 3 and 4, Metamora and Peoria; October 5, on to Pekin. Douglas may or may not have loaned people money and written poems but he too was on the move after Urbana: he hit Onarga; Kankakee; Hennepin; Henry; Metamora; Pekin; Oquawka; and Monmouth. 20

As Douglas dashed from town to town, smaller Republican presses such as Galena's *Weekly North-Western Gazette* goaded him. On September 21st, the *Gazette* had reprinted a piece from the St. Louis *Democrat* charging that Douglas "coolly assumed that he was the standard-bearer of the National Democratic party," but the Senator "was totally oblivious of the fact that the President is thundering excommunications against him every day," and "giving the offices which were held by his friends to his enemies, because they are his enemies." The *Gazette* went with the subtle approach in its next edition, headlining its piece on the Little Giant, "STEPHEN ARNOLD DOUGLAS: THE TRUTH IS NOT IN HIM," and opining that "none but mean, dirty little politicians" would tell the lies that Douglas had told of Lincoln. Quoting the Buchananite Washington *Union*, the Galena newspaper told readers that Douglas was "a vagrant politician" who was "the nominee of no party," the representative of no political organization. In contrast, Lincoln, wrote the *Gazette*, was "the very soul of honor," whose speeches had "used up the Little Giant" while giving the challenger "a national reputation which any man could be well proud of." The Republican weekly predicted that "with Trumbull and Lincoln as its Senators," Illinois would "not rank second to any State in its influence in our National Councils." The *Gazette* contrasted this with the supposed "Moral Bravery" of the incumbent, who "valiantly 'pitches into the nigger'. . ." Although the territories "should be kept free for the European emigrants and the white inhabitants of this country, he summons all his courage. . .shakes his shaggy locks, and amid the roar of his *cannon*,. . .he threshes the nigger in the fence, and the nigger in the field, and the free nigger and the nigger slave. . ." The *Gazette* sneered, "This is not only moral bravery, but it is statesmanship!!" Slaves were "utterly powerless to affect any change in their condition, and because they are weak and wholly unable to defend themselves, our Little—oh, how little—Giant exercises the immense powers of his mind in abusing them" as though "a dozen stalwart Irishmen should 'mount' a little boy, and ask a medal for their bravery, as if a man should beat a woman, and then demand a public ovation for his heroism."   21

And Quincy's *Daily Whig and Republican* charged that "Douglas is as persistent in the urging of his false and slanderous charges against Lincoln and the Republicans, as a blind bat is in flying against stone walls." The editors challenged "the little champion" to produce one legitimate reason why "Abraham Lincoln is not a better man, or an honester politician, or that he would not prove a more able or faithful Senator, than Douglas has proved himself."   22

Of course, small Democratic papers such as Freeport's *Weekly Bulletin* happily took up such a challenge. When Freeport's Republican *Journal* complained that Democratic editors were editing Lincoln's speeches so as "to read absurdly," the *Bulletin* jeered that the speech was "delivered *absurdly*. . .the whole thing was *absurd.*" It also raised an issue thus far left untouched: "In place of Judge DOUGLAS being the recipient of large sums from the Illinois Central Railroad Company, it turns out that Lincoln is hired and paid large fees to do any act that can rid the company of taxation, and saddle the same upon the people." The paper alleged that "For one case, the company paid Lincoln $5,000." (In fact, the railroad had coughed up the money after Lincoln had sued for fees due him in a case in which he had represented the Illinois Central.) And the *Bulletin* dripped sarcasm in its October 7 piece entitled "THE DECENCY PARTY." Lincoln's party, "convinced of the weakness and inability of Lincoln to reply to Judge Douglas, has been resorting to regular ruffianism in attempting to break up meetings Mr. D. was addressing." Citing the "blackguardism" of Republican crowds at Moline, the *Bulletin* urged their opponents, a party "that claims so much decency, if it wishes respectability," to "act as becomes white men—half civilized, at least." 23

For its part, the September 24 Jacksonville *Sentinel* returned to a trusty Democratic theme: white supremacy. The local Republican paper, the *Morgan Journal* had taken "open grounds in favor of Lincoln's doctrine of negro equality," and a Lincoln supporter had said in a speech "that a certain colored barber of this place, in all the attributes that constitute the man, was the superior of Judge Douglas." The *Sentinel* sputtered, "Oh, they don't advocate negro equality, not them!" Warming to the subject, the paper ran a piece entitled "BY THEIR WORKS YE SHALL KNOW THEM," warning readers that Republicans were trying to persuade central Illinois voters that the party did not support black equality. But, "they seek to reverse the Dred Scott decision, which would break down all the state barriers to negro citizenship. The clause in our state constitution requiring the Legislature to pass laws prohibiting the emigration of blacks and mulattoes into the state, was but carrying out in advance the doctrine of the Dred Scott decision." The *Sentinel* reported the roll call vote on an 1857 attempt in the state legislature to repeal the state's black code. All Democrats and Know Nothings had voted no; all but two Republicans had voted yes. 24

The heat rose, for the race would be decided in the "great battle ground" which lay "between the parallel of Peoria and the parallel of Alton," wrote the

Chicago *Tribune*. Informing its northern Illinois readers of the "fierceness and intensity," the "frenzy" of the struggle in this region, the Republican organ declared that "American politics have never developed so close and heated a campaign as the one now in progress within this parallelogram." Breathing hard, the *Trib* reported that "Every inch of ground presumed to be doubtful is contested with the energy of desperation." Moreover, "The eyes of the Union are riveted on the combatants," as Americans ignored "all other objects of political interest," for all knew "that the history of the Republic is shaping itself around the Illinois battle field." And the *Tribune* predicted that "whichever way the beams shall fall . . . that way will the nation incline in 1860," a presidential election year. Republicans, former Whigs, and Americans—the anti-immigrants, the "Know Nothings"—*must* elect Lincoln senator, for they would be "making the history of their country for many years to come." 25

All of this intensity could be draining. After the invasion by Douglas, Lincoln, and their rapidly expanding tail of journalists, bandsmen, and supporters had torn through Urbana and Champaign, the *Central Illinois Gazette* professed a certain level of exhaustion. Crediting local Republicans for listening "with much respectful attention" to Douglas, and pronouncing Lincoln's two-mile parade—especially its "lady equestriennes"—"one of the finest things we have ever seen," the *Gazette* professed relief that "things are beginning to settle down once more to their customary routine. The farmers have returned to their ploughs, the merchants to their places of business and the Editors of the Gazette are particularly well pleased to find themselves again under the shade of their own vine and fig-tree, with nothing to do but to provide for the intellectual recreation of their own rapidly increasing circle of weekly readers." 26

There would be no such respite for the two candidates, who descended on Galesburg one day after heavy rains and falling temperatures tested the willingness of the locals to attend the debates. By early Thursday morning, October 7, frost lay on the ground as cannons boomed. A campaign that had begun in the searing heat in Ottawa seemed to have found its way to early winter, and the roads to town were muddy and treacherous for the wagons and ox carts and buggies and feet that carried the curious and the committed to the campus of little Knox College amid harsh, howling winds that tore banners and sent hats flying and whisked campaign signs "pell mell all over town." Nonetheless, amid testing conditions, a crowd of perhaps 20,000—the largest turnout of all seven debates—swelled the town's population to four times its normal size. Many had slept in tents. 27

Douglas hit town at 10 a.m. on the eleven-car Burlington train; the local artillery company welcomed him. He rode in a carriage pulled by six white horses. Galesburg's Republican newspaper, the *Semi-Weekly Democrat*, reported that "a portion" of the students of Lombard College presented the Senator with a "beautiful banner" which was a "true circle of silk," and in his "well prepared but somewhat fulsome address," George Elwell "said the circle was emblematic of Mr. Douglas' course." And "So it was," snickered the *Democrat*, but "in a different sense from that meant by them." 28

Lincoln arrived at about the same time, and, reported the *Democrat*, the delegation that led the Republican into town was "of monstrous length. . . 'mammoth' would not describe it." T. G. Frost made a welcoming speech, and then the Republican ladies of Galesburg—represented by the "queenly" Miss Ada Hurd, riding at the front of (you guessed it) a troop of equestrians--presented Lincoln with "the most beautiful banner of the day." This was all part of what the Republican paper called "the most beautiful ceremony of the day." 29

The "rousing" Monmouth delegation caught the *Democrat's* eye with its banners. "Somebody down there is great on crayon sketches, as the banners of this delegation were of the most amusing kind." 30

These included a crayon sketch of Douglas and Georgia Senator Robert Toombs "erasing the clause referring the Kansas Constitution back to the people." In another, Douglas stood on a "Dred Scott platform" with one leg "giving away beneath." And in a banner entitled "'Coming form [sic] Egypt'. . . Douglas, roaring with rage, is being punched up with Lincoln's cane." 31

Other banners survived the wind long enough for the *Democrat's* man to report them. One had Douglas attempting to ride two donkeys, "Popular Sovereignty" and "Dred Scott." Kicking their heels, they pitched the Little Giant to the ground. In another, three figures swiped a chair from under Douglas, "dropping him plump upon the floor, at which he exclaims, 'Oh, my place!'. . .The *'place'* Mr. Douglas referred to was doubtless the portion which came into contact with the floor." A four-sided banner from the Macomb Lincoln Club read, "We honor the man who brands the Traitor and Nullifier." "Small fisted Farmers, Mud Sills of Society, Greasy Mechanics for A. Lincoln" "The dose of milk Abe gave Dug down in Egypt made him very sick." (South Carolina's Senator James Henry Hammond had earlier that year taunted northern workers as part of the "mud-sill class," little better than slaves.) Harking back to Lincoln's House Divided speech, Douglasites carried a "well-painted banner" with a roaring lion on one side and a dog on the other: "Douglas the dead Lion, Lincoln the Living Dog." According to the *Democrat*, the 'best banner upon the ground" featured a painting of a locomotive engine named "Freedom" trailed at high speed around a curve by a long line of "Free State cars. . .with the warning, 'Clear the Track for Freedom', while sticking upon the track a little in advance of the train was Douglas' ox car laden with cotton. His negro driver had just taken the alarm and springing up in terror exclaims, 'Fore God, Massa, I bleves we's in danger!'" The writer found "ludicrous" a double-sided rendition of Douglas attempting to bring Lincoln to milk in Egypt. On the other side, "Like Mr. Sniggs, in his first effort at milking a cow, he gave the customary command to '*histe*' the foot. Abe *histed*, and Douglas and his pail are seen 'laying around loose.'" The *Democrat* added that "Star spangled banners were numberless," and that "Lithographs of Douglas abounded." On the east side of Old Main, the central building of Knox College, a wide banner called, "KNOX COLLEGE FOR LINCOLN." 32

At approximately 2:30 p.m., the two candidates rode alongside one another in carriages to the college grounds. The awful wind had caused a hasty relocation of the debate platform from open ground to the east exterior wall of Old Main, the handsome brick building central to the campus. Off to the east stood a dormitory, fronted by a large pile of coal to see the students through the months of prairie cold; by day's end, legendarily, the coal pile would be flattened into the mud by the crush of citizens straining to hear the candidates above the moaning winds. Later the coal was dug up and put to use. 33

Local legend says that the only way for the debaters and dignitaries to mount the platform was to climb through a window, for the platform blocked the door. Lincoln is supposed to have joked: "Well, at last I have gone through college!" 34

Douglas would lead off. He knew the region well, for he had once represented a nearby district in the House of Representatives. Galesburg had then been a bit of an abolitionist hotbed, with its church (the product of the Presbyterian/Congregational union) and its small colleges. The coming of the railroad had brought workingmen, especially Irish workingmen, and the town had become a little less anti-slavery, a bit more a political toss-up. The Buchaneers' presence in Egypt made places such as Galesburg extra important to the Senator's shaky prospects of returning to Washington. 35

Taking a throat lozenge from a little box, he offered one to Lincoln. 36

Douglas shouted into the wind that "Four years ago I appeared before the people of Knox County for the purpose of defending my political action upon the Compromise measures of 1850, and the passage of the Kansas-Nebraska Bill in 1854," and he reminded them further that he stood by "a great fundamental principle, that the people of each State, each Territory, have the right, and should be permitted to exercise the right, of regulating their own domestic affairs in their own way, subject to no other limitations than that which the Constitution of the United States imposes upon them."

And then Douglas claimed something that he had not mentioned thus far in the debates. Here, in free soil (if not exactly abolitionist) Galesburg, Douglas did what he had chastised Lincoln for having done: he played to the locals. He invoked the Lecompton constitution fight, reminding the 20,000—or at least those that could hear him—that he had blocked Kansas' admission as a slave state.

"In my opinion, the attempt to force Kansas into the Union under that Constitution was a gross violation" of that principle. In fact "I led off in the fight against the Lecompton Constitution—conducted that fight until the effort was abandoned of forcing Kansas into the Union under it." He looked out over the flags, the banners, the signs whipping and curling in the gusts.

"During the whole of the fight, I can appeal to all men, friends and foes, Democrats and Republicans, northern men and southern, that I carried the banner aloft, and never allowed it to trail in the dust, and never lowered the flag until victory perched upon our banner." The *Times* reported cheers as Douglas paused. (The Little Giant's oratorical style, self congratulatory and florid, stood in contrast to Lincoln's, and never more than here; it is literally impossible to imagine Lincoln uttering that sentence. Still, however self-important he may have sounded, Douglas had cleverly claimed to have carried "our" banner.)

Douglas then called out that another "fundamental principle" of American government was that "all States of this Union, old and new, free and slave, stand on exact equality." He drove it home: "Equality among the States is the cardinal principle on which all of our institutions rest."

Lincoln did not jump out of his seat to contest this point; that sort of thing had not gone over well in Ottawa, a safe region, and it would have been even riskier here. But it is doubtful that Douglas ever said anything in the debates, *anything*, with which Lincoln would have disagreed more lustily. Douglas's assertion, that the equality of states was the founding principle of the republic, stood in direct contrast to everything that Lincoln would ever say, at least between the 1854 Peoria speech and the end of his life. For the equality of *men*, not of political units called states, stood as "our ancient faith," "the sheet anchor of American republicanism," the "electric cord" that bound the nation together. Trying hard to convince the crowd of his free-soil bona fides, Douglas had offered his challenger an opening, one that Lincoln would seize a little less than one hour later. 37

But Douglas still had forty-five minutes to indict the Buchanan administration, a wise move in western Illinois. Noting that his supporters had been cashiered from federal offices and replaced by Buchanan loyalists, Douglas charged that, "They are making speeches—these postmasters are—all over the State against me, and in favor of Lincoln." But that did not matter, for the Senator had bravely done the right thing: ". . . I submit the question to you whether if it had not been for me, that Constitution would have been crammed down the throats of that people against their consent." The crowd cheered him on his self-congratulatory way, even as the wind picked up the aroma of burning martyr.

"The very men that acknowledge that I was right in defeating the Lecompton Constitution now form an alliance with the postmasters, with the federal officers, with the professed Lecompton men to defeat me because I did right."

Someone yelled, "It can't be done!"

Douglas continued, "Mr. Lincoln would never dream that he had a chance of success but for the aid he is receiving from the federal officers." Douglas asked what the citizens thought of a party that would make "an unholy and unnatural combination to beat a man merely because he was right." You all know, he shouted, "the axe of proscription is suspended over the head of every Democratic office holder in Illinois, unless he goes for the Republican ticket against me and my Democratic associates." (The *Times* reported it as "the axe of decapitation and proscription." Binmore and Sheridan also reported cries of "The people are with you," and "let them threaten.")

Douglas spoke the truth. The Lecompton Constitution would not have been defeated without his leadership; the Buchanan administration was purging Douglas loyalists; and the Republicans and the Buchaneers were in bed together.

And yet it all reads so unattractively. When Douglas wasn't congratulating himself for his bravery, leadership, and adherence to principle, he was whining about the "unholy and unnatural" forces arrayed against him. Each point individually or the two together might move these people to vote for Democrats loyal to Douglas. But it's hard to imagine that the hardy souls who had braved withering conditions would have had much patience for the paired themes of aren't-I-wonderful and woe-is-me. Perhaps sensing this, Douglas changed front.

It was time to turn to two old reliables: Lincoln's geographically-shifting views, and the old favorite, race. The Senator recalled Lincoln's Chicago speech, which had included an inquest on what "all men are created equal" meant. Changing a word or two, Douglas pretended to quote his challenger: "If one man says it does not mean a negro, why may not another say it does not mean a German?" He continued, probably sneering, evoking Lincoln's suggestion that we "'discard all this quibbling about this man and the other man, this race and that race, and the other race being inferior,'" and that "'we should once more stand up declaring that all men are created equal.'"

"That's right," someone hollered.

"Yes," answered Douglas, "I have no doubt you think it's right, but the Lincoln men down in Coles, and Tazewell, and Sangamon don't think it's right."

A snappy retort, greeted with applause.

Lincoln had concluded his speech to the "Chicago Abolitionists," cried Douglas, with "'I leave you, hoping that the lamp of liberty will burn in your bosoms until there shall no longer be a doubt that all men are created free and equal.'"

As Republicans shouted back, "Good, good" (and Democrats shouted, "Shame"), Douglas again played off the crowd.

"Now, you say 'good' on that, and are going to vote for Mr. Lincoln because he holds that doctrine."

"That's so," called Lincoln's friends.

"Now," said Douglas, closing the trap, "I am not going to blame you for supporting him on that ground, but I will show you in immediate contrast to that, what Mr. Lincoln said, in order to get votes down in Egypt, where they didn't hold that doctrine." Democrats applauded in anticipation.

When Douglas quoted from Lincoln's Charleston denial of racial equality, Republican loyalists shouted, "Hurrah for Lincoln," and "Good for Lincoln."

"Yes," shot back Douglas, "here you find men who hurrah for Lincoln, and say he is right when he discards all distinction between the races, or when he declares that he discards the doctrine that there is such a thing as a superior and inferior race. . .And down South with the Old Line Whigs, with the Kentuckians, the Virginians, and the Tennesseeans, he tells you there is a physical difference between the races making one superior, the other inferior, and he is [in] favor of maintaining the superiority of the white race over the negro.

"Now, let me ask you, how can you reconcile these positions?"

Douglas had not to this point been nearly this effective on the theme of Lincoln's evasiveness, nor had he handled a crowd so well; he seemed to have learned from the embarrassing dust-up at Freeport.

He thundered, "I would despise myself if I thought that I were seeking your votes by concealing my opinions, or advocating one set of principles in one part of the State and a different class in another part of the State." (This despite his newly-featured lead-off theme of Douglas, Slayer of Lecompton.)

Let there be no mistake about one fundamental: "I tell you that in my opinion this Chicago doctrine of Mr. Lincoln's declaring that negroes and white men were included alike in the Declaration of Independence,"--he rose to high dudgeon--"is a monstrous heresy."

Again, the contrast. In Peoria four years earlier Lincoln had used the adjective "monstrous" when he said that he hated the Kansas-Nebraska Act, "because of the monstrous injustice of slavery itself." To Douglas, racial equality was a monstrous idea; to Lincoln, slavery was a monstrous reality. 38

When the founding fathers signed the Declaration, Douglas shouted, "They referred to white men, men of European birth and European descent, when they declared the equality of all men."

He looked down into the audience.

"I see a gentleman here shaking his head. Let me remind him that when Thomas Jefferson wrote the Declaration he was the owner, and continued to the end of his life the owner of a large number of slaves. Did he intend to say that his negro slaves were created his equals by Divine law, and that he was violating the law of God every time [sic] of his life by holding them as slaves?" Was Jefferson a hypocrite?

The crowd cried back, "No, no." (Ask that question today to a group of history students, and see what answer you get.)

Nearing a close in what had been a strong performance, Douglas stayed with the Founding. What if Lincoln had been a delegate to the 1787 Constitutional Convention, and had proclaimed his "house divided" doctrine there? "Would not the twelve slaveholding States have outvoted the one Free State and under his doctrine have fastened slavery under a Constitutional provision to every inch of the American Republic?" And any attempted constitutional amendment to eradicate slavery would fail today, too, for want of the super majorities needed in Congress and among the states, despite the preponderance of free states.

The only thing to do, the "one path of peace in this Republic," was "to administer this Government as our fathers made it, divided into free States and slave States, allowing each State to decide for itself whether it wants slavery or not."

To loud applause, Douglas sat. Perhaps Lincoln did not have the gentleman; not just yet.

"I Think It Will Take a Better Answer Than A Sneer"

On the heels of Lincoln's erratic performance in Charleston, Douglas's opening posed a real threat to Lincoln's hopes. The Republican began haltingly.

"A very large portion of the speech which Judge Douglas has addressed to you has previously been delivered and put in print," called Lincoln, and the crowd laughed.

Lincoln paused; he had not wanted to start in this way; he hadn't meant to be funny.

"I did not mean that for a hit on the Judge at all."

Hitt reported renewed laughter still. But Lincoln was not going for a laugh. "If not interrupted," he had wanted merely to point out that since the debates had already been reported in detail, he would not go over points already made in four other towns.

Why did he hasten to disavow a "hit" at his opponent, when in town after town, supporters of both men bayed "Hit him again" as a call of approval? Why not just score a point with this crowd accidentally, and leave it at that? Why in effect admonish a crowd whose votes you needed? Especially when it was true that Douglas changed his speech very little from place to place?

In 1840, Lincoln had won notoriety in Springfield for the "skinning" of one Jesse B. Thomas, an unmerciful attack on a former Whig turned Democrat. Imitating his rival's voice and mannerisms, Lincoln drew forth a delighted, almost savage response from the audience, and Lincoln poured it on, resorting to "intense, scathing ridicule." Reduced to tears, Thomas fled the stand. By 1858, this sort of take-no-prisoners verbal assault had ceased to be Lincoln's style. (Cross the line Lincoln certainly had with poor Thomas. Billy Herndon would later write that Lincoln confessed that "the recollection of his conduct that evening filled him with the deepest chagrin. . .He felt that he had gone too far, and to rid his good-nature of a load, hunted up Thomas and made ample apology.") The memory of the skinning may have made Lincoln cautious in the use of invective against Douglas; he would needle the great man, but with care. When the Galesburg crowd thought that he'd zinged his rival, Lincoln made haste to assure them they were wrong. 39

What did Lincoln look like that blustery day? What did he sound like? Billy Herndon offered this sketch of Lincoln as a public speaker:

When he began speaking, his voice was shrill, piping, and unpleasant. His manner, his attitude, his dark, yellow face, wrinkled and dry, his oddity of pose, his diffident movements—everything seemed to be against him, but only for a short time. . .As he proceeded he became somewhat animated, and to keep in harmony with his growing warmth his hands relaxed their grasp and fell to his side. . . He never sawed the air nor rent space into tatters and rags as some orators do. He never acted for stage effect. He was cool, considerate, reflective. . .He always stood squarely on his feet, toe even with toe. . .As he proceeded with his speech the exercise of the vocal organs altered somewhat the tone of his voice. It lost in a measure its former acute and shrilling pitch, and mellowed into a more harmonious and pleasant sound. His form expanded, and notwithstanding the sunken breast, he rose up a splendid and imposing figure. In his defense of the Declaration of Independence—his greatest inspiration—he was 'tremendous in the directness of his utterances.' 40

Douglas had strongly contended that Thomas Jefferson and the other Founding Fathers had not intended to include blacks under the fundamental truth that all men are created equal. Lincoln would not let that go.

"I believe the entire records of the world from the date of the Declaration of Independence up to within three years ago, may be searched in vain for one single declaration from one single man, that the negro was not included in the Declaration of Independence." Lincoln shouted, "I think I may defy Douglas to show that he [Jefferson] ever said so, therefore, I think I may defy Douglas to show that any President ever said so—that any member of Congress ever said so—that many man ever said so. . ." And he built to the applause line, ". . .until the necessities of the Democratic party had to invent that declaration."

Applause.

"And I will remind Judge Douglas," he called into the prairie winds, "and this audience, that while Mr. Jefferson was the owner of slaves, as he undoubtedly was, he, speaking on this very subject used the strong language that he trembled for his country when he remembered that God was just."

A timely and well-chosen quote from *Notes on the State of Virginia*, a quote Lincoln must have committed to memory. But here came the stinger:

"I will offer the highest premium in my power to Judge Douglas, if he will show that he, in all his life, has ever uttered a statement akin to that statement of Jefferson's."

The *Times* reported "applause" on that line. Hitt heard "great applause and cries of 'Hit him again,' 'good,' 'good.'" Lincoln had drawn blood here on campus: the most charitable thing Douglas had ever said publicly about blacks was that just because they were inferior didn't mean that they had to be slaves; pretty thin beer compared to Jefferson's anguished, eloquent admission.

Something seemed to have happened within Lincoln in the three weeks between Charleston and Galesburg. He appeared at once more confident, more upright, and more morally certain. Today, Lincoln had already taken the high road, disavowing any intent to mock Douglas' tendency to say the same things again and again. And he had—in one of the important central counties, strongly and unequivocally asserted that Jefferson had intended blacks to be included in "all men are created equal." This in the face of a clever, sneering Douglas attack on that very notion.

Did Lincoln in a sense hijack the Declaration, imputing to Jefferson a commitment to racial equality that the Virginian never held? If so, he did this more boldly in Galesburg than in any of the debates thus far. And if he did this, it was certainly an act of supreme self-confidence for a former one-term Congressman, an underdog candidate for the US Senate, in a race that had gained unprecedented newspaper coverage. For Lincoln to refashion Jefferson's words, to improve upon them, that suggested real audacity. 41

At the same time, what Lincoln did not say suggested an important change. Nowhere in the Galesburg debate did Lincoln return to his earlier disclaimers that he did not mean to make voters or jurors of negroes, nor to promote interracial marriage, which had in the first four rounds always been bound to his endorsements of "the right to eat the bread which she has earned." This may have been due to Lincoln's sense that Galesburg retained some of its old abolitionist character; certainly Douglas worked under that assumption, as evidenced by his narrative of his own heroism in the fight against the Lecompton Constitution.

But it may also have been traceable to those three weeks, and to events a decade and-a-half earlier. In the early 1840s, Lincoln's ambitions had gotten the better of him. A young man in a hurry, he had skinned Thomas. He had also mocked a political opponent named James Shields in print, been forced to row to an island in the Mississippi to duel Shields (cooler heads had prevailed), and broken off rather badly his engagement to Miss Mary

Todd of the Lexington, Kentucky Todds. In the small world of Springfield politics and society, none of this was secret, and Lincoln was mortified. Billy Herndon later wrote that Lincoln had fallen into such a depression that his friends kept razors out of his reach. But he survived it, and came out at the other end of the wilderness with a firmer sense of himself, and more able to hear and obey "honor's voice." 42

Had something like this happened in the run-up to Galesburg? Could Lincoln have been entirely happy with those first five minutes in Charleston? Sure, he had gotten big laughs from the Coles County throngs, but were those the sorts of laughs you wanted, even if it won you votes? And if you lost—a distinct possibility whatever Lincoln may have predicted in his more optimistic moments—could you live with yourself, knowing that you'd taken the low road, only to come in second? And for that matter, who knew if you would get a second chance? Lincoln had learned early in life that death could come without warning; he had lost both of his natural parents, his older sister, and one son by 1858, and seems to have taken nothing for granted in terms of his own longevity. If you died and Charleston represented your final words on the subject of human equality, how would you be remembered, if at all? 43

Although Lincoln told racist jokes to friends, it's hard to find examples in his public speeches of him holding up for ridicule the notion of equality, and so much of what Lincoln said and wrote urged people to take seriously the belief that at some level, all people were equal regardless of race. Modern readers feel surprise and disappointment at Lincoln's performance in Charleston, and not just because he endorsed only a limited equality for blacks; it was the tone, the ungenerous, mocking, contemptuous, superior tone that many of us react against. And maybe Lincoln reacted against it, too. Maybe.

And perhaps the Democratic press had told the truth about what had happened on September 20 at Sullivan. Maybe Lincoln's friends had acted irresponsibly; maybe they had tried to break up the Douglas rally. Had the campaign gotten out of hand? In a friendly Quincy newspaper, one Republican had commented that, "I am afraid that someone will be killed before it is over, as everyone is excited." If Lincoln—beginning to sense that "we have the gentleman"—had gotten caught up in the moment, and been part of that Republican phalanx, then realized his mistake and fled before hundreds of pairs of eyes, that was the embodiment of dishonor. And Lincoln would have known it and realized it and regretted it.

After the affair at Sullivan, he had come home, back with Mary and Bob and Willie and Tad at the corner of 8th and Jackson. He had been away for so much of the summer; Mary had again been a single mom. It had been his estrangement from Mary in the early 1840s, coupled with some dishonorable political conduct, that had caused friends to deny Lincoln razors, but which had also led him to catharsis. Did something similar happen now? Off the trail momentarily, returned (if only briefly) to his family, helping a questionable character get a few sticks of furniture, then spending three days in the not especially critical town of Winchester, writing affectionate poems to two sisters. . .did Lincoln have time to think, reflect, and to listen to honor's voice? (Or was it the voice of Mary, maligned in history, but for years a discerning watcher of politics and often an in-house advisor to Lincoln?) 44

Whatever it was, Lincoln had found his new voice just in time, for Douglas had done his best work thus far in his opening outside Old Main. Having taken on Douglas's reading of the Declaration, Lincoln then refuted the senator's charges of Republican evasiveness. Picking up on Douglas's charge that in Tazewell County, Republicans had not advertised their party's name at a rally featuring Lincoln, the challenger called, "I have the honor to inform Judge Douglas that he spoke in that very county of Tazewell last Saturday, and I there on Tuesday last, and when he spoke there he spoke under a call not venturing to call the meeting Democratic."

As Republicans applauded, Lincoln couldn't resist. "Now, Judge," he said loudly to Douglas, seated behind him, "what do you think of yourself?"

Laughter, cheers, and according to the *Times*, defiant cries of "Hurrah for Douglas."

In fact, shouted Lincoln, if there were a meeting called of the national Democratic party, "Judge Douglas and his friends would not go there; they would not suppose themselves invited; they would understand it to be a call of those hateful postmasters."

To laughter and applause, someone yelled at Lincoln—not entirely inaccurately—"A call of your allies, you mean."

Just as Lincoln was defending his party against Douglas's charge that Republicans made "odious distinctions between the free and slave states," reported the *Times*, a group of men broke off from the crowd, "running off to see some kind of hubbub" at the crowd's perimeter. A tussle? Whatever it was, Lincoln, taking notice, said, "Well, that is very beautiful."

The difference between himself and Douglas, contended Lincoln, was that the Democrat favored "eradicating" and "pressing out of view, and out of existence, all preference for free over slave state institutions," so, "consequently, every sentiment that he utters, discards the idea that he is against slavery, every sentiment that emanates from him discards the idea that there is any wrong in slavery. Every thought that he utters will be seen to exclude the thought there is anything wrong with slavery."

Lincoln spoke the truth; Douglas's most anti-slavery statement thus far had been this: just because blacks are profoundly inferior does not mean that they *must* be slaves.

He rolled on. The Judge "insists, upon the score of equality, that the owner of slaves and the owner of horses should be allowed to take them alike to new territory and hold them there," which was true if there was no difference between livestock and blacks. But "I believe that slavery is wrong, and in a policy springing from a belief that looks to the prevention of the enlargement of that wrong, and that looks at some time to there being an end to that wrong. The other sentiment is that it is no wrong, and the policy springing from it [is] that there is no wrong in its becoming bigger, and that there will never be any end of it."

He closed: "There is the difference between Judge Douglas and his friends in the Republican Party."

Honor's voice? Or the voice of a brief hiatus from the grinding, dusty, windswept road trip, a hiatus in which Lincoln had time to think about what he really believed, to think about the person he really wanted to be as this campaign sped to its climax? Whatever the case, hijacking the Declaration or not, Lincoln had committed himself to a line of attack on Douglas and on slavery (cleverly linking the two) that was first and foremost a moral one. Even if few could hear him in that howling wind, Hitt and White and Binmore and Sheridan—and Douglas—could hear him, and now he was on record in the Chicago papers and beyond; the slavery question, which was the central question of the campaign, would be argued by one side primarily along moral lines.

Lincoln turned to less grave concerns. As for Douglas's charges that Lincoln and company were collaborating with the Danites, Lincoln joshed: "I have said upon former occasions, and I do not choose to suppress it now, that I have no objections to the division in the Judge's party." Lincoln shouted that when it came to the "unholy and unnatural alliance between the National Democrats and the Republicans" he wanted "to enter my protest against the judge being perceived as an entirely competent witness upon that subject." The *Tribune* reported cheers.

Still cooling off from his strongly moralistic attacks on Douglas's position on slavery, Lincoln did some political needling. He returned to the 1854 Springfield resolutions that had provided the Little Giant with his now-discredited seven Ottawa questions. Reminding the audience that Douglas had promised to "investigate the matter," Lincoln noted that one month after Douglas had gone to Springfield, ostensibly to conduct the investigation, "so far as I know he has made no report. . ." Lincoln shouted, "I have some curiosity to see and hear whether the fraud"—Hitt reported applause at the word "fraud"—"was committed, and the perpetuation of it was clearly traced to the three." These were Charles Lanphier, editor of the *Illinois State Register*, Thomas Harris, the incumbent Douglas Democrat candidate for the House in the Springfield district, and Douglas himself. Lincoln contended that this trio had committed a similar "forgery" in the campaign of Harris against Richard Yates, and that Douglas had tried it before in floor debate with the hated Lyman Trumbull in 1856. At Ottawa, they'd turned on Lincoln. "It has been clung to, and played again and again as an exceedingly high trump by this blessed trio."

Hitt reported "roars of laughter and tumultuous applause, and cries of 'Give it to him.'" But it was hard to see what this had to do with being a United States Senator.

So back to slavery; more specifically to Chief Justice Taney's contention that "the right of property in the slave is distinctly and expressly affirmed in the Constitution." When I asked Douglas his view of this dubious contention, and its potential as a precedent to re-inject slavery into the free states, asked Lincoln, how did he respond? "He contented himself with sneering at the thought that it was impossible for the Supreme Court to ever make such a decision, and sneering at me for propounding the interrogation." Lincoln argued that one could "search in vain" for a place in the Constitution where such right was "distinctively and expressly affirmed," but that since the Court had ruled it so, "the conclusion inevitably follows that no State law or constitution can destroy that right."

It was the familiar House Divided theme again, Stephen, Franklin, Roger, and James teaming up to cause us all to wake up one morning only to learn that the Court had made Illinois a slave state.

But Lincoln gave it one twist. Douglas had sneered at the challenger's question, but "I think that it will take a better answer than a sneer to show that those who have said that the right of property in the slave is distinctly and expressly affirmed in the constitution [sic] are not prepared to say that no constitution or law of a State can destroy that right." Furthermore, the Dred Scott decision—"in the opinion of one very humble man"—would never have been made had the Democrats—"the party that made it"—not won the 1856 election. And "the new Dred Scott decision," the one that would truly nationalize slavery, "will never be made if that party is not sustained in the next election." And it was sure to be made—"as to-morrow is to come"—if Douglas and the Democrats triumphed less than one month from now. Douglas's religious devotion to the 1857 ruling would bind him to whatever came next, argued the Republican, and that would have calamitous impact on Illinoisans, for "as he teaches men—and he has a great power to teach men—he has a great power to make men say it is right if he says so. . .he is preparing the public mind" to accept this next ruling, "without inquiring whether it is right or wrong." Douglas would achieve this through "his maxims that he does not care whether slavery be voted up or be voted down; that whoever wants slavery has a right to have it; that upon the principle of equality it has a right to go everywhere." The Judge, "whether purposely or not" was "preparing the public mind for making the institution of slavery national."

Returning to a quote from the Ottawa debate--Clay's admonition about slavery advocates "blowing out the moral lights around us"—Lincoln charged Douglas with doing just that, and with "muzzling the cannon" that sounds the celebration of Independence Day each year. Lincoln shouted that through Douglas's failure to join with Lincoln—and by implication with Jefferson and Washington and John Adams and Henry Clay—the Senator had begun blowing out those lights. This professed advocate of the sacred right of self government would, if not stopped by you shivering, damp people, you voters of Illinois, end up snuffing the lamp of liberty. The *Tribune* reported "Great applause" and cries of "Yes, yes," and "That's so."

Lincoln began to close. The challenger loosely paraphrased Douglas's support for "the acquisition of territory so fast as would need it" without regard to the slavery question. The Senator would, recalled Lincoln, "leave the question of slavery to be settled by the people of the territory."

A voice called out, "That is perfectly right."

"Maybe it is; let us consider it a while." If Douglas got re-elected, and could convince people not to care about slavery's growth, "the next thing he goes for grabbing Mexico and Central America, and the adjoining islands, each one of which promises an additional slave field, and it is to be left to the people that we get to settle the question of slavery in them." But Lincoln doubted that Douglas really wanted this for Mexico, "for the Judge has a great horror of mongrels"—the *Trib* reported laughter here— "and I understand that not more than one of eight are white. I don't know, but I don't suppose he is in favor of these mongrels settling this question, which would bring him somewhat in collision with this inferior race. . ."

Withdrawing the needle, Lincoln turned serious. Senators do vote on wars, on treaties, on territorial acquisition, and so it mattered who Illinois sent to cast those votes. Lincoln shouted that, "this slavery question has been the only one that has ever threatened or menaced a dissolution of the Union, that has ever disturbed us in such a way as to make us fear for our own liberty. . ." (He was reading history selectively; the War of 1812 and the Tariff and Nullification crisis of the Jackson era had also raised secession prospects.) And "I say in view of these facts, I think it it [sic] an exceedingly important question for this people to consider, whether we shall enter into a policy of the acquisition of new territory without regard to the question of slavery." Without saying so, Lincoln implied that as Senator he would view skeptically any new expansionist efforts; here was a clear difference with his opponent.

Having spoken for just shy of an hour and twenty minutes, having met a forceful Douglas assault with an equally forceful reply, and having found more clearly than at any other time in the debates his moral voice on slavery, Lincoln sat.

The *Times* reported no crowd reaction; the *Tribune* "three tremendous cheers for Lincoln from the whole vast audience" given "with great enthusiasm" as "their favorite retired."

"I Began This Contest Treating Him Courteously"

If Douglas had checked his watch, expecting Lincoln to go for ten more minutes, he'd been brought up short. The *Times* reported that the Senator's loyalists roused him with six cheers given "with great spirit." He had delivered a powerful opening, one that might have elicited another uneven Lincoln response; but the challenger had returned fire. Lincoln was not finished off. Douglas would need to immediately strike back with a powerful response. But instead. . .

"Now, gentlemen, the highest compliment you can give me during the brief half hour I have to conclude is your entire silence. I desire to be heard rather than applauded."

Someone yelled, "Good," according to the *Times*.

When Douglas noted that Lincoln's first criticism had been the sameness of Douglas's speeches, the Senator added, "I wish I could say the same of his speeches."

An outburst of laughter, applause, and calls of "good," "you have him," and further proof that the debates were not held on the rarified floor of the US Senate. Here, no matter how much Douglas might insist, the audience would participate; they had endured much to get here and they'd stood in that October wind for nearly three hours. They claimed a part in the debate.

Undeterred, Douglas shouted, "The principal complaint I make of him is, that he makes one speech North and another South," one in the "abolition counties" and another in those opposed.

"That's so," someone yelled, reported Binmore. "Hit him over the Knuckles."

"I have proved that he has different sets of principles" for Chicago and Jonesboro.

The *Tribune* reported cries of "It's not so," and what it termed "great confusion" in the crowd.

Attempting to make himself heard amid the gusts and the freshly-aroused crowd, Douglas shouted, "Here I understand him to re-affirm the doctrine of equality—that by the Declaration of Independence, the negro is declared the equal to the white man. He tells you to-day that the negro was included in the Declaration of Independence, which says all men are created equal."

"We believe it."

"You believe it," replied Douglas. "Very well."

The *Times* (though not the *Tribune*) wrote that, "Here an uproar arose, persons in various parts of the crowd indulging in cat calls, groans, cheers, and other noises, preventing the speaker from proceeding." Douglas's call for entire silence had worked as well as a principal's request that we hold all applause until the last of the graduates have received their diplomas. How bad did it get?

Trying to restore order, Douglas yelled, "Gentlemen, I ask you to remember that Mr. Lincoln was listened to respectfully, and I have a right to insist that I shall not be interrupted in reply."

Lincoln rose.

"I hope that silence will be observed," called the Republican.

Douglas restarted, perhaps flustered, perhaps remembering his rough handling at Freeport, anxious not to have that happen again.

"He asserts to-day, as he did in Chicago, that that," he stuttered, "the negro was included in the clause of the Declaration of Independence which says that all men were created equal," but ". . .how came he to say at Charleston to those Kentuckians that the negro was physically inferior to the white man, belonged to an inferior race, and he was for keeping him always in that inferior condition?"

"He's right," hollered a Republican.

"Is he right now, or was he right at Charleston?"

Listeners called out, "Both, both, both," and Douglas moved on to Lincoln's charge of fraud and forgery by Douglas, Lanphier, and Harris in regard to the 1854 Springfield resolutions first introduced by the Senator at the Ottawa debate. Sneering that Lincoln had "dared to talk about fraud" in light of his shifting views on racial equality, Douglas noted that the broad truth was simple: Republicans *did* support those extreme resolutions now, in 1858, whether Lincoln was physically present at the spot where the drafting took place. (This of course gave the Democrat a chance to drag in the Mexican War.)

Defending both Lanphier and Harris, Douglas fumed, "I do not believe that there is an honest man in this State that don't abhor with disgust his insinuations of my complicity with that forgery, as he calls it," and Douglasites cheered and applauded.

"Does he wish to push these things to the point of personal difficulties here?

"I began this contest," called Douglas as he looked out over the thousands, "treating him courteously, kindly, and spoke of him in words of respect. . .I desired to conduct the contest with him like a gentleman, but I spurn the insinuation of there being a complicity in fraud merely because the editor of a newspaper"—Lanphier would take the fall—"has made a mistake as to the place where the thing was done, instead of the thing itself."

And the thing itself included a plank "that there should be no more Slave States admitted into this Union even if the people wanted them. Lovejoy stands pledged against any more Slave States."

"So do I," yelled someone.

"So do you," shot back Douglas. So did Farnsworth and Washburne and "the candidate for the Legislature, who is running on Lincoln's ticket in Henderson and Warren. . .and I am informed, though I do not know the fact certainly, that your candidate stands pledged to the same thing."

"Good for him."

"Now you Republicans all hallow 'hurrah for him' and yet Mr. Lincoln tells you that his conscience won't enable him to sustain that doctrine."

To what the *Times* called "immense applause," Douglas clinched his point: "I wonder if Mr. Lincoln and his party has not presented the case that he has cited in Scripture, that a house divided against itself cannot stand."

As his supporters applauded, Douglas returned to Lincoln's "house divided" speech and its stated assumption that the Taney Court awaited the chance to issue a "second" Dred Scott ruling to make Illinois a slave state.

"Mr. Lincoln knows," he assured the crowd, "that there is no member of the Supreme Court that holds that doctrine."

Then why would the Republican make the assertion?

"It looks," called Douglas, "as if there was an effort to destroy public confidence in the highest judicial tribunal on earth." And that was dangerous business, for, if Lincoln could persuade people to ignore the Court's rulings, "He will have changed this Government from one of laws to that of a mob, in which the strong arm of violence will be substituted for the decisions of courts of justice."

Urged on by cheers, Douglas shouted, "He says the decision is binding on all Democrats, but not on Republicans."

Lincoln, charged Douglas, was urging the raising of mobs to defy the Constitution, but, in stark contrast, "I stand by the laws of the land."

"I stand," he drew himself up, "by the Constitution as our fathers made it, by the laws as they are enacted, and by the decisions of the Courts upon all points within their jurisdiction, as they are announced by the highest tribunal on earth," and, he closed, "any man that resists these must resort to mob law and violence, and overturn the government."

Binmore reported that "When Senator Douglas concluded, the applause was perfectly furious and overwhelming."

"The Strong, Earnest Faces of Our Men. . ."

As many thousands of people left Galesburg, the partisan press returned to their customary hi-jinks. Freeport's Republican *Weekly Journal* jeered on October 14 that the incumbent had "repeated his stale nonsense concerning the Declaration of Independence." Bloomington's *Daily Pantagraph* reported that the Galesburg *Democrat's* editor had compared the *Times'* transcript of Lincoln's remarks to what the Republican actually had said, and had found "ONE HUNDRED AND EIGHTY" changes, which the *Pantagraph* called "Mutilations." On the Democratic side, the Chicago *Times* wrote that Republicans had to wrap Lincoln "'in flannels. . .to restore the circulation of blood in his almost inanimate body.'" (Shades of the lugging off in Ottawa.) Meanwhile, big city reporters from the east showed signs of losing interest, accusing the two gladiators of indulging in "'twaddle'" and "'quibbles'" and "'mutual recrimination of the vulgarest sort.'" 45

Reading the transcripts leads to "none of the above." Both men had done well, and in some ways Galesburg represented the best front-to-end performance thus far. Certainly the debaters gave a stalwart, large, heroic crowd that had endured harsh conditions a worthy performance. The press had its own agenda, be it partisanship or regional snootiness, and its recollections cannot be taken that seriously.

Which does not mean that the articles are worthless. The newspaper accounts help us to gauge the intensity of the campaign, and as organs of the political parties they offer an insight into the styles of Democratic and Republican leaders. They help us to ascertain the broad themes in this race, and the strategic adjustments made by both sides.

But they are in a sense no more reliable accounts of "what really happened" than were 1929 recollections of octogenarians solicited by the folks who dedicated Leonard Crunelle's statue of "Lincoln, The Debater" up north in Freeport. Casting a wide net, the Freeport committee hauled in the reminiscences of some men and women who had not been at Freeport, but who had attended the October debate in Galesburg.

What sorts of things did they remember about the three-hour long oratorical clash? What *do* eyewitnesses recall about historical events such as the debates?

G.W. Gale's father was on the Lincoln reception committee, and thus "the appearance of the speakers I remember well," but "of the debate itself I understood little," partly because Gale was ten at the time. What he did remember was the "banners and flags, girls representing the states in the rack wagons, a noisy crowd whose enthusiasm and cheers for their candidate not even the chilly wind could restrain." Gale recalled that "our mothers worried, fearing that the girls in what then seemed thin costumes would suffer from the exposure." J.A. Widney, a Civil War veteran, also remembered "a load of thirty-three girls all dressed in white and all Democrats and all for Douglas." Lydia A. Samuels, whose parents were Kentucky-born Republicans, went "From Henderson in a float drawn by our horses, thirty-three girls to represent the states, all dressed in white, and one black to represent Kansas." Writing in the era of short-skirted flappers, the spry 88-year-old Union Army veteran Captain J. C. Hogue also recalled the presence of many women, but "the ladies wore those awful full long skirts, capes, mitts, poke bonnets, shoes, etc." 46

Miss Emma Scott claimed to hold a "vivid mental picture of that throng, the delegations with their decorated wagons and beautiful horses, bands, flags," and she added, "the speakers too, but I was too young to grasp the significance of their speeches." And yet Miss Scott could remember that when Lincoln rose to speak, Douglas had said "'How long, O Lord, how long!' to which Lincoln replied, 'The days and the years of the wicked are short.'" J. M. Dennis remembered also that Douglas quote. Although hard of hearing at 83, Dennis was "yet able to sing the old songs of those days." Lydia Samuels, remembering how "red in the face Douglas got" as he "finally resorted to personalities," recalled that the Democrat had said that Lincoln "sold at the bar," and that Lincoln had answered back, "'When I was on one side of the bar my friend Mr. Douglas was on the other.'" Still, as J.C. Hogue reported, "the voices of the speakers carried very little beyond the first few seats of the crowd." The fact that few could truly hear the debaters, and that neither the Republican nor Democratic phonographers reported the "How long, O Lord" comment or the needling about tending bar (which did in fact happen at Ottawa) reminds us that memory can embellish dialogue at least as well as 180 mutilations by the party press. 47

So of what use are these remembrances, those of 1858 newspaper reporters and those of 1929 senior citizens, mere children when the two great men came to Galesburg? If you discount the intentional embellishments and the unintentional imperfections of memory, what are you left with?

The thousands of people, the bands, the girls, the flags, the harsh conditions which seem not to have deterred anyone from participating; the two candidates, competing for the respect of men and--because of their possible influence upon their enfranchised husbands--disenfranchised women. Most of these men and women hailed from remote farm communities, and their respect, their favor would determine which aspirant would go to Washington to shape the nation's foreign policy, its judiciary, and its response to the burning political and moral question of its time. Neither man would exercise that power without the support of people like the thousands gathered outside Old Main on that raw October day.

And those thousands may have heard more than we credit them for. Both Binmore and Hitt reported frequent reactions from the crowd, and although 83-year old J.H. Dunn allowed that "Douglas was very hoarse, his voice rough and harsh and carrying only a short distance in the great crowd," he also wrote in 1929 that "Lincoln's clear tenor voice carried to the very outskirts." And Dunn, who parenthetically reported that "the mother and I are well past 83 years, both going strong," recalled one other detail, haunting in its definition: "Memory lets me see again the strong, earnest faces of our men, striving to clutch every word" as the winds whipped the American flags. Considering the whirlwind that buffeted Illinois and the other states within the next decade, those strong-faced men were well-advised to listen closely to the man with the clear tenor voice. 48

CHAPTER SIX: "THE SUCCESSIVE ACTS OF A DRAMA"

"Why It Touches Me Some"

In just over a week the debates would end; Douglas and Lincoln would meet in the Mississippi River towns of Quincy on Wednesday, October 13, and Alton on the 15th. "The political excitement in this state is tremendous," reported the semi-weekly edition of Greeley's New York *Tribune*. "No previous canvass ever came up to it. The Presidential contest of '56 was calm in comparison. The whole population, female as well as male, are excited." Lincoln had less than a month to topple the Senator, and that meant more travel and more speeches. The day after the Galesburg debate he hit Toulon, and on the ninth, a Saturday, he spoke at Oquawka Junction "for hours." Crossing the Mississippi, he spoke in Burlington, Iowa on the evening of that same day, then spent Sunday at the home of Iowa's governor James M. Grimes outlining his remarks for Wednesday's showdown in Quincy. Then he re-crossed the river for a Monday speaking engagement in Monmouth. Heavy rains reduced the roads to bogs, and a triumphal procession from Oquawka to Monmouth had to be cancelled. But Lincoln made it to his destination. And again, the people of Illinois came out despite the conditions. 1

Before the speech, the Monmouth Republican Glee Club serenaded the candidate. There's no record of what they sang, but it could have been this number from the *Lincoln Campaign Songster* of 1858:

Uncle Abe, Uncle Abe! here we are again.
We've got a platform now we think that will not bend or strain,
Beat the drum, unfurl the flag, freedom is for all,
And so we'll fling it to the breeze as in the ranks we fall.

Ho, Uncle Abe! Listen Uncle Abe! and see,
We sing for you, work for you, hurrah for liberty! 2

Cole Porter it wasn't. But it could have been worse, as in the case of this Douglas ditty:

> When Saxon raid,
>   With brand and blade,
> O'er Scotia's borders came,
>   And gave the land,
>   With bloody hand,
> To the pillage and the flame;
>   'Twas thus rang out
>   The welcome shout,
> From mountain and from brae;
>   "God and our right!
>   Stand firm and fight!
> A Douglas to the fray!" 3

Immigrant voters, always a concern of both camps, would be an important target in Adams County, and especially in Quincy, the county seat. The third largest town in Illinois, Quincy's 14,000 residents could read a Republican and a Democratic newspaper. The city was also ethnically diverse. Although it lacked a large Irish community, by 1860 one in four residents of the city traced their roots to Germany; the city even had a German-language newspaper. Some of those Germans were Jews (Quincy has the fifth oldest synagogue in the nation), and perhaps one hundred free blacks lived in this city which sat not far across the river from Hannibal, Missouri. Although state law barred black children from attending public school, the city's school district set up a separate school for African-Americans on North Ninth Street in the year of the Dred Scott ruling. One year later, leading black families founded Bethel A.M.E Church at Ninth and Oak. Quincy was cosmopolitan by Illinois standards; the Quincy House, where Douglas lodged, was the most modern hotel west of Pittsburgh. 4

Located in the critical central belt of Illinois, the city had an abolitionist history. After the 1837 murder of abolitionist printer Elijah Lovejoy downriver in Alton, the abolitionist theologian David Nelson transformed his Presbyterian Mission Institute on Quincy's outskirts into what Missouri historian Terrell Dempsey terms "a hotbed of abolitionist activity" that was "a well-used stop on the Underground Railroad." Institute students spent weekend nights on the riverfront searching for runaways to aid, and when few fugitives materialized, in July, 1841 two seminarians and the school's mechanic ventured across the river to slave state Missouri, bungled an attempt to free a slave, and ended up arrested, tried, and convicted by a jury that included young Samuel Clemens' father. They got twelve years in the state penitentiary. The next year, Dr. Richard Eels, an associate of Nelson's, found himself hauled before state Supreme Court judge Stephen A. Douglas for having harbored the runaway slave Charley. The owner, Chauncey Durkee, tracked the slave to Eels' home. Douglas found Eels guilty and fined him, but not before anti-abolitionists in Quincy held a mass meeting to signal their reliability to their neighbors across the river. The meeting resolved that God never intended "two people so widely different as blacks and whites. . .to mingle together in the enjoyment of the same civil, political, and social privileges" and that the meeting would "oppose to the utmost of our power all schemes having this object in view." 5

Quincy and surrounding Adams County were politically complex. New Englanders and Germans dominated the former, southern migrants the latter. The district was at once abolitionist and anti-abolitionist, nativist and immigrant, a region once represented in Congress by Douglas himself, but an area where Whigs had once been competitive. Both men felt they had a shot in this district. 6

The competition to get right with immigrant voters had raged since August. The Democratic Freeport *Weekly Bulletin* kept up a drumbeat of attacks on Republican cohabitation with the anti-immigrant American (or Know Nothing) Party, accusing Lincoln and company of hypocrisy. Having failed to "deceive and gull" the Irish to support them, Republicans "begin to show their hatred for that portion of our community." To illustrate, the *Bulletin* quoted the Chicago *Press and Tribune's* account of a Douglas rally: "'A body guard of five or six hundred Irish Papists stood close by him, yelling at all he said, perfectly indifferent whether it was sound sense or wild raving.'" And the Freeport paper noted that Connecticut Republicans had recently called for full voting rights in that state for Indians and blacks, but had resolved that all immigrants reside in the Nutmeg State for 21 years before being allowed the vote. "They would grant the negro rights that foreign born white citizens would be deprived of," wrote the *Bulletin*. "Let no foreigner vote for a party that would place a negro above the white man." The Republicans "bespatter the federal office holders, actual or expectant, who have bolted the regular nominations of the democratic party, with the most fulsome adulations, and laud them as the most *incorruptible* of patriots," meanwhile "seeking *publicly* to identify themselves with the Know Nothing party. . . a party which makes the 'particular spot' in which a man was born, as well as his religion, a qualification of citizenship. . ." The *Bulletin* asked "Naturalized citizens" whether they could vote for a party "which, if it ever has the power, will not only deprive you of a participation in the administration of the affairs of the government of your adopted country, but will prevent your fathers, brothers . . . and friends who may hereafter seek an asylum from oppression in this country, from enjoying any of the privileges of citizenship until they have served a probation of at least two thirds of an ordinary life time?" 7

These were legitimate questions for immigrants—chiefly the thousands of Germans and Irish Catholics migrating to America by the mid-century. And Republican papers such as Lincoln's hometown Illinois *State Journal* legitimized Democratic charges. Reporting that *The Catholic Tablet* ("one of the most bigoted and ferocious of the journals devoted to the interests of the Holy Mother—the Church of Rome")—had urged its readers to elect Douglas, Lincoln's hometown paper added, "We expected as much. The union, for ten years past, between popery and slavery propaganda in the United States has been so intimate, and, we must say, profitable, that we have no reason to suppose the Senator's quarrel with the President would break it up. . ." The Republican paper charged that as "the old principles of the founders of the Republic. . . were departed from by the Democracy. . .when the crudities and insanities of Calhoun took the place of their humane and patriotic maxims, Catholicism, another form of despotism which has been transplanted to American soil, struck hands with the new doctrines that were promulgated, and since that time Popery and Slavery have been the hard masters of the American people." But there was hope, asserted the *Journal*, for when Catholicism "desired to encroach upon the great principle which lies at the base of our government—when it should attack the common school system upon which the stability and virtue of the State depend—when it would thrust its communicates into places of patronage and power—when it would proscribe and beat down Americans because they were born on American soil, and because they would not yield allegiance to those of Rome—everywhere it has appealed in vain." 8

That suggested that there was little to worry about, but, warned the *Journal*, Catholics, "the wheel horses and leaders of the bogus Democratic strength," held a hatred for "the Protestant Bible and the Protestant faith." Further, when Douglas killed the Missouri Compromise "Catholic citizens held up their hands and raised their voices in loud approval of the traitorous act. When Kansas was dragooned by the bloody borders of Western Missouri, and the myrmidons of Federal power gathered from the most disreputable places in the South, no token of disapproval came from the Catholic people or the Catholic press." 9

The *Journal* explained:

And now, in this tremendous contest going on in the nation, wherein the Republican and American parties on one side are endeavoring to uphold the purity and preserve the humanity of the American Constitution, as the fathers wrote it, and wherein, opposed to them, the sham Democracy are seeking to ingraft upon it the dogma that slavery may take possession of and blight all the Territories (and hereafter all the States) without the authority and in defiance of the local law, almost to a man the members of the Roman Catholic Church—particularly those who owe their birth to Ireland are arrayed side by side with the nullifiers and disunionists of the South.

. . .The alliance, so mighty for evil, must be opposed by an alliance more powerful for good . . . When the party which is attempting the propagation of slavery by fire and the sword—the weapons which, from time immemorial, the Church has punished heretics—gets it death wound, the ascendancy of Catholicism goes with it. 10

The Republican paper reassured its readers, "We make no attack upon any man's religion." Perish the thought. 11

Articles such as these would not make it any easier for the Republicans to win over the Adams County Germans, although by 1858 American Nativists increasingly made distinction between desirable German Lutherans and undesirable Irish Catholics and their German co-religionists. Thus Lincoln's alliance with Gustave Koerner (while at the same time reaching out to former Whigs who had gravitated toward Know-Nothingism; a morally questionable double game.) 12

The speech that Lincoln gave in the Monmouth mud also pointed up the continuing tendency of the partisan press to "report" events subjectively. The Chicago *Press and Tribune* reporter wrote, "Of his speech I will only say that it lasted three hours, and that during that time the whole audience seemed perfectly wrapt in attention, and that in power, pathos and eloquence I have never heard it equalled," as Lincoln charged that Douglas "'is a pretty man to undertake to wrap the mantle of Clay around him.'" 13 The Democratic Monmouth *Review* saw it differently. Lincoln "referred to the Mexican war, while he was in congress, giving aid and comfort to the enemy, and against his own country, pronouncing it unholy, unconstitutional, God abhorred, and not begun on the right '*spot.*' This he made as clear as mud. . ." The speech "was not marked by the 'abilities of a Statesman, or the dignity of a would be Senator,'" and was coldly received by the small crowd present. 14

According to the Democratic press, Douglas's return to Quincy drew a warm reception. Arriving at the train station at 10 p.m. on October 12, the Senator stepped out to what Democratic newspapers called an "'extensive and brilliant'" parade by torchlight. The Republican press predictably termed the procession "'a miserable fizzle'" produced by "a small sized Irish mob.'" Although Lincoln came to town the next morning to his own welcoming parade, Carl Schurz allowed that Douglas's parade was the more impressive by far; after all, the Little Giant "'had plenty of money to spend on such things.'" 15

D. F. Spencer, writing in 1929, but contending that he could remember the events "as vividly as though it was yesterday," recalled that Quincy had a club of "Wideawakes," of which he was a member, who wore "capes of black oil cloth with the name in honor of Lincoln. Then we had the Hickory Club in honor of Douglas. They wore black pants and a red shirt. We all had torches and drilled with them every night for two weeks before Lincoln and Douglas arrived." (The Republicans must have been disappointed when Lincoln arrived from Macomb on Wednesday morning, not Tuesday night.)

Remembering that Tuesday night of the 12th as though it were yester-day, Spencer wrote that when Douglas arrived at Quincy, the Senator "was well loaded with booze, and to your surprise, perhaps, Mr. Lincoln took him by the arm and helped him into the bus, and they were taken to the Quincy House." If Spencer was right, Lincoln's miraculous appearance at Douglas's side—the night before the Republican's arrival in town--makes the Quincy railroad depot sound like the road to Emmaus. (Spencer may well have accurately described Douglas's condition. Joseph Smith III, son of the Mormon martyr, reported that in a speech at nearby Carthage, the Senator "showed unmistakeable signs of intoxication, was unsteady on his feet, and his words were pronounced with difficulty." Hancock County Democrats got out the hook midway through the address.) 16

In 1925, the Illinois State Historical Society published recollec-tions of the debate setting, Washington Square, which overlooked the Mississippi and fronted the county courthouse. One citizen remembered that the square was "bounded by a stretch of irregular and unhandsome wooden awnings," and that the square itself was "weedy and unkempt." Around the square "truant cows, who then had the right of way now com-manded by the automobile, escaped the farmers' watchful eye, got a taste of the hay or corn or oats in the wagons, to be driven off by farmers and dogs and boys." 17

William A. Richardson, Jr., the son of Douglas's loyal lieutenant (and Quincy's congressman) William Richardson, recalled that, "A little south and east of the center stood the old liberty pole, from the top of which the flag was given to the breeze on that beautiful day. In the southeast corner the grass was worn off in lines and patches by the young men and boys in playing town ball—the catcher standing in the path near the southeast gate." 18

Richardson remembered that the streets surrounding the square were macadamized, "but the stones had a way of hiding under a coating of dirt or mud." And, no doubt, manure. 19

Richardson's written remembrances showed a real fixation on women's fashion. Asking, "How would you have liked to have seen that crowd?" Richardson remembered "the jests and the jokes and the railieries that were roughly given, and the loud laugh that went with each discomfiture," the jostling and pushing of "squirming boys, dressed in grotesque imitation of men." But he recalled most vividly "those ladies in pompous and aggressive bonnets and large, loose, and balloon-like cloaks or mantles, or shawls with plenty of pattern, and skirts with many flounces." Richardson recalled that "Ladies dressed in a fashion that had the quality of making 'young women appear middle aged.'" He continued, "How would you like to have seen some one pat one of those demure little girls under the chin? Those serious-looking little girls with their hair worn down to their necks, brushed severely back with a rubber comb. Those prematurely old girls in their long paletots. Those ridiculous looking little girls with their frocks stuck out like little balloons, and their long, frightful pantalets that came almost to their shoes." And what of one of "the belles of that day" wearing a "huge silk skirt of flopping flounces over her tilting crinoline, her black skirt flounced jacket with its wide sleeves and wide, wide undersleeves and collar, with her wealth of jewelry on her person," and "her hair drawn flatly over her ears and fastened in a shapeless lump and encased in a net at the back of her head, with her unbecoming hat and veil?" Still, wound up Richardson, "in spite of all that downright ugliness, in spite of this fashion that had lost the art of dressing, some of these girls. . .were pretty and charming and bewitching." (Richardson spent less time on the men, but he mocked the "dandies," who wore long-hair "covered with hair oil, roached in front and brushed down all around and turned up on the inside at the bottom," dressed in garish broadcloth coats, vests, peg-top trousers, gold chains, "high chimney-pot hats" and carrying canes.) 20

However they dressed, there were moments involving members of the audience that seemed to have been scripted for the movies. 10,000 to 15,000 citizens of Illinois, Iowa, and Missouri crowded Washington Square to bursting. When local dignitaries packed the debate platform, a railing gave way and politicians and the bench they sat on tumbled to the ground. Then a bench reserved for ladies collapsed under the sheer weight of all those crinolines and flounces and pantalets. 21

And then there were the boys. Mike Cashman, twelve at the time, remembered:

"We had been having a high old time chasing through the crowd and creating havoc in general. Deciding to rest, we perched ourselves on the handles of an old pump fire engine. . . Well, there we sat, raising old Ned and enjoying ourselves to the utmost, just as the notion struck us. Just as things were getting along in great shape we heard a rough voice exclaim, 'Ye little devils, get your hides off that fire engine 'fore I skin ye alive.' Maybe you think we didn't skedaddle." 22

The man who would try to grab the attention of this three-ring circus would have as his primary mission raising old Ned for the incumbent senator from Illinois. Getting everyone's attention might be the first task.

"I have had no immediate conversation with Judge Douglas," began Lincoln, "but I will undertake to say, that he and I are perfectly agreed that your entire silence when I speak, and when he speaks, will be most agreeable to us."

To which a number of people let fly a forerunner of a venerable American ballpark cry:

"*Sit down in front.*"

The *Times* reported "considerable commotion."

Returning for what he hoped would be the last time to the question of founding platforms and resolutions of the Republican party, Lincoln noted that in May, 1856, "elements. . . which have since been consolidated into the Republican party" met in Bloomington, and adopted a platform, as did the national party later that year. The state party which had nominated Lincoln had "adopted again their platform" in June of 1858, "and I have supposed in entering upon that canvass I stood, generally, upon this platform." He asserted that thus far, no Democrat had "laid his finger upon anything in it that he called wrong."

And yet Douglas continued to try to link him to an 1854 resolution adopted "not [at] a local convention that embraced my residence, nor one that reached nearer I suppose than 150 or 200 miles of where I resided; nor one in which I had taken any part at all--"

"*Sit down in front.*"

"—He also introduced other resolutions, passed at other meetings" shouted Lincoln above the din, passed before the formation of the Republican party, "and now insists, as I understand him, that I am in some way responsible for them. . ." (At Jonesboro Lincoln had confronted Douglas with similarly tortured ties to Democratic resolutions, and Douglas had predictably disavowed responsibility for them.)

Even worse, at Galesburg, Douglas "undertook to establish that I am guilty of a species of double dealing with the public" by making different sorts of speeches in northern Illinois than in the south. But, Lincoln protested, I said "substantially the same thing" at Charleston as at Ottawa.

True only to a point. At both venues Lincoln had reassured his audience that he was not contending for the social or political equality of blacks and whites. But at Charleston he never contended that in the right to eat the bread that they have earned a black man or woman was the equal of every white, Judge Douglas included. Douglas's charge had merit, not on the basis of what Lincoln had said, but what he had not.

Still fighting past battles, Lincoln returned to the question of the "forged" Springfield resolutions of 1854. Douglas had charged that Trumbull had employed forged evidence in an 1856 Senate floor debate over Kansas. In Charleston, during that tedious segment on the Trumbull-Douglas feud, Lincoln had challenged Douglas to "put his finger" upon any piece of Trumbull's evidence that was forged, and "Judge Douglas did not dare to say that any piece was a forgery," to which the *Tribune* reported cheers and laughter.

"So it seems that there are some things that Judge Douglas dares to do and some that he dares not to do."

Laughter and "great applause," according to Hitt.

A voice sang out, "It's the same with you."

"Yes, sir, it is the same with me!" Lincoln called, "I do dare say forgery when it is true, and I don't dare say it when it is not."

Amid applause that Hitt called thunderous, voices shouted:

"Hurrah for Douglas."

"Hurrah for Lincoln."

"Hit him again."

"You don't hit very hard."

"Give it to him, Lincoln."

All of the commotion showed that the Quincy crowd reacted more to tone than substance. After all, the question of forged evidence had little directly to do with the responsibilities that the winner would assume in the Senate, nor did the forgery question explore in any meaningful way the territorial slavery question. But Lincoln was on a roll, and he decided to keep rolling.

"I tried to suggest to him that he was not quite clear of all suspicion" in the fraudulent 1854 resolutions.

"I dared to do that much, and I am not a very daring man, but I dared that much, and," he needled, "I am not much scared about it."

People laughed and applauded.

But he wasn't done; still fighting the battle of Galesburg, Lincoln shouted, "When the Judge says he would not have believed that Abraham Lincoln would make such an attempt as that, it reminds me that he entered upon this canvass with a purpose to treat me courteously, why," he said, "it touches me some."

The *Tribune* reported "great laughter" at Lincoln's gag line.

"—it sets me to thinking," called Lincoln.

"I was aware, when it was first agreed that Judge Douglas and I were to have these seven joint discussions, that they were the successive acts of a drama, perhaps I shall say, to be enacted not entirely in the face of an audience like this, but in the face of the nation, and not for anything in me, in the face of the world, and I was anxious that they should be conducted with a dignity and a degree of good temper that should be befitting the vast audience before which it was conducted."

But as early as his speech in Bloomington in early summer, Douglas had charged Lincoln with speaking out of both sides of his mouth.

"Now, I understand that to be an imputation upon my veracity," and it had continued at Ottawa, at Jonesboro and at Galesburg.

". . . I do not understand but he does impeach my honor, truth, and candor, and because he does this I do not see that I am bound, if I see truthful grounds for it, to keep my hands off of him." The onetime wrestler from New Salem vowed, "I know that I will not be the first one to cry hold. I know it originated with the Judge, and when he quits," shouted Lincoln, "I probably will."

The crowd laughed.

"But I shall not ask any favors at all."

Still going, still having left alone issues of policy, Lincoln called, "He asks me, or rather, asks the audience, if I wish to press this matter to the point of personal difficulty. I tell him no. He did not mis-state, in one of his early speeches, when he called me an amiable man, though perhaps, he did when he called me an intelligent man."

"He did so," called a voice according to the *Times*.

"It really hurts me to suppose that I have wronged any man on earth. I tell him no. I very much prefer, when this canvass shall be over, to be on terms of friendship, let it result as it may."

A voice called out, "We don't want to hear your long yarns."

"Now is my friend entirely sure that these people agree with him," called Lincoln. According to the *Times*, an "uproar" followed, and Lincoln shouted, "Don't waste my time."

Having ingratiated himself with the crowd in a spitting contest with Douglas, Lincoln finally turned to substance; he sensed that it was time to return to first principles.

"We have in this nation this element of domestic slavery," he began. "It is a matter of absolute certainty that it is a disturbing element. . .it is a dangerous element. Why keep up controversy in regard to it?"

Noting that the controversy sprang from a difference of opinion, Lincoln reduced the conflict to one "between the man who thinks slavery wrong and those who do not think it wrong. . ."

He continued, "We, the Republican party, think it wrong. We think it is a moral, social, and a political wrong." And further, "We think it is a wrong, not confining itself merely to the person or the States where it exists, but it is a wrong outspreading, that extends itself to the interest of the whole nation."

What did Lincoln mean when he charged that slavery's spread extended itself to the whole nation's interest? At one level, he certainly must have had in mind the threat to the territories as the homes of "free, white people." But seven years after the debates, he would speak of a terrible war as the woe due Americans north and south for the sin of "American slavery." He offered no clear indication of what "the interest of the whole nation" meant, but he had by now come to the realization that Northerners who sat by and let slavery grow were morally responsible for a vast moral evil. Did he yet suspect they might pay a price? When he saw the tents pitched by the Galesburg crowds, the uniformed marching bands, the militia companies that met him in Quincy and in the other towns, could he in his mind's eye foresee a time when bands, tents, and uniformed, armed bodies of men would mark the bloodiest event in his nation's history?

Since slavery was wrong, Republicans would support policies similar to those regarding any other wrong, "in so far as we can prevent it from growing any larger, and so that in the run of time there may be some promise of an end of it."

"Amen," shouted a voice.

But there were limits. Called Lincoln, "we have no right to disturb it where it does exist. We think that the Constitution would permit us to disturb and abolish it in the District of Columbia, but we are unwilling to do that on the terms which we do not suppose the nation would agree to very soon—the gradual emancipation of the slave, with compensation to unwilling owners."

Lincoln here covered his flank; he had been saying these sorts of things all along, since Ottawa.

He turned to Dred Scott. Noting the Republicans' opposition to the ruling, he added, "We do not propose that when Dred Scott is decided to be a slave, that we will raise a mob to make him free; we do not propose that when any one—or one thousand—or any number in his condition shall be decided in like manner, that we will disturb that decision," he shouted, "but we do oppose it as a political rule that shall be binding upon the man when he goes to the polls to vote, or upon members of Congress, or upon the President, to favor no measure that does not actually tally with the principle of that decision," for Republicans believe that "it lays the foundation of spreading the evil into the States themselves. . ."

Time grew short; he would need this district with its former Whigs, its abolitionists, and its perhaps wavering Democrats. Speaking slowly, deliberately, he drove to a conclusion. 23

"There is a sentiment which holds that slavery is not wrong," Lincoln began, "it goes for a policy that does not propose dealing with it as dealing with a wrong."

Who held to such a policy?

"That is the Democratic policy—that is the Democratic sentiment," and "the leading man—I think I may do my friend Judge Douglas the honor of calling him the leading man in the advocacy of the Democratic party—has never said that it is wrong."

Perhaps pausing to let that sink in, Lincoln underscored it:

"He has, I believe, the honor of never saying that it is right or wrong."

Hitt reported laughter at the notion that any American politician of the late 1850s could possible have no public position on the morality of slavery.

Lincoln asked each anti-slavery Democrat in the crowd to ponder that. And he continued, addressing free-soil Democrats:

"You say it is wrong—do you not object to anybody else saying so?"

He bore in.

"You say it must not be opposed in the free States because it is not here, and it must not be opposed in the slave States because it exists there. It must not be opposed in politics because it will make a fuss; it must not be opposed in the pulpit because it is not religion. . ." to what the *Trib* heard as cheers, Lincoln crowned the absurdity: ". . . in short, there is no suitable place to say anything wrong against that thing that is wrong."

He pressed on.

"If Judge Douglas says that whatever community wants slaves has a right to have them, his logic is correct if he does not believe it a wrong. When he says that slave property, and horse and hog property ought to be allowed to go together to a territory upon principle, it is true if there is no difference between them, perhaps; but if one of them is right and the other wrong then there is no equality between right and wrong."

"Douglas is right!" someone shouted.

"That is just the question we are going to try," said Lincoln.

His time was about up.

"So turn it any way you can in all the arguments that sustain the Democratic policy, and in that policy itself there is a careful, studied exclusion of the idea that there be any wrong" in slavery. And whenever all who did think it wrong unified, "I think we may see how we shall get an end to this slavery agitation."

According to Hitt, Lincoln sat to prolonged cheers.

He had asked Douglas a question in its way more probing than the famed Freeport question: *Is slavery wrong?*

"I Tell You Why I Can't Do It"

As "tremendous applause" died down following Douglas's introduction, he intoned, "Unless entire silence is observed it will be impossible for me to be heard." Douglas's voice showed signs of wear and tear. "My friends can do me no higher favor than to preserve silence through the whole of my remarks, omitting all expressions of applause or approbation."

"We cannot help it, Douglas," hollered some uncooperative but honest soul.

"I desire to be heard rather than applauded. I wish to address myself to your reason, to your sense of justice, and not to your passions."

Douglas turned to what he persisted in calling the Springfield resolutions of 1854.

"I regret," he called, "that Mr. Lincoln should have deemed it proper for him again to have indulged in gross personality, and to have resorted to insinuations and charges," and furthermore, "I tell him, too, that it will not do to charge forgery on Charles H. Lanphier or Thomas L. Harris. No man on earth that knows these men or Lincoln could believe Lincoln on oath against either of them." Democrats applauded and cheered; Douglas had for the first time accused Lincoln of personal dishonesty. By now, each candidate showed signs of irritation with the other.

And, about those resolutions.

"I quoted them at Ottawa only for the purpose of asking Mr. Lincoln where he stood on that platform. . .I read them and put those questions. He refused then to answer."

Laughter; "He was afraid," someone hollered.

"Subsequently, one week later he did answer a part of the points, and on the other he has never answered to this day."

At this, Hitt reported "great confusion" in the crowd; the *Times* heard cries of, "No, and never will," "Never can," and cheering. Douglas had ignited the Democrats in the crowd. But. . .

"My friends, if you are my friends, you will be silent, instead of interrupting even by your applause."

"We can't help it," Binmore heard someone yell.

"I ask him," continued Douglas, "Will you admit Kansas to the Union with just such a constitution as the people want—with slavery or without, as they shall determine? He didn't answer. I have put the question to him from time to time again—he won't answer it." And it wasn't just Kansas.

"I ask him again, will he vote to admit New Mexico. . .either with slavery or without it, as they shall decide? He won't answer."

As the crowd cheered, the Times reported someone yelling, "He's afraid."

What about Oregon?

"He won't answer," called Douglas.

Washington Territory?

"He won't answer."

And the "new states to be carved out of Texas"?

"He won't answer."

An effective, slashing attack, even if Douglas had not persistently posed these questions in all or even most of the five debates prior to Quincy.

What was more, what with the Kansas-Nebraska Act and the *Dred Scott* ruling, the playing field had been tilted, for slavery could not be barred from any of these territories.

And then there was Lincoln's two-facedness. As at Galesburg, Douglas had cited Lincoln's Chicago speech to ask why, if rights could be denied blacks they might not be denied to Germans. He reprised the line in an obvious attempt to damage Lincoln among Quincy's largest immigrant group, and to contrast Lincoln's northern Illinois remarks with those outside the northern counties. Why, cried Douglas, "can't he avow his principles the same in the North and in the South, in every county, if he has the conviction that his principles are just?" Lincoln "could not be a Republican if his principles could stretch alike over all the country." In fact, those principles "cannot even cross the Missouri River in your ferry boat." (Douglas must have meant the Mississippi River, but the line got applause and laughter.)

He then raised a fair question.

"He says that he is not now, and never was, in favor of interfering with slavery where it exists in the States. Well, if he is not in favor of that, how does he expect by his policy to bring it into a condition of ultimate extinction?"

Binmore heard a voice, "Hit him again."

"How can he extinguish it in Kentucky, Virginia, in any slave State, by his policy, if he won't pursue a line of policy that would affect it in the states?"

Noting that Lincoln *had* said that he would bar slavery in the territories, Douglas opened a tortured line of argument.

This would confine slavery to the southern states alone, and what would that mean? "[T]he natural increase will go on until the increase is so plenty that they cannot live on the soil. He will then hem them in until starvation awaits them. . ." Lincoln could only "extinguish" slavery "by extinguishing the negro race, if he drives them to the point of starvation; and that is the humane remedy, the Christian remedy, that he proposes for the great crime of slavery."

Now, Douglas confronted Lincoln's pointed question.

"He tells you I won't argue the question of whether slavery is right or wrong. I tell you why I can't do it."

Douglas had gone right up to the edge of commenting on slavery's morality, for the first time in this race. Now he would explain why he could not do so.

"I hold that under the Constitution of the United States, each State of this Union has a right to do as it pleases on the subject of slavery."

That was it? Because states get to choose whether they would allow slavery, a United States Senator and leading party figure could not speak on the morality of slavery?

"It is none of my business whether slavery exists in Missouri or not. Missouri is a sovereign State of this Union, and has the same right to decide the slavery question for herself that Illinois had to decide for herself."

This was a form of moral relativism way ahead of its time. Not only could the Senator do nothing about Missourians' collective decision to establish slavery in their state, he could not even say whether he thought it a moral decision. All Douglas would say was that he "approve[d] the line of policy which Illinois has adopted on this subject."

And practically, all of the breath that Lincoln expended on the morality of slavery was worth nothing as a potential US Senator. "Why, is he going to discuss the rightfulness of slavery, when Congress cannot act upon it either way [?]" asked Douglas. "He is going to discuss the merits of the Dred Scott decision, when under the Constitution a Senator has no right to interfere with the decisions of the judicial tribunals."

That didn't mean that Senator Lincoln wouldn't try.

"When I used to practice law with Lincoln, I never knew him to get beat in a case in the world, that he did not get mad at the Judge and talk about appealing it."

The crowd laughed at Douglas's recollection of Lincoln the Sore Loser.

"And when I got beat in the case, I generally thought the Court was wrong; but I never dreamed of going out of the court house and making a stump speech against the Judges, merely because I found out I didn't know the law as well as they did."

The *Times* reported great laughter.

Lincoln, called Douglas, "because he is a Republican," held that "he is not bound by the decision of the Court. . .Well, it may be that Republicans don't hold themselves bound by the laws of the land and the Constitution of our country, as expounded by the courts," but "Democrats are bound by it because they cannot resist it. A Democrat cannot resist the constitutional authorities of his country. . ."

"*Good*," someone yelled.

". . .A Democrat is a law-abiding man. A Democrat stands by the Constitution, by the laws, by the constituted authorities, and relies upon liberty as protected by law, and not upon mob or physical violence."

As a counter statement to Lincoln's articulation of Republican principles, Douglas's words had the virtue of simplicity. But the argument was a little hard to sustain, given Andrew Jackson's defiance of Supreme Court rulings on the Bank of the United States and the Cherokee, and in the face of Democratic involvement in the murder of the printer Elijah Lovejoy in Alton twenty-one years earlier.

He pressed on, venturing into areas that promised controversy should the Senator ever seek slave state votes for president, reminding the crowd that slavery could not go into Kansas or any other territory if the residents of the territory passed "unfriendly legislation," just as "unfriendly legislation" similar to Maine's temperance laws could cause purveyors of liquor to have to dump their booze in the gutter upon reaching the territorial border. (An interesting argument for a fellow with a reputation for hard drinking.) And in a comment that foreshadowed more grief than Douglas could perhaps have known as he stood on a platform in Adams County on an autumn day, he responded to Lincoln's query about a congressional fugitive slave code for the territories:

"I would not vote for a code of laws for or against slavery in any Territory by Congress. I will leave the people of each Territory to decide that question for themselves."

The *Times* reported cheers in response to Douglas's declaration, the sort of declaration that—coupled with his return to the Freeport Doctrine—he had not uttered in Jonesboro or Charleston.

But, much as he chided Lincoln for regional pandering, Douglas had begun to see a need for just such positioning. At Galesburg and again here at Quincy, he reminded his audiences of the ways in which he had not been—and would not be--an agent of the slave power conspiracy. Hadn't he led the fight against the Lecompton Constitution? Wasn't he on record as defending the right of anti-slavery territorial settlers to enact legislation unfriendly to slavery? Hadn't he declared his opposition to a federal fugitive slave code for the territories? None of these were at variance with Douglas's political philosophy, the philosophy of the Jacksonian Democratic party, a philosophy which celebrated local self-government. But he proclaimed this element of that philosophy in places such as Galesburg, Freeport, and Quincy. When he visited areas further south, the emphasis swung to another, less attractive aspect of Jacksonian ideology: white supremacy.

This commitment to self-government may have made him enemies, cried Douglas, among them the Buchanan administration and its house organ, the Washington *Union*, but he would "cling firmly to that great principle of self-government" no matter what the political consequences.

He had to do this; Douglas deemed it critical to the survival of the Union. For if "every State of this Union will only agree to mind its own business, and let slavery alone, there will be peace forever between us."

Douglas continued, "In this State we have declared our policy that a negro shall not be a citizen. [The *Times* reported: "All right."] We have also declared that he shall not be a slave. We have a right to adopt that policy. Missouri has just as good a right to adopt the other policy."

He explained, "I am now speaking of rights under the Constitution. I am not speaking of moral or religious right. I don't discuss the morals of the people of Missouri, but let them settle that for themselves." Looking out at the Missourians, Illinoisans, and Iowans arrayed below him, Douglas declared, "I hold that the people of the slaveholding States are civilized men as well as we. They have consciences as well as we. They are accountable to God and to posterity and not to us, and it is for them to decide the moral and religious right of their slavery question for themselves within their limits. . ."

No smart aleck thought to ask Douglas if this rule would apply were Missouri to legalize cannibalism. But the Little Giant was not quite finished with his discussion of the peculiar institution.

"Let each State mind its own business, and let its neighbors alone—then there will be no trouble on this question. If we will stand by that great principle, then Mr. Lincoln will find that this Republic can exist forever divided into free and slave States, as our fathers made it."

Forever.

If we just followed that principle, America would, as he had said before, "become the admiration and terror of the world," it could "perform its great mission—that destiny which Providence has marked out for us." The nation could "receive, with entire safety, that stream of intelligence flowing from the Old World into the New, filling up the prairies, cutting down the forests, building up cities and towns, railroads and internal improvements, thus making this the asylum of the oppressed of the world." (Terror of the world, cut down the forests, develop the open space. . .again, Douglas was a man ahead of his time.)

On something of a roll, the Senator called, "[I]t don't become Mr. Lincoln, or anybody else, to tell the people of Kentucky that they have no conscience—to tell them that they are living in a state of iniquity—to tell them that they are cherishing an institution to their bosom in violation of the law of God. Better for him to adopt the doctrine of, 'Judge not, lest ye be judged.'"

The Senator then revealed an understanding of the Union that almost suggested that the states were sovereign nations. Douglas sounded like modern-day isolationists who oppose the US government sending resources to Bangladesh as long as some Americans live in squalor.

"Let him perform his own duty at home within our limits, and then he will have a better fate in the future. I think there are objects of charity enough in all the free States to exhaust the pockets, and the sympathies, too, of all the benevolent that we have, without going away in search of negroes of whose condition we know nothing. We have objects of charity at home—let us perform our own domestic duties. Let us take care of our own poor, our own suffering, and make them comfortable and happy, before we go abroad to meddle with other people's business."

(Did Douglas really "know nothing" of the blacks' condition? As manager of that Mississippi plantation he took some pride in the quality of care he insisted the slaves be given.)

The ninety minutes were up. Although the crowd had been raucous, the Senator ended graciously, thanking the people for "the kindness and courtesy with which you have listened to me." He called, "It is something remarkable that in an audience as vast as this, with men of opposite politics and passions highly excited, there should be such courtesy towards not only one another, but towards the speaker, and I feel that it is due to you that I should express my gratitude for the kindness with which you have treated me."

To loud applause—the *Times* counted nine cheers for the Little Giant— Douglas retired.

"We Are Getting A Little Nearer the Issue. . ."

Binmore and Sheridan allowed that Republicans greeted Lincoln with three cheers, but since "his party kept up a perfect bedlam. . .there was such confusion on the side of the platform occupied by Republican marshals that great difficulty was experienced in hearing him."

Which meant that only handfuls of the crowd may have heard Lincoln pounce.

"I wish to return to Judge Douglas my profound thanks for his public announcement here to-day to be put on record, that his system of policy in regard to the institution of slavery contemplates that it will last for ever."

Somehow or other, enough people heard Lincoln's direct hit on Douglas' gaffe to break out in cheers of, "Hit him again."

"We are getting a little nearer the true issue of this controversy, and I am profoundly grateful for that one sentence."

With one-half hour to go in his penultimate debate with the incumbent, Lincoln seemed confident, jubilant even. What had begun in Ottawa as the Douglas-Lincoln debates seemed to have radically changed character.

"Judge Douglas asks why can't the institution of slavery, or the Union part free and part slave continue as our fathers made it, forever?"

Lincoln had a ready answer for that question. "I insist that our fathers did not make this nation half slave and half free. . . I insist that they found the institution existing here, and didn't make it so, but left it so because they did not know the way to alter it at that time, and that is all."

Republicans cheered him on.

"When Judge Douglas undertakes to establish that the fathers of the government as a matter of choice undertook to make the Union part slave and part free, he assumes to insist upon what is historically a falsehood."

Noting that the Founders had in fact barred slavery from the Northwest Territory and had later criminalized the Atlantic slave trade, Lincoln shouted over the din, "When Judge Douglas asks me why it cannot continue forever as our fathers made it, I ask him and his friends, why they could not let it remain as our fathers made it?"

Lincoln had only twenty-odd minutes with which to work. Time for a change of topic and for a slight change of tone, from opportunistic to humorous.

"The Judge has informed me, or this audience, that the Washington *Union* is laboring for my election to the United States Senate." Lincoln called, "That is news to me, not very ungrateful."

He turned toward the Democrats on the platform, and eyed one W. H. Carlin, a Danite.

"I hope Carlin will get elected to the State Senate and will vote for me for United States Senate."

Carlin called out, "Carlin don't fall in."

To laughter, Lincoln responded, "Carlin don't fall in."

The Republican innocently declared, "I am glad of all the support I can get anywhere, if I can get it without practicing any deception for it."

Noting that Douglas had spent much of his speech proclaiming the rightness of his Lecompton stand, Lincoln called, "I say to Douglas, 'give it to them just all you can.'"

Hitt reported laughter and cheers. Lincoln had noticed other Danites on the platform.

"And on the other hand I say to Carlin and Jake Davis and our man Wagley up here, give it to Douglas. . ." There were "roars of laughter," reported the *Trib*, ". . .just pour it into him. You know him and he knows you. It is a fair fight, just clear the way and let them have it."

Lincoln seemed to have ignited all three components of the crowd, Republicans, Douglasites, and Danites; the *Times* reported cheers of,

"Hurrah for Douglas, for Jack Davis and Border Ruffian Jake." The *Tribune* reporters heard, "Good for you," and "Hurrah for Lincoln."

Lincoln would not disengage on Dred Scott, his third topic as the sun began to sink over the Mississippi. Douglas, shouted Lincoln, "is desirous of knowing how we are going to reverse the Dred Scott decision."

Lincoln looked out over the crowd. "Well, now, Judge Douglas ought to know! Did he not, and his political friends find a way to reverse a decision of that same court in favor of the constitutionality of the United States Bank?"

(This was a reach. In 1832, Douglas's political hero Andrew Jackson had vetoed the re-charter of the Second Bank of the United States, which had itself been ruled constitutional by John Marshall's Supreme Court in 1819. Douglas may have supported the veto, but he was not directly involved in killing the Bank.)

And then Lincoln moved to a more legitimate example of Douglas's handiwork regarding the judiciary. When in the early 1840s the Illinois Supreme Court had ruled against a Democratic governor who had attempted to place limits on the Secretary of State, Douglas had taken the lead in passing a court re-organization bill; when the smoke had cleared away, Douglas had gone from state legislator to—*voilà*—State Supreme Court Justice!

"[D]id he not go and make speeches in the lobby and show how it [the original Court ruling] was villainous, and did he not succeed in sitting on the bench, getting his name of Judge in that way?"

Hitt heard "thundering cheers and laughter."

"If there is any villainy in opposition to Supreme Court decisions commend it to Judge Douglas's consideration. I know of no man in the State of Illinois who ought to know so much villainy it takes to oppose a decision of the Supreme Court as our honorable friend S. A. Douglas."

Although the *Tribune* reported "Long continued applause," the *Times* heard someone yell, "Hurrah for Douglas then."

Lincoln kept moving. Next topic, unfriendly legislation.

Perhaps too conscious of the dwindling time, Lincoln began a slightly confused inquest designed to ask whether territorial legislators sworn to uphold the Constitution could legally enact laws unfriendly to slave owners. The reality, the hard reality was that although "Judge Douglas had sung paeans to his popular sovereignty doctrine," the Taney Court "has squatted his popular sovereignty out of the way."

To what Hitt called, "uproarious laughter and applause," Lincoln shouted, "To still keep up that humbug about popular sovereignty he has at last invented this sort of do-nothing sovereignty"—more laughs—"of the people excluding slavery by doing nothing at all."

Continuing laughter, reported the *Times.*

"I ask you is this not running down his popular sovereignty doctrine to death, till it has got as thin as the homeopathic soup that was made by boiling the shadow of a pigeon that was starved to death?"

"Roars of laughter," according to Hitt.

But it was an impossibility; two bodies could not occupy the same position at the same time: "The Dred Scott decision covers the whole ground and while it stands there is not room for even the shadow of a starved pigeon to occupy the same ground."

Someone on the platform yelled, *"Your time is almost out."*

According to the *Tribune,* this triggered a reaction.

"Go on, go on, we'll listen to you all day."

"Well," Hitt quoted Lincoln, "I'll talk to you a little longer."

Still locked in a competition to get right with Henry Clay, Lincoln noted that the great man had held that in the organization of new societies amid the territories, slavery should be banned under the principle that "all men are created equal."

"Now, when I sometimes in relation to the organization of new societies in some new countries where the soil is clean and clear," advocate the identical policy to that of Clay, "Mr. Douglas will insist that I want a nigger wife. . ."

(How did Lincoln use that word? Did he use it to pander to the white supremacists in the crowd, proving as he had earlier in the campaign that he was one of the boys when it came to blacks? Did he lapse deep into his Kentucky native tongue, where "negro" might have come out as 'nigra?" Or did he employ the term to lampoon his opponents' use of it, to make Douglas look overheated and irrational? The transcripts offer no clue, although Hitt reported that there was "Great laughter" immediately following those words.) 24

Never does Douglas understand, shouted Lincoln "that there can be any middle ground on this." Then it was into familiar territory, as Lincoln noted that he'd lived half a century without a black slave or a black wife, "and I think I can live fifty centuries for that matter without having either."

Still time? Then one last shot at the "forged" 1854 resolutions, and one more shot at the Senator, for whom Lincoln was beginning to feel real irritation.

Douglas "wants to know why I won't withdraw a charge in regard to a conspiracy to make slavery national, as he has withdrawn the one that he has made" on the resolutions.

"May it please his worship," spat Lincoln, "I will withdraw it when it is proved false like that was proved false on him."

A moment later, Lincoln sat down, as "a deafening cheer went up that was continued with unabated enthusiasm for some minutes," according to Hitt.

Perhaps they were cheering what had happened since Galesburg; if Illinoisans had attended the Douglas-Lincoln debates beginning in the

August heat in Ottawa, now, as the harvest approached, something had changed. Having experimented with a variety of approaches in the first four debates, Lincoln had put together three powerful hours in the past six October days, toe-to-toe with the greatest man in American politics.

He had remade the series into the Lincoln-Douglas Debates.

"Go Home and Keep Quiet Till After the Election"

Both men remained in Quincy that night. Lincoln stayed in the home of Quincy Republican Orville Browning (who was not himself in town; Browning doubted Lincoln's capacity to make much of a run against the Little Giant, and played little role in aiding the challenger's campaign, although Lincoln and Browning were friends.) Douglas and Adele spent another night at the hotel. The next night, both men booked passage on the steamboat *City of Louisiana*; 115 miles south lay Alton. No one left any account of what went on that night on the river; it's up to our imagination as to whether they avoided one another, conversed, prepared for the next day's showdown, or caught up on their sleep. 25

Nearing their close, the debates began to attract criticism. The Democrat James Gordon Bennett's New York *Herald* jeered on October 13 that, "the best thing that Douglas and Lincoln can do, is to close up their debates . . . go home, and keep quiet till after the election." The *Herald* charged that the two had "exhausted the field of legitimate debate" and "descended into the dirty arena of personalities." The New York paper predicted that before long, Lincoln and Douglas might resort to "'the noble art of self defense' unless their friends take them away." Earlier, a Virginia paper had similarly forecast "a pugilistic encounter" to cap what it called "the most malignant and reckless contest which ever disgraced the annals of American history." Just after the Charleston debate, the Cincinnati *Commercial* had written: "Few debates less dignified in their external manifestations, or containing so little that was worthy to be remembered, have fallen under our observation." And the *Commercial* joined with papers in other corners of the nation in condemning Illinoisans' provocative campaign to rest control of Senate seats away from the state legislature. The Cincinnati *Gazette* reminded its readers that "Washington was no speechmaker, neither was Jefferson," and the editors doubted that "the stump is the best way by which to judge candidates and their principles." A more impressed Chester Dewey would agree that the challenge to the Constitution's mode of choosing senators made this a moment "without parallel in the history of electioneering campaigns in this country." 26

Ahead lay the yet faintly bloodstained Alton riverfront.

CHAPTER SEVEN: "IT IS THE ETERNAL QUESTION"

"Why Cannot We Thus Have Peace?"

The *City of Louisiana* docked in downtown Alton, along the Mississippi's east bank, at 5 a.m. on Friday, October 15. The two candidates awakened to the day that would hold the last of their face-to-face meetings in this race. 1

The riverfront had deep historical meaning. For it was up the river from nearby St. Louis that Elijah Lovejoy, a Maine-born abolitionist and nativist newspaper editor, had come to town in 1837. The printer's reputation had preceded him and anti-abolitionist mobs had more than once attempted to silence him by seizing his newly-arrived printing presses at Alton's docks then throwing the presses into the Mississippi. 2

In August of that year Lovejoy called a state antislavery convention at Alton, to be held in October. But the Democratic state Attorney General, an anti-abolitionist provocateur, helped to arrange a counter-meeting of "colonizationists." In fact, the meeting drew large numbers of white supremacists, slavery supporters and riverfront toughs who had already menaced Lovejoy. Two decades later, that attorney general would acquire the nickname "For-God's-Sake" as a desperate Stephen A. Douglas pled for help in the 1858 Senate race. Usher F. Linder would play a central role in the disturbances that scarred the name of this river town perched above the Mississippi. 3

When inevitably tensions rose in the late autumn, Linder ignited a fire, asking in a November 3 public meeting, "whether the interests and feelings of the citizens of Alton should be consulted or whether we are to be dictated to by foreigners" such as Lovejoy. In a wild speech, Linder questioned Lovejoy's sanity. Abolitionist Edward Beecher would later call the attorney general's performance, "Unequaled by anything I ever heard for an excited, bitter, vindictive spirit." To close, Linder pushed through a resolution that, "discussion of the doctrines of immediate abolitionism, as they have been discussed in the columns of the Alton *Observer*, would be destructive of the peace and harmony of the citizens of Alton, and that, therefore, we cannot recommend the reestablishment of that paper." 4

This was in effect a get-out-of-town notice from a fairly dangerous group of men, but Lovejoy, who was nothing if not stubborn, refused to leave. His wife was pregnant with their second child, and furthermore he had decided, "to make my grave at Alton" in the cause of freedom of the press and immediate abolition. And a new press was on the way, to arrive within days. Soon the press was quietly installed in the warehouse where Lovejoy planned to resume publishing, and residents "learned that Lovejoy would not leave under any circumstances and that the leading state and city officials did not seem to frown on violence." Linder, the top law-enforcement official in the state of Illinois, would leave town early the next morning but not before remarking, "Elijah Lovejoy will be killed in two weeks." 5

Linder got his wish. On the night of November 7, a mob of men who had liquored up at Alton's Tontine Tavern set out, forming a line, "almost like a military line" to attack the warehouse where Lovejoy's newest press sat, guarded by Lovejoy himself and a handful of allies. This added another element to the collision, for Lovejoy was no William Lloyd Garrison, no pacifist fighter against slavery. Empowered to defend themselves by a local government that claimed it lacked the capacity to quell the threatened street violence, Lovejoy and his supporters bore arms themselves, and used them.

But it didn't last long. When Lovejoy himself emerged to attempt to staunch a fire on the warehouse roof midway through the battle of Alton, two physicians who read the Hippocratic Oath rather narrowly, Doctors Horace Beal and James Jennings, took aim and dropped the printer. Five bullets found their mark. (A third doctor, Thomas Hope, claimed afterward to have shot Lovejoy also.) Lovejoy's brothers, Owen and John, at home with their sister-in-law, saw the printer's riderless horse coming and knew something had gone terribly wrong in the defense of the *Observer's* right to publish. 6

Although it was not the first case of anti-abolitionist violence in the free states (Garrison had for instance nearly been killed in the streets of Boston in 1831), the murder of Lovejoy caught the attention of Americans north and south, including young Abraham Lincoln, who noted it as an example of the "rising mobocratic spirit" in America in an 1838 speech to the Springfield Young Men's Lyceum. It also troubled Garrisonians, who had foresworn violence in their war against slavery. Although decrying the murder, Garrison, Samuel J. May, Wendell Phillips, and Sarah Grimke doubted that slavery could be ended with muskets. 7

At the same time, as much as a modern commentator has written that today's Alton citizens "are proud to say that in 1837 Elijah Lovejoy died defended his printing press and the First Amendment with his life," the murder also stained the city's reputation. In no other free state town had an abolitionist, albeit an armed abolitionist, died in the struggle to end slavery. Alton suffered economically. Its reputation for lawlessness diverted river traffic to St. Louis, and property values tumbled; this in a town that had once hoped to become one of the great cities of the West. 8

Alton had also been the site of Lincoln's abortive duel with James Shields in 1842. Shields, born in County Tyrone, took umbrage at some mocking letters that Lincoln may have conspired with Mary Todd to publish in the *Sangamo Journal*, and he'd challenged Lincoln. (Lincoln actually took the rap for a particularly offensive letter written by Mary and Julia Jayne after Lincoln had gotten the ball rolling with his own epistle. It was the honorable thing to do and it might have cost him his life.) On September 22, Lincoln, Shields, and seconds met in Alton. (Dr. Thomas Hope, never one to miss a shoot-out, was Shields' second.) They rowed out to Sunflower Island--also known to some as Bloody Island--on the Missouri side of the river, for dueling was illegal in Illinois. As so often happened in these affairs, cooler heads prevailed, apologies were made, and the whole party rowed back to Alton. Some locals gathered on the east bank to see "a bloody corpse" in the boat. It was in fact a log covered with a red shirt, and Lincoln and Shields and company got a good laugh. They sure knew how to have a good time in those days. 9

The Alton near-duel, in one historian's words, "had some unanticipated benefits" for Lincoln. First, the incident "helped him understand how painful the unintended effects of his undisciplined sense of humor could be." And second, the tempest led to "the renewal of his engagement to Mary Todd, who was touched by his chivalry in covering her contributions to the . . .letters." (For his part, Shields would serve in the Mexican War, become a loyal Douglas Democrat, represent Illinois and Minnesota in the U.S. Senate, and have more battlefield success against Stonewall Jackson than would his fellow political generals, John C. Fremont or Commissary Banks in Jackson's dashing Shenandoah Valley Campaign. Not that that was saying much.)

Still, the duel "remained one of Lincoln's most painful memories," writes David Herbert Donald, one that neither he nor Mary ever willingly spoke of again. 10

Thus it must have been with at least some unease that Lincoln stepped off the steamer in Alton; the place carried for him an embarrassing memory and it had a history of being rough on anti-slavery outsiders. Perhaps it helped that for the first time in the seven debates, Mary would be on hand, along with the Lincolns' eldest son Robert. (Perhaps. Outside of Thomas Lincoln, no two members of Lincoln's family get worse press than do high-strung Mary and humorless Bob.) The Sangamon-Alton railroad's special half-price train from Springfield carried the two, Bob in the blue and gold tunic and white pants of the Springfield Cadets militia unit. 11

Douglas's second wife, Adele, had accompanied the Senator to all of his meetings with Lincoln. It was widely held that Adele's good looks did not hurt Douglas with undecided voters. Adele was also a Catholic, and she and Douglas had been married in the Church; Douglas' sons attended a Jesuit school in Georgetown. In an election where religion was a factor, some nativists held this against Douglas, especially because of Douglas' mocking attacks on church basement abolitionist lecturers, and his "malignant attacks on the Northern minister" as Chicago's *Congregational Herald* termed it. On balance, however, Adele's steady presence probably worked to the Senator's favor, partly on appearances (she had turned him into a well-dressed man, and she was an attractive woman) and partly because he had to behave himself at least moderately well after hours in her presence. 12

In contrast, Mary had spent August, September, and the first half of October as a single parent to three boys, at least two of whom, Tad and Willie, were renowned for being a handful. (Billy Herndon, who positively dreaded visits by the Lincoln boys to the law office, famously said that their father indulged them so that if they were to shit in his hat he'd chuckle and think it was clever.) Mary remains a controversial figure among historians, who tend to either defend her or savage her. But even though neighbors once swore they saw her chasing hubby across the backyard wielding a carving knife, no one doubts that she loved Lincoln and craved for him electoral success. Just ask Senator and Mrs. Lyman Trumbull of Alton. When Trumbull nosed out Lincoln for the Senate seat in 1855, Lincoln had nevertheless maintained a strong political relationship with the new senator. But Mary had cut off Julia Jayne Trumbull, her former co-conspirator in the 1842 letters that had landed Lincoln in the duel on Bloody Island. Suffice to say that life in general was not easy for Mary Todd Lincoln, and that the past two-and-a-half months could not have been a picnic, not with her husband paying little or no attention to his family. 13

Three days earlier the German political leader Gustave Koerner had seen Douglas arrive in Quincy, and professed to be "shocked at the condition he was in. His face was bronzed, which was natural enough, but it was also bloated, and his looks were haggard, and his voice almost extinct. In conversation he merely whispered." Although accounts suggest that Douglas looked better upon arriving in Alton (despite the 5 a.m. arrival time), Koerner sensed that the campaign was wearing on the Senator, who would cover close to 5,000 miles over three months before it ended. Still, the Democrats staged a spirited rally marked by "martial music and artillery fire." (The artillery fire did not come from Douglas's railroad flat car, for Douglas had eschewed the railroad for the steamboat. Nonetheless, the Dixon *Republican and Telegraph*, noting the absence of the six-pounder jeered that the Little Giant had found that Lincoln "is all the pounder he needs.") 14

When the Republican welcome to Lincoln proved underwhelming, Lincoln knew who he had better take care of, so he asked Koerner to locate Mary and reassure her. Koerner had attended Kentucky's Transylvania University, and had known Lexington-bred Mary for a long time, and Lincoln urged him to "go up and see Mary. Now tell Mary what you think of our chances. She is rather dispirited." Koerner walked over to the Franklin House on State Street, and met Mary in the Lincolns' second floor room, and temporarily settled her fears by predicting that "we will carry the state and we are tolerably certain of carrying the legislature." 15

Part of the problem was that the novelty had worn off of the debates. Alton had expected crowds similar to those in Quincy and Galesburg, but on this day only about 5,000 people showed up; an indicator of the flagging interest was the dollar discount on steamboat service from St. Louis. Illinoisans may have reached the saturation point, which coincided with harvest season. 16

This didn't stop the newspapers from continuing their harassment of the two candidates. The two Freeport papers continued to abuse Lincoln and Douglas and sometimes one another; an October 14 exchange over which candidate was truly the tool of the Illinois Central Railroad caused H.M. Sheetz, the Republican editor of the *Weekly Journal* to ask, "Has the editor of the Bulletin no fear of death and a just retribution, that he utters such glaring falsehoods?" For his part, W.T. Giles, the *Bulletin's* editor, dredged back up the Mexican War. Lincoln's Spot Resolutions "were in substance that our nation was wrong, and that it was the duty of Congress to withdraw troops from Mexico, and that if the soldiers' bones were left to bleach on the plains, or they met a bloody grave, they had merited it at the hands of the Mexicans." In another article quoting abolitionist disenchantment with Lincoln, the *Bulletin* concluded that "The old fellow is a *moral coward. . .*" Meanwhile, the Dixon *Republican and Telegraph* returned fire on Douglas, asked its readers to "look at the hypocrisy of this time-serving demagogue" who had in Galesburg not once used the word "Black" in reference to Republicans. In Egypt, Douglas had resorted to "insolent, bullying language and billingsgate, but when speaking in the north becomes as mild as a kitten and begs for the support of even those hateful Republicans." The voters may have been cooling off with the coming of autumn, but the editors showed no sign of moderation. 17

By 2:00 the candidates sat on a platform next to the newly-constructed town hall, surrounded by local pols; the Mississippi rolled south, quietly curving around the island where Lincoln had once been ready to fight for his life, as on shore the noise of vendors and the buzz of the crowd carried up to the speakers' platform, which stood not far from the warehouse where Elijah Lovejoy had lost his own. 18

Douglas went first. Drinking in what the friendly *Times* termed "long and loud bursts of applause," Douglas flexed his ragged vocal chords when a local Danite, the ubiquitous Dr. Hope, putative shooter of Lovejoy, erstwhile second to James Shields, sang out:

"Judge, before you commence speaking, allow me to ask one question of you please."

"If you will not occupy too much of my time," said Douglas.

"Only an instant."

"What is your question?"

Hope shouted, "Do you believe that the territorial legislatures ought to pass laws to protect slavery in the territories?"

Douglas said, "You will get your answer in the course of my remarks." The Buchanan Democrats had served notice. They would force Douglas to again articulate his opposition to the South's newest demand, a federal fugitive slave code for the territories.

Over the course of that first hour, Douglas struggled to make himself heard, not because of a particularly boisterous crowd, but because of his failing voice, worn thin over the miles, from Chicago to Cairo, from Charleston to Sullivan. The hours-long speeches, the reception committees, the hand shaking, the hours spent standing and talking, the cigar smoke, the unfamiliar beds in the private homes and hotels, the jouncing carriage rides, the clacking of thousands of railroad ties passing beneath the Illinois Central cars, the inability to shake Lincoln. He was close to spent. 19

Douglas hit predictable lines. He of course admonished the audience at one point ("Gentlemen, your silence is more acceptable to me than your applause, for I desire to address exclusively your judgment"); he worked in the line about the Declaration's signers never intending to assert the equality of "negroes, the savage Indian, or the Fejee Islander," and he nicked Lincoln for holding to principles that could not be proclaimed all over the nation. He waxed eloquently if predictably about the Framers' genius in designing a system that could adapt "to the Green Mountains of Vermont" and the "rice plantations of South Carolina," "the beautiful prairies of Illinois" and the "mining regions of California." He reprised his call-and-answer routine on Lincoln's unwillingness to say whether he would vote yes on a slave-state Kansas, Oregon, Washington, or Southwest, and he got the desired responses.

And he reiterated the most startling thing he had said at Quincy. Just after Dr. Hope's attempt to derail the Little Giant, Douglas turned yet again to the house divided doctrine. In speeches given even before the debates had begun, rasped Douglas, the senator had said, "and [I] have often repeated it, and now again assert that in my opinion this government can endure forever divided into free and slave states as our fathers made it." Lincoln had heard him right.

The long journey to Alton and that 5 o'clock reveille had left the incumbent a little fuzzy. But he shook it off, and before long was reminding his audience that under the founders' guidance, a number of states soon ended slavery, until the free states had "become the majority of the whole Union, having the power in the House of Representatives, the power in the Senate, and consequently the power to elect a President with Northern votes without a Southern State." (This was literally true, but the Senator did not mention that in the Senate the South enjoyed power disproportionate to its population, or that in the House Southern states got a bonus count in determining representation, as 3/5 of the slaves were counted in figuring state population. Nor did Douglas mention that the White House had been occupied by a long train of slaveholders and Northern "Doughfaces" such as Buchanan and Pierce, who would always protect the white South. And he omitted the fact that slaveholders made up a majority of Roger Taney's Supreme Court.)

With northerners having gained "ascendancy under the operation of that great principle of local self-government" Republicans now insisted that, "because we have the power, we will make a warfare against the

Southern States, until we force them to abolish slavery everywhere." That line drew applause, "great applause" if Binmore and Sheridan are to be trusted.

And then Douglas shifted targets. After months of slugging it out with Lincoln, Douglas opened a second front. He had chided Buchanan in past, indirectly by defending his own Lecompton stance, indirectly by taking issue with the Washington *Union,* indirectly by noting the attacks made on him by newly-appointed postmasters in unholy alliance with the Republicans. Now, however, he went whole hog after the President.

Returning to earlier vows to "fight the Lecompton Constitution to the death," Douglas croaked that "there is no power on earth which has a right to ram a Constitution down the throats of an unwilling people." He continued, "Most of the men who denounce my course on the Lecompton question object to it, not because I was right, but because it was expedient at one time, for the sake of keeping the party together, to do wrong." To cheers, Douglas declared, "There is no other safety except always to do right and trust the consequences to God and the people, and I am not going to depart from principle in that instance, nor do I ever intend to do it."

And that might have been that. Douglas did hold that principle close to his heart, and the fraudulent Kansas constitution violated it, as did the attempt to buy off the Kansans via the so-called English bill (which would have relaxed statehood requirements had the settlers reversed field and ratified the Lecompton plan.) Douglas had made similar points in the earlier debates as part of a larger attack on his challenger. But before the eyes of the 5,000, that challenger became part of the background scenery as Douglas found a new target.

"I have no personal difficulty with Mr. Buchanan or his cabinet," began the Senator, and you could tell what that would mean. Douglas had once said that he had no such difficulty with Lincoln, either. But the President "undertook to say to me, if you don't vote as I tell you" on Lecompton, "I tell you I will take off the heads of your friends."

The crowd laughed.

"I said to him in reply: 'You did not elect me. I represent Illinois. I am accountable to Illinois as my constituency and to God, but not to the President, nor any other power on earth.'"

The *Times* reported "vociferous applause" amid shouts of "Good, good."

"And this warfare is made on me because I wouldn't surrender my convictions of duty—because I would not abandon my constituency and receive orders from the executive authority how I should vote under oath in the Senate of the United States."

"Never do it," Binmore and Sheridan heard someone call. "Three cheers."

And because the Senator had taken this stand, Buchanan had targeted Douglas's friends, so that "every post-master, every route-agent, and every Federal office-holder in the State is removed" when having expressed a preference for Douglas over Lincoln.

"I hold that any attempt to control the Senate by the executive is subversive of the principle of our Constitution," he shouted. "And whenever you recognize the right of the Executive to say to a Senator: 'Do this, or I will take off the heads of your friends,' you convert this Republic into a despotism," he continued, "you destroy the independence of the Representative and convert him into a tool of Executive power."

In Charleston, Douglas had taunted his opponent, claiming that he had assumed that he was running against Lincoln, not Lyman Trumbull. But now Lincoln might have turned the tables, and protested that Douglas had forgotten that his opponent was indeed Lincoln, not Buchanan. Why did Douglas shift the spotlight?

He may have been confident that the Senate race was in hand, and that he would have to challenge Buchanan for the presidential nomination in 1860. The Washington *National Era* seems to have thought this the case. Attacking the Buchananite Washington *Union's* denunciation of Douglas's claim of being a Democrat, the *Era* noted that Mississippi's Senator Albert Gallatin Brown (later a Douglas nemesis) had called Douglas "'a better Democrat than nine-tenths of those in the free states who abuse him.'"

The paper mentioned Douglas's support from the Richmond *Enquirer*, and posited that "Mr. Douglas is no Republican but very likely he *is* in the way of Mr. Buchanan for a second term of the Presidency." Looking ahead to just such a clash in 1860, Douglas may have decided to close his campaign as he had opened it in Chicago, with an attack on the man who stood most directly between himself and the White House. 20

Or, as he showed at Galesburg and Quincy, was Douglas still concerned that the centrist voters of middle Illinois found him insufficiently free soil? Over the past week Douglas had spent unprecedented time, energy, and voice reminding his debate audiences of his noble stand against the Lecompton Constitution.

Or was it a clever appeal to those elusive "Old Line Whigs" that both camps pursued with relish? The ideological theme of executive power and its tendency to corrupt the people's legislators had a rich history in American politics, stretching back to the Revolution. Executive officers, it was thought, had a natural tendency to try to buy off legislators by letting them in on patronage decisions, and by doing so, executives attained dominance, killing off republican government. British Whigs had opposed this, and the American revolutionaries liked to call themselves Whigs, too. And when Andrew Jackson had overdone it in killing off the Second Bank of the United States, a Whig Party formed, under the leadership of the man whose presence shadowed these debates, Henry Clay. 21

Since Ottawa, both candidates had sought again and again to get right with Clay. Douglas's attack on Buchanan's corrupt, overheated use of executive power may have been designed to strike a chord with one-time Whigs who had long distrusted presidential power. And this was a perfect way to introduce the next portion of his opening, in which Douglas yet again walked selectively through history. Before, in his words, "it became necessary to organize the Territories of Kansas and Nebraska," the "Whigs and Democrats united in establishing the compromise measures of 1850." They had together applied to the Utah and New Mexico territories the principle "that the people of each State and each Territory should be perfectly free to form and regulate their own domestic institutions to suit themselves." We Democrats and you Whigs basically agreed on the big issues, asserted Douglas. And even the corrupt Buchanan had once been with us, Douglas reminded the audience, as he quoted Buchanan's 1855 letter accepting the Democratic nomination. The Kansas-Nebraska Act, Buchanan had written "'is founded upon principles as ancient as free government itself, and in accordance with them has simply declared the people of a territory like those of a State shall decide for themselves whether slavery shall or shall not exist within their limits.'"

Douglas sought out a face in the crowd.

"There, Dr. Hope, is an answer to the question you put." As Douglas loyalists applauded, the Senator added, "whether he considers it an answer or not, James Buchanan has answered that question."

The hour was nearly up; Douglas could rest in just a few minutes.

He promised, "I will never violate nor abandon that doctrine" of self government, "even though I stand alone."

Binmore and Sheridan heard a voice: "Hurrah for Douglas."

"I have stood and resisted the blandishments and threats of power on the one side, and seduction on the other"—Douglas didn't elaborate on *that*— "standing immovable for that principle, fighting for it when assailed by Northern mobs, and fighting for it when denounced by Southern hostility."

He had one prescription for the thousands arrayed before him, and by implication for the nation.

"I say to you that there is one, and but one, path of safety for this country, and that is to stand immovably by that principle which declares the right of each State, and each Territory to decide this question for themselves . . .If the people of all the States will stand on that principle, and let each State mind its own business, attend to its own affairs and let their neighbors alone, there will be peace between the North and the South and the whole Union."

He closed with a question.

"Why cannot we thus have peace?"

The "cheer after cheer" that "rose in the air" no doubt came from citizens who defined peace as the absence of strife. A little over a century later, an imprisoned descendent of slaves would define peace differently as he scribbled away in an Alabama jail. Peace, wrote Martin Luther King, was less about the absence of conflict than about the presence of justice. Given the "monstrous injustice" endured by nearly four million enslaved blacks, it is hard to see how Douglas's recipe for peace could have worked for long. [22]

"The Eternal Struggle Between Right and Wrong"

The *Times* reported "a great confusion of cries and cheering" when Lincoln rose to speak. Binmore and Sheridan heard many "hurrahs for Douglas" mixed in with similar cheers for Lincoln, as well as voices urging everyone to pipe down and let the candidate speak.

Lincoln began.

"Ladies and Gentlemen—"

"There are no ladies here."

Amid laughter, Lincoln answered, "You are mistaken. There is a fine chance of them back here."

Professing pleasure that Douglas had spent so much of his time attacking the President, Lincoln added that "This is the seventh time that Judge Douglas and I have met in these joint discussions, and the Judge, upon that subject, has been gradually improving."

Laughter, and a voice calling out, "That's so."

Milking the line, Lincoln called as he had at Quincy on both parties to the conflict to prosecute the struggle "in the most vigorous style," and likened his position to that of a wife who found her not entirely pleasant husband attacked by a bear: "I say, 'go it husband and go it bear.'"

"Great laughter," reported Robert Hitt.

Noting Douglas's use of Buchanan's acceptance letter, Lincoln applied the needle again. Douglas had once strongly supported the Missouri Compromise, and had then killed it in the Kansas-Nebraska bill, so "I want to know if Mr. Buchanan has not as much right to be inconsistent as Judge Douglas?" As the crowd laughed and cheered (according to the *Tribune*), Lincoln asked, "Has Judge Douglas an exclusive right to be inconsistent? Has he a monopoly?"

Lincoln turned serious, contending that despite Douglas's charges, the Republican had never criticized the Dred Scott ruling for its passages on black citizenship, but because the ruling "was a portion of a system to make slavery national in the United States." He accused Douglas of today garbling Lincoln's Chicago speech before "an audience with strong sympathies by birth, education, and otherwise with the South," in order "to place me in a strong Abolition attitude."

Lincoln pulled out an old speech of his own given in Springfield in 1857. He had quoted old speeches before, with underwhelming results, in Ottawa and at Charleston. But it was important for this audience to understand what Lincoln meant when he said that "all men are created equal' applied to blacks.

He shouted that the Declaration's authors:

. . .intended to include all men, but they did not intend to declare all men equal in all respects. They did not mean to say that all were equal in color, size, or intellect, moral development or social capacity. They defined with tolerable distinctness in what respect they did consider all men created equal—equal with certain inalienable rights, among which are life, liberty, and the pursuit of happiness. This they said and this they meant. They did not mean to assert the obvious untruth that all men were then actually enjoying that equality, nor yet that they were about to confer it immediately upon them. In fact, they had no power to confer such a boon. They meant simply to declare the right so that the enforcement of it might follow as fast as the circumstances should permit. They meant to set up a standard maxim for free men [Lincoln had said "free society" in 1857] which should be familiar to all and revered by all, constantly looked to and constantly labored for, and even though never perfectly attained, constantly approximated and thereby constantly spreading and deepening its influence and augmenting the happiness and value of life to all people of all colors everywhere. 23

Sure, people like John C. Calhoun had denied this fundamental truth of the American nation, and Douglas's Indiana crony Senator John C. Pettit had "in that rather coarse expression" termed it "a self-evident lie." But until three years ago, "there had never lived a man, who ventured in the sneaking way of pretending to believe in the Declaration then to say, that it did not include the negro." But that changed; "the first man that ever said it was Chief Justice Taney in the Dred Scott case, and," Lincoln built to the laugh line, "the next to him was our friend Judge Douglas," and, he said, his voice rising over the cheers and laughter, "now it is becoming the catch word of the entire party. . ."

And the ruling also flew in the face of the reasoning of—you guessed it—Henry Clay. The Republican again brought forward Clay's words ("If a state of nature existed, and we were about to lay the foundations of society, no man would be more strongly opposed than I should be to incorporate the institution of slavery among its elements.") Then Lincoln asked, "What have I done in regard to the Declaration of Independence that I have not the license of Henry Clay to do?" Lincoln assured his audience that his op-position to slavery "is in relation to laying the foundation of new societies. I have never sought to apply this principle in those old States where slavery exists for the purpose of abolishing slavery in those States." He shouted, "It is nothing but a gross perversion to assume that I have brought forth the Declaration of Independence to ask that Missouri shall free her slaves. I will propose no such thing at all." But Lincoln, acting in the spirit of Clay, would oppose Dred Scott because it injected slavery into the "new societies" of the west. (Of course, Clay had in 1820 and in 1850 supported legislation that conditionally opened regions of the west to slavery, through the 36'-30 line in the former case, and through popular sovereignty in the latter. Clay was allowed his inconsistencies, too, it seemed.)

To cries of "good," to a single voice hollering "We want white men; we don't want niggers," to applause, Lincoln took aim at the Nebraska bill.

Why, Senator John Crittenden of Kentucky, Clay's political heir and a politician whose endorsement both candidates coveted, had said "that there was a falsehood in it, that there was no slavery agitation at the time the bill was introduced, and that the bill itself was the means of stirring it up again." Furthermore, what of the "collateral object" of the bill, to give to the settlers a power that they had not had before, the power to decide on slavery themselves, by majority rule?

"I will put it to you now," shouted Lincoln to the 5,000: "have you ever known of a people on the face of the earth that ever had as little to do with the application of this principle as in the first instance of its use, the people of Kansas, in the application of this same right of self-government in its main and collateral objects?"

Hitt heard "loud applause."

"It has been nothing," spat Lincoln, "but a living, creeping lie from the time of its introduction to this day."

That drew applause. (Even if Lincoln had misstated the facts when citing Kansas as the site of the doctrine's first use. The Compromise of 1850 had put popular sovereignty into the New Mexico and Utah territories, and there had neither been a Bleeding New Mexico nor a Bleeding Utah.)

Reacting to Douglas's predictable attack on the house divided doctrine, Lincoln sought to convince the crowd of a critical distinction. Judge Douglas does not need to explain to me the importance of local self-government and the usefulness to the Union of the variety of soil, climate, and topography from state to state, called Lincoln. For "if we raise a barrel of flour more than we want, and Louisiana raises a barrel of sugar more than she wants," both states benefit from trading these. That's to be celebrated, for "it makes a mutual commerce, it makes us better friends, it brings us together," and furthermore, "I understand that these differences and varieties are the cement in part that bind the Union together, and instead of being the things that divide the house, and tend to throw it down, they are the props tending strongly to hold it up;" so this was to be encouraged and furthered.

Lincoln looked out over the 5,000.

"I ask if there is any parallel between these things and the institution of slavery among us."

Time for another rhetorical question: Have we had any strife "about the cranberry laws of Indiana, or the oyster laws of Virginia, or about the timber laws of Maine and New Hampshire, or about the fact that Louisiana produces sugar and we produce flour and no sugar. Have we had quarrels about these things?"

But what about slavery? When have we had "perfect peace" on that question? "We have had peace whenever the institution of slavery remained quiet where it was, and we have had turmoil and difficulty whenever it has made a struggle to spread out where it was not."

Like Douglas, Lincoln revealed an understanding of peace defined only as the absence of conflict, not the presence of justice. For the slave, these periods of perfect peace were no doubt nearly indistinguishable from the periods of conflict over slavery's spread, a political and moral question that they were not entitled to debate and that usually impacted their nightmar-ish day-by-day existence not at all. But to a white voting public which could not have wanted more sectional conflict, Lincoln's formulation made a strong argument against the man who had reignited "slavery agitation" in 1854.

And the Douglas policy had not limited its destructive effect to politics alone. Lincoln called on his audience to reject what we early twenty-first century Americans consider one of the gravest of sins: Denial.

"Does it not enter the church, please? What divided the great Methodist Church, North and South? What makes the disturbance in every Presbyterian General Assembly that gets together? What made the disturbance in this city a few years ago in the Unitarian church? What sets them by the ears in the great American Tract Society, not splitting it yet but surely to split it?" Lincoln cried, "It is this thing that so operates upon the minds of men as to stir them upon all the relations of life not merely in the political world, but in the moral and religious. . ."

Lincoln may have heaved upward as he asked the clincher question:

"[I]s that, however, to be assuaged by pretending that it is an exceeding small thing and that we ought to quit talking about it?"

The *Tribune* reported "great cheers and laughter."

"But," probed Lincoln, "where is the statesmanship in saying that you can quiet that disturbing element menacing us with the only danger to our Union—where is the philosophy and statesmanship that rests upon the belief that we are to say and do nothing about it?"

Now he was pounding at one of the founding tenets of the great Jacksonian Democratic party, the notion that the Union would be most secure if northerners and southerners agreed to disagree on slavery, and to keep discussion off the floor of Congress and out of national campaigns. That had been a reason for the gag rule, for Democratic platforms for decades, for the Nebraska bill. 24

"I ask if it is not a false philosophy and false statesmanship that undertakes to build up a system of caring nothing about a thing that everyone does care a great deal about. . ."

"Yes, yes," the people cried, according to the *Tribune*.

"We insist that it be kept from the territories," shouted Lincoln. "Judge Douglas insists that we have no right to say anything about that; but I think we have some interest in that as white men." For if a slaveholder migrated into a territory alongside a free laboring migrant, the slaveholder "has it all his way" and you, the free laborer, "have no part in the matter."

"Now, irrespective of the moral question," continued the Republican, "I am still in favor of the new territory being kept free, into which free white men may move, fix their homes and better their conditions in life." This "free labor ideology" occupied a central role in the thinking of Republicans, especially northwestern Republicans such as Lincoln, for they had in many cases lived the experience.

But there were of course immigrant votes to be contested, and Lincoln proclaimed, "I am in favor of that—not merely—I must say it here as I say it elsewhere—not merely for our own people that are born among us, but I am in favor of an outlet for free white people, for new homes in which all free white men from all over the world may find place, and better their condition in life." That got applause, according to the Democratic *Times*.

The middle autumn sun, so bright on this clear October day when Douglas had confronted Dr. Hope's question, now lay low over the rolling Mississippi. Lincoln had perhaps twenty minutes to go; twenty minutes left in his best hope to unseat the Little Giant, twenty minutes' speaking time in these "joint discussions." It was time to return to the theme that had emerged after those uneasy three weeks coming out of Charleston, the theme that he had first proclaimed into the prairie gusts outside Old Main in Galesburg, the theme he furthered down by the riverside at Quincy. Given the choice between Douglas and Lincoln, why should Illinoisans support the Republican over the Democrat?

He began with a familiar line, alerting the audience that now he was onto "the real issue."

That real issue, "springs from a sentiment in the mind, and that sentiment is this: on the one part it looks upon the institution of slavery as being wrong, and on the part of another class, it does not look upon it as being wrong." And if slavery is not only wrong, but also a threat to our Union and liberties, what makes sense? To spread it, to make it bigger? "You may have a cancer upon your person, and you may not be able to cut it out at once, lest you bleed to death, but you may not treat it as a wrong by spreading it over your whole body."

Douglas, Lincoln said yet again, believed that there was nothing particularly wrong with slavery. And he was not alone, for "everything in the Democratic policy, in the shape it takes in legislation, in the Dred Scott decision, in their conversations, everyone carefully excludes the thought that there is anything wrong in it whatever."

And there it was. Illinoisans had a real choice, between one candidate who hoped for slavery's end and another who cared not whether slavery lived or died.

Lincoln now reached back into the speech that had so enchanted the Quaker Abraham Smith and so troubled the Know Nothing W.M. Chambers, the speech that had set up the terrible choice, the politician's choice, the speech that had led Abraham Smith to paint this race as one between the Kingdom of Heaven and the Kingdom of Satan; Chicago and the Tremont House seemed so long ago.

Lincoln might have taken a deep breath; he too had a choice to make. Hitt heard Lincoln say:

> That is the real issue. That is the issue that will continue in this country when these poor tongues of Judge Douglas and myself shall be silent. It is the eternal struggle between these two principles--right and wrong— throughout the world. They are the two principles that have stood face to face from the beginning of time; and will ever continue to struggle. The one is the common right of humanity and the other the divine right of kings. It is the same principle in whatever shape it develops itself. It is the same spirit that says, "You work and toil and earn bread, and I'll eat it." [Loud applause.] No matter in what shape it comes, whether from the mouth of a king who seeks to bestride the people of his own nation and live by the fruit of their labor, or from one race of men as an apology for enslaving another race, it is the same tyrannical principle. 25

Lincoln tied the struggle against slavery to a longer historical theme, the struggle of all people everywhere to be free, as he had in July, in Chicago. But this was not friendly Chicago; this was Alton, bloody Alton, in the critical downstate region. And this was middle October, only weeks away from the vote. Sounding the theme of racial equality, Lincoln had subtly but powerfully placed the struggle to put slavery on the course of ultimate extinction alongside the American Revolution, the French Revolution, the Latin American wars for independence, the liberal revolutions recently waged in Europe in 1848. In an even larger sense, the slaves and their advocates occupied the same ground as the people who waged the Glorious Revolution in England, and as the people who forced King John to sign Magna Carta; Lincoln implied that the slaves were on the same side as Christ in his challenge to the local authorities and the Roman empire, and to Moses challenging Pharaoh. They had all challenged some version of the "divine right of kings," which shared with slaveholding "the same tyrannical principle. . .you work and toil and earn bread" and I, the monarch *or* the slaveholder, will eat it. Lincoln, the ex-Whig, stood for the right to rise for all people, white and black.

And Douglas, the great democrat, stood on the side of the divine right of kings.

In July, from little Norwich, New York, the Chicago power broker Charles H. Ray had written Lincoln, "you are like Byron, who woke up one morning and found himself famous." Even in this remote corner of western New York "I have found hundreds of anxious enquirers burning to know all about the newly raised-up opponent of Douglas." But Ray had stern advice for the prairie Byron: "leave nothing undone which may promise to give you a vote. . .no false delicacy must keep you from trying to win by any legitimate means in your power." Ray wrote, "You have a chance which comes to but few men of each generation. It is for you to make the most of it." 26

Clever advice it may have been, but something in Lincoln knew that when the poor tongues of the two candidates were forever silenced, the *real* issue, embodied in the question around which this campaign centered, would live on: *What do* you *mean, what do* we *mean, by the words, 'all men are created equal?'* No election result would outlive that question's importance for the people of this nation.

Having soared to his oratorical peak in these debates, Lincoln, as if unready to assume moral leadership once and for all, as if remembering to leave nothing undone to gain a vote, reverted briefly to the lesser Lincoln of the early debates, repeating lines that he had used elsewhere, promising that there would be peace if we only returned to the policy of the "wisest and best men of the world;" asserting that intentionally or unintentionally Douglas had been the leading figure in the retreat from that policy; and assuring ex-Whigs that Lincoln himself could be trusted on fugitive slave legislation.

He supported such a law, he called, despite the fact that Republicans like him "have no great taste for running after niggers," because "I do not understand that the Constitution which gives that right can be carried out if that legislation is withheld." If—and it was only if—"I believed that the right to hold slaves in a territory was as firmly fixed" as the right to retrieve runaway slaves, "I would be bound to give the legislation necessary to support it" for "no man can deny his obligation to give legislation [protecting] slave property in the territory, who believes there is a constitutional right there."

So what did Douglas's espousal of "unfriendly legislation" as a means by which territorial settlers could freeze slavery out signify?

Simply this: "There is not such an abolitionist in all the States as Douglas."

And with that odd, second-rate ending, Lincoln sat. For him, the Lincoln-Douglas debates were over. The *Tribune* reported "loud and enthusiastic applause," but the *Times* appraised it differently. Lincoln, "being run down, stopped, having several minutes to spare."

". . .Than For All the Niggers in Christendom"

In contrast, "Senator Douglas' re-appearance in front of the stand was the signal for a general yell of applause," reported Binmore and Sheridan, "which fairly shook the earth, and startled the old Mississippi which was rolling along in all its majesty within a few hundred yards of the stand."

Proving himself yet again the political equivalent of the uncle who doesn't think you've understood his joke unless he repeats the punch line three times, Douglas immediately reacted to Lincoln's branding him an abolitionist.

"If he could make the Abolitionists of Illinois believe it, he would not have much show for Senate."

The crowd laughed.

"Make the Abolitionists believe the truth of that and his political back is broken."

The crowd laughed.

"The back of his party is broken when Abolitionism is withdrawn."

No reports of laughter that time. Douglas moved on.

Noting that Lincoln applauded the "war" between the Democratic factions, the Senator fell back on a trusty old friend.

He rasped that, "there is something really refreshing in the thought that Lincoln is in favor of prosecuting any war vigorously."

The laughter suggested that everyone knew what was coming.

"It is the first war I ever knew him to be in favor of prosecuting."

More laughter.

"It is the first one I ever knew him to believe to be either just or constitutional."

Laughter and cheers.

"When the Mexican War was waged and the American army was surrounded by the enemy in Mexico, he thought that was unconstitutional, unnecessary, and unjust."

Continued laughter, and according to the *Times*, cries of "That's so," "you've got him," and "he voted against it."

"He thought it was not commenced on the right spot."

Douglas was having fun. He mentioned the exchange between Lincoln and Orlando Ficklin over in Charleston. When Ficklin had recalled that Congressman Lincoln had supported the Ashmun Resolution declaring the war "unconstitutional, unnecessary, and unjust," Lincoln, Douglas explained, had answered "'Yes, I did.' Yes, he confesses that he voted that the war was wrong—that our country was in the wrong—that consequently, the Mexicans were in the right."

"And remember," intoned Douglas, "that this was done after the war began. It is one thing to be opposed to a declaration of war, and another thing to take the side of the enemy against your own country, for the war was commenced." Instead, Lincoln had "follow[ed] the lead of Tom Corwin," head of the anti-war faction in the House. The troops were "surrounded by the dangers, and the guns, and the poison of the enemy, and then it was that Corwin made his speech, stating that American soldiers ought to be welcomed to hospitable graves with bloody hands." The resolutions of Ashmun and Corwin and Lincoln "were sent to Mexico,"—Douglas didn't say by whom—and read to the Mexican troops to show "that there was a Mexican party in the Congress of the United States."

It's no surprise shouted Douglas, that a man capable of these actions "would rejoice in the war being made on me now," and the crowd applauded.

"And in my opinion no other man would rejoice in it."

Hitt heard the cry, "Go it, Stephen," and "All right, my covey."

It was clever, give Douglas that. He had needled Lincoln on the Mexican War all along, but never had he launched such a concerted attack on Lincoln's patriotism, and this was an attack that Lincoln could not answer before a joint audience, an attack that he could not answer to Douglas's face. And although in one sense the Mexican War was a dead issue, having ended twenty years earlier, a fundamental requirement for being a United States Senator would seem to be patriotism. Was Lincoln unpatriotic?

Having impugned the challenger's patriotism, the Little Giant then attacked his claim to the all-important Clay legacy. Let me take you yet again back in time, urged Douglas, this time to 1848.

Henry Clay was of course one of the greatest Senators and by far the most hapless presidential candidate ever. He had lost bids for the White House in 1824, 1832, and (the one that really hurt) 1844. 1848 found the Whigs desperate to reclaim the White House after William Henry

Harrison had committed suicide-by-inaugural address and been succeeded by a Whig in name only, John Tyler. The party had to choose between a freshly-minted war hero in Zachary Taylor or Clay, who had famously reacted to his 1844 upset by saying, "I'd rather be right than President." The Whigs would rather have had the Presidency, and in 1848 Lincoln spoke up publicly for Taylor.

He "made a speech in favor of throwing Clay overboard," charged Douglas, citing a Clay associate, General James Washington Singleton. "Singleton testifies that Lincoln's speech did have the effect to cut Henry Clay's throat," and that "Lincoln rejoiced with great joy when he found the mangled remains of the murdered Whig statesman lying cold before him, and now he tells you he is an Old Line Clay Whig." In contrast, Douglas had worked closely with Clay in 1850 in "putting down the strife" that Lincoln and Seward and Chase and Joshua Giddings had ginned up through their support of the Wilmot Proviso. So, Clay men, implied Douglas, your duty is clear.

The Senator had thus far launched withering attacks on Lincoln's past conduct, but he had not addressed the slavery question. Now he would. Noting Lincoln's mistake in contending that territorial slavery had been the only question ever to divide the sections, Douglas asked, what about the 1832 Tariff and Nullification crisis? What about the divisions over the War of 1812? "Was that the slavery question?"

"He complains," shouted Douglas, "that I don't look forward to the time when slavery shall be abolished everywhere." I'll tell you what I *do* look forward to, called Douglas: "I look forward to the time when each State shall be allowed to do as it pleases." To applause, he said it again. If a state "chooses to keep slavery forever, it is its business, and not ours."

And that represented properly-ordered priorities. For. . .

"I care more for the great principle of self-government—the right of the people to rule themselves—than I do for all the niggers in Christendom."

He'd used the line before, in August. As then it brought down applause and cheers.

"I would not dissolve this Union; I would not endanger its perpetuity; I would not blot out the great unalienable rights of the white man for all the niggers that ever existed."

It wasn't clear how the unalienable rights of whites would be threatened by barring slavery from the territories, unless God granted every white man the natural right to own slaves, but the line drew applause.

The sun sank lower over the Mississippi. Douglas would try one last attack on the territorial question. "Now what is the principle on which he proposes to govern the Territories? Give them no representation and then call on the Congress to make laws controlling their property and domestic concerns, without their consent, against their will." Reaching, Douglas termed this "the identical principle of the party of George III, and the Tories of the Revolution."

And—I'll explain it slowly, Lincoln, I know you're a Republican—the Taney Court had merely said that slave property carried into the territories was no different than any other property; you had the right to bring it in, but the property once in was subject to the local laws.

"Suppose," began Douglas, "one of your merchants would take $100,000 worth of groceries," meaning alcohol, "into Kansas. You have a right to go there under the decision, but when you get there, you find the Maine liquor law in force. You cannot use it—cannot sell it. It is subject to local laws, and that law is against you." Douglas looked out over the crowd, about to make his point.

"What can you do with it?"

A voice hollered at the Senator, "You would drink it."

To the end, the people of Illinois reserved the right to act in this comic drama.

According to the *Times*, "for some minutes after he concluded the applause was perfectly deafening and overwhelming," according to the *Times*.

As the crowd began to disperse, Douglas's Danite questioner, Dr. Hope, moved to the platform and demanded in a loud voice to be heard, as he was a candidate for the U.S. House of Representatives. The Missouri *Democrat* reported that Douglasites "set up a storm of yells." These "rowdies and drunkards kept up a continual shout for Douglas." One of the Little Giant's loyalists brandished high a quart of whiskey and screamed out an invitation for the 'Douglas boys' to 'come and drink.'" They finished the quart with dispatch. Meanwhile, according to Charles Lanphier's *Illinois State Register*, Hope "had scarcely thrown back his oily locks and opened his mouth, before he was greeted by a torrent of noise of every description, such as 'Hurrah for Douglas,' 'Hurrah for Lincoln,' 'Dry up,' 'You're a hopeful case', etc." An angry Hope "danced over the platform" and shook his fists and head at the hecklers. The good doctor soon "disappeared (after speaking half an hour and making a fool of himself) off the stage in a most theatrical manner; that is chasing an individual who was making noise. During all that time the crowd was convulsed with laughter." 27

And on that comic opera note, the debates were history.

"To Mar the Beauty of His Eloquent Passages"

All along, the two sides had spat gall at one another over the accuracy with which rival papers reported the candidates' words. Harold Holzer's invaluable "unexpurgated" edition of the debate transcripts explores the possibility that the Democratic Chicago *Times* polished up Binmore's and Sheridan's shorthand for Douglas, leaving Lincoln's words raw, the way he said them, and that the Chicago *Daily Press and Tribune* did the same thing in reverse, improving Lincoln's language and leaving Douglas's words in a rougher, more natural state. 28

By the time of the Quincy debate, the Democrats had also printed a pamphlet version of the Ottawa debates, and Lincoln reacted angrily to a transcription that made him seem like a babbling idiot next to an eloquent Douglas. (For his part, Holzer wonders if Lincoln, so good at delivering a prepared text, but so unsteady when unscripted, truly "won" the debates on the basis of delivery.) 29

Binmore, Sheridan, Hitt and White thus became targets in their own right. The Republican *Daily Pantagraph* of Bloomington, for instance, sputtered that the *Times* men had committed multiple mutilations of Lincoln's words. The *Pantagraph* charged that "we find the last half hour of Lincoln's Alton speech—the portion where he pitches into Douglas the heaviest—more horribly garbled. . .Many sentences are dropped out which were absolutely necessary for the sense; many are transposed to read wrong end first; many are made to read the exact opposite of the orator's intention. . ." There was a reason for this: "the whole aim has been to blunt the keen edge of Mr. Lincoln's wit, to mar the beauty of his eloquent passages, to destroy the force of his irresistible logic and break the blows that he rained down upon the head of his pro-slavery opponent. . ." In short the *Times* sought to make Lincoln appear "a half-witted booby." Who was responsible? The Little Giant himself, for the crime was perpetrated "under Mr. Douglas' own eye and direction by that wheat-rust colored, bandy-legged reporter he takes with him to do up his dirty work." 30

Whether or not the Republicans had a legitimate complaint, the transcripts published just days after each debate by both Chicago papers made it outside Illinois. At least one Southern leader, Governor Henry A. Wise of Virginia, having followed the action in the newspapers, was moved to write Douglas, "I see you standing alone, isolated in a tyrannical proscription which would alike foolishly and wickedly lop off one of the most vigorous limbs of the National Democracy," but for "firmly fronting the foe and battling to maintain conservative nationality against embittered and implacable sectionalism," Douglas deserved his countrymen's esteem. "Fight on, fight on," Wise wrote, "never yield in death or victory." 31

Douglas never would.

Chapter Eight: "But it Hurts Too Much to Laugh"

"Put In Your Best Licks"

Sixteen days left. "These debates are now closed," readers of the Rockford *Republican* were told in a clipped piece from the Chicago *Journal*, and the people of Illinois would now choose. "We, as the friends of Mr. Lincoln, feel perfectly satisfied—and more than satisfied—with the noble fight he has made, and we rest in the confidence that the November election will show that the verdict of the people will be in his favor." On October 29, The Chicago *Press and Tribune* called Lincoln's "the most brilliant, and as the event will prove, most successful political canvass ever made in this country." On the same day, the *State Gazette* of Burlington, Iowa reported that "the whole nation is watching with the greatest anxiety," adding that "No State has ever fought so great a battle as that which Illinois is to fight" on Election Day. "Its result is big with the fate of our Government and the Union." Back in Washington, the National *Era* used early state election results to needle Douglas for his tendency to claim victory under any circumstances: "If the Democrats succeed, as in Missouri, Douglas shouts, 'We routed the black Republicans.' If the Republicans succeed, as in Ohio, Pennsylvania, Indiana &c., he shouts, 'We have rebuked the administration!'" The *Era* predicted, "In a short time, he will be claiming the election of Lincoln." And J.H. Jordan of Cincinnati assured Lincoln that whatever the result, "you are not fighting in vain . . . thousands of eyes outsight of your own State, are turned to you . . . You are beginning to be looked to as the Champion of the West." 1

The Dixon *Republican and Telegraph* reprinted a piece from Quincy's *Whig and Republican* charging that Douglas had financed his campaign with a $52,000 mortgage on his Chicago property, with "Fernando Wood, the notorious Tammany Hall politician, of New York . . . the principle mort-gagee." Douglas hoped to carry the election, explained the Quincy paper, by buying votes. "He pays for the puff he gets in the newspapers. He carries around with him hirelings whose business it is to manufacture crowds and enthusiasm. The occupation of this toady is the same as that of the man who is hired to puff some quack medicine into notoriety . . ." Douglas "carries a big cannon with him, to give him a puff wherever he goes, and he pays for *that*." And the Senator "has somebody to go around and shoot it for him, and *he* pays for that also." But, predicted the correspondent, "it won't win after all. He will spend his $52,000 for nothing, but is bound to lose '*my place*' likewise." The Tammany rumors circulated beyond Illinois. F. C. Fay of Canton, Ohio, wrote Lincoln that although "a stranger to you . . . I deem it my duty" to let Lincoln know that "Douglas was backed up by the N.Y. Tammany Society and if Necessary Tammany would expend a million dollars in order to carry Douglass election . . . your voters are to be bought up and corrupted . . ." 2

The candidate, for his part, believed that he could make it. From Rushville, on October 20, he wrote to Republican state central committee chairman Norman B. Judd: "I have a high degree of confidence that we shall succeed, if we are not over-run with fraudulent votes to a greater extent than usual . . . If we can head off the fraudulent votes, we shall carry the day." 3

Both candidates maintained ramming speed over the last two weeks. The Republican made speeches at the town of Lincoln; Meredosia; Mount Sterling, and Rushville, all between Saturday the 16th and Wednesday, the 20th. Taking one day off, he hit Carthage on the 22nd, Dallas City the next day, and Macomb the day after that. On the 27th he spoke at Vermont, on the 29th at Petersburg, and on the 30th at Springfield to close the campaign. Douglas, trying to regain his health, soldiered bravely on, speaking at Gillespie on the 16th and Decatur the next day; there he drew a crowd of 6,000. Taking one day off, he raided Lincoln's backyard, giving a speech in Springfield on October 20. He then brought his road show to Atlanta, then to Bloomington (where he drew 8,000) and then to Peoria. In the final week he spoke at Toulon, Geneseo, and Rock Island. On November 1 he crossed the finish line with a speech in Chicago before an "immense number of citizens." From the windows of that city's Garrett Block "were hung out almost innumerable banners and transparencies; and bonfires were blazing on State Street," which was no small feat given the omnipresent rain. The *Times* had two days earlier announced the Little Giant's arrival by assuring readers that "He is in excellent health and spirits. Notwithstanding his many speeches, his voice is in excellent order." (The Democratic *Times* expressed its own concern about voter fraud: ". . . if we can have an honest vote on Tuesday we will have no fault with the judgment of the people.") 4

Newspapers such as the Freeport *Weekly Journal* took nothing for granted. The *Journal* reminded its readers that "Our U.S. Senators are not elected by the direct vote of our people, but by our legislature," and that the state legislators elected by Stephenson County voters *"may elect or defeat Abram Lincoln."* So Lincoln supporters needed to get to the polls and vote for "JOHN H. ADDAMS for Senator, and JOHN A. DAVIS for Representative—both good men and true." 5

Lincoln's loyalists continued to come out in large, pugnacious crowds. The *Tribune* wrote of the challenger's Macomb rally that "the weather was dreary and foggy during the morning, but the enthusiasm of the Republican host defied the elements." In fact, the train carrying Republicans had to "run by several stops" rolling north out of Quincy, as the cars were full of Lincoln enthusiasts, among them the Quincy Blues militia unit. In Macomb, "the streets were muddy, the sidewalks slippery and overhead things decidedly damp." But Republican intensity shone brightly. When a delegation from the northern part of the county marched around the Macomb town square, "a squad of Douglas riff-raffs" tried to block them, reported the Chicago *Press and Tribune*. "An old gentleman, near sixty years of age, jumped in among them and in rather less than no time four of the drunken bullies were sprawling in the mud." The *Tribune* added that "The people kept pouring in notwithstanding the rain kept pouring down," all to hear Lincoln as he "completed the Quincy debate in which Douglas was so unmercifully threshed. . ." 6

Voter enthusiasm was a good sign for the Republicans, but Lincoln's anxiety showed through, both in the brief notes and letters that he scribbled and in some of his speeches. Henry C. Whitney had written on October 14 to Lincoln to warn of "extensive colonization schemes" in "out of the way precincts." In an October 20 letter to Norman Judd, Lincoln fretted about an incident that had occurred in Naples days earlier:

> . . .On alighting from the cars and walking three squares. . .I met about fifteen Celtic gentlemen, with black carpet-sacks in their hands.
>
> I learned that they had crossed over from the Rail-road in Brown county, but where they were going no one could tell. They dropped in about the doggeries, and were still hanging about when I left. At Brown County yesterday I was told that about four hundred of the same sort were to be brought into Schuyler, before the election, to work on some new Railroad; but on reaching here I find [John] Bagby thinks it not so.
>
> What I most dread is that they will introduce into the doubtful districts numbers of men who are legal voters in all respects except *residence* and who will swear to residence and thus put it beyond our power to exclude them. They can & I fear will swear falsely on that point, because they know it is next to impossible to convict them of Perjury upon it.
>
> Now the great remaining part of the campaign, is finding a way to head this thing off. Can it be done at all?
>
> I have a bare suggestion. When there is a known body of these voters, could not a true man, of the *"detective"* class, be introduced among them in disguise, who could, at the nick of time, control their votes? Think this over. It would be a great thing, when this trick is attempted on us, to have the saddle come up on the other horse.
>
> I have talked, more fully than I can write, to Mr. Scripps [the publisher of the Chicago *Press and Tribune*], and he will talk to you. 7

Lincoln closed with a stiff-upper-lip assurance that, "If we can head off the fraudulent votes we shall carry the day." Billy Herndon's cousin J. Rowan Herndon agreed, at least as regarded his Adams County hometown of Columbus: "Now abe i Will tell you what we are Doing for you in this town we Will give you a mjority of 2 to 1 and that is hard to Beat I have counted all the legal votes and you get 2 to 1 Sertin and some Dutfull the duglasites are stedfast the Lincolites is the same way." But "Old Row's" assurances aside, would there be enough "Lincolites" in the critical central Illinois precincts to counteract Democratic schemes? 8

Lincoln's nervousness had already caused him to go public with the presence of those Irishmen in Naples, in a speech at Meredosia on the 18th.

The Democratic Jacksonville *Sentinel* jeered, "Doubtless Mr. Lincoln enter-
tains a holy horror of all Irishmen," wrote the *Sentinel's* correspondent, "and
other adopted citizens who have sufficient self-respect to believe themselves superior to the negro. What right have adopted citizens to vote
Mr. Lincoln and his negro equality doctrines down? He would doubtless
disenfranchise every one of them if he had the power." The *Sentinel* reported
that "Dr. Wackly" (actually Dr. W.J. Wackerle) "an influential German"
had opined nights before that Lincoln was a Know-Nothing, and that at
Meredosia Lincoln had "retorted on the Dr. in severe, personal manner." 9

As Election Day drew closer, Lincoln's gnawing anxiety persisted. To
Judd he wrote on the 24th: "Just out of Hancock. Spoke three times in
that county. *Tight*, with chances slightly in our favor." He added, "Heard
nothing new about fraudulent voters since I spoke to Mr. Scripps." To John
Moses, a State Senate candidate from Scott, Pike and Calhoun counties,
Lincoln wrote:

Throw on all your weight. Some things I have heard make me think your
case is not so desperate as you thought when I was in Winchester. Put in
your best licks. Yours in haste

A. LINCOLN— 10

On the same day, Lincoln dashed off this note to Alexander Sympson:

Since parting with you this morning I heard some things which make
me believe [George] Edmunds and [Milton] Morrill will spend this
week among the National democrats trying to induce them to content
themselves by voting for [Danite congressional candidate] Jake Davis,
and then vote for the Douglas candidates for Senator and Representative.
Have this headed off if you can. . . 11

Increasingly worried about charges that he was a closet nativist,
he wrote to Edward Lusk, an ex-steamboat operator and farmer from
Meredosia that "I am not, nor ever have been, connected with the party
called the Know-Nothing party, or party calling themselves the American Party." He added "*Certainly* no man of truth" could associate Lincoln
with the Know-Nothings. (Although as early as June 24, Lincoln's partner
and stalwart friend Billy Herndon had himself written to Lyman Trumbull

that the Nativists, "The Fillmore boys," were falling into ranks with the Republicans, "they knit close—close as shattered ice of a cool night on a mill pond, forming a solid sheet of ice over which the Republicans may march to victory.")   12

The pace sometimes left Lincoln dizzy. One week earlier, on October 18, he had written to Thomas J. Henderson: "I have concluded to speak at the place that you name (I forget the name of the place) on the 27th, and you may give notice accordingly." Lincoln eventually turned up as promised, in Vermont, Illinois.   13

Lincoln manned the bridge, shouting directions to the crew, afraid that the victory would be stolen, hatching zany schemes to turn the tables on the Democratic plan to "colonize" Irish railway workers to swing counties, and exploiting the back channel to the Danites. The candidate's fretfulness did not seep into the Republican newspapers, which professed confidence that the best man would win. The friendly half of the press continued to throw valedictory bouquets his way and brickbats at the Little Giant.

The Chicago *Journal's* assessment was that "Mr. Lincoln has shown him-self Senator Douglas' superior in soundness of reasoning, in intellectual resources, and in statesmanlike dignity—and in only three respects has Douglas exhibited superiority over Lincoln." And what three areas were these? "[W]ordy equivocation, impudence of pretension, and unmanly person of controversy." Douglas's speeches had been "full of spleen, ver-bose nonsense, and weak falsification," but Lincoln's had been marked 'by fairness, logical argument, and commendable manliness of spirit."   14

Had the voters reached the saturation point on these sorts of assessments of the two candidates? Not by the looks of things. The furious charge to the finish line witnessed still more boosting and still more vilification. And some late surprises.

One came in the November 1 Chicago *Press and Tribune*, a single day before the election. The Republican paper alleged that on the Mississip-pi plantation once inherited by his first wife and that he now managed in absentia, Illinois' senior senator presided over a force of slaves kept in truly miserable condition, "their backs scarred by the lash, their bodies pinched by hunger, their limbs bent by incessant labor." Not only was Douglas figuratively eating the bread derived from their labor, but the Little Giant "derives from their toil the cash with which he is endeavoring to convince the people that slavery ought to live forever." Louisiana Senator John Slidell—Bruce Catton would refer to him as Buchanan's "chief hatchet man"--was supposedly the source of this information, passed through the Danite Dr. Daniel Brainerd to the *Tribune*. The *Tribune's* implication? Just that Douglas could talk all he wanted about standing up to Buchanan on Lecompton, but his plantation management proved conclusively that he was as much the slaver as any Southern leader. 15

The Democrats had sprung their own surprise, and here Lincoln's assailant was a friend, Ottawa's Judge T. Lyle Dickey. Concerned about what he saw as the radical abolitionist drift of the Republican campaign, Dickey had earlier written to Kentucky Senator John Crittenden, urging the senator to support Douglas. When Clay had died early in the decade, Crittenden had lifted the standard of centrism, nationalism, Union, and Whiggism (as well as a certain aversion to foreigners.) More than any single individual, Crittenden represented in voters' minds the Clay legacy.

Both candidates had tried hard to get right with Henry Clay, and getting right with John Crittenden could advance that cause. Crittenden's endorsement would be critical, so critical that on July 7 Lincoln had written to Crittenden, assuring the Senator that he did not believe rumors of a pending Crittenden endorsement of Douglas. The Kentuckian had written back confidentially on the 29th that in fact he favored Douglas' re-election, for his leadership in the Lecompton crisis would make his re-election a blow to Buchanan. 16

Dickey had stuck in the knife by writing to Crittenden and asking his opinion on Senator Douglas. The Kentuckian wrote back on August 1, acknowledging that "in conversation last April he had expressed a warm admiration for the course of that Senator, and that he had said, 'in substance, that the people of Illinois little knew how much they rally [sic] owed him,' &c." Crittenden's letter also professed an aversion to interfering in the Illinois race, a demurral at once so senatorial in style and so very disingenuous. 17

The Douglas forces held onto the letter, and then released Crittenden's note in the final days of the race. Allan Nevins contended that "A multitude of old-time Whigs in Southern Illinois heeded Crittenden's voice." This bombshell eroded the Danite vote in Egypt and it probably cost the Republicans dearly among old-line Whig voters in the central belt. 18

The 29th found Lincoln a little over twenty miles from home, in Petersburg, where he gave one of his last speeches of the campaign. Again the skies opened and at a flag station on the route to Springfield, Lincoln found himself taking refuge in a box car with a German-American reporter from New York, Henry Villard. As the two men talked, Lincoln admitted to Villard that as a young man his highest ambition had been to win a seat in the state legislature, but that now Mary told him that he *would* become a United States Senator, and, one day, President of the United States. As Villard told the story, the homely face grinned, "Just think of such a sucker as me as President." 19

Ambition seems to have been much on the challenger's mind during these frantic final days; somehow, amid the angling for position, the boxing out, the letters dashed off to former steamboat operators, the need to react to late implants in the Chicago papers, Lincoln seems to have reflected on the question: Why am I doing this?

On Saturday, October 30, before 5,000 or more of his neighbors, finally back home in Springfield, Lincoln tried to answer that question. He called out that he was "surrounded by friends—some *political, all personal* friends, I trust," and noted that "I have borne a laborious and, in some respects to myself, painful part in the contest." 20

This was new. He had never before admitted to being pained. What had pained him? Was it the adversarial nature of the seven debates? The thousands of miles of travel? The very unkind things written in unfriendly newspapers? The hecklers? The time away from home? The financial sacrifice? Lincoln elaborated a little, noting that he and his friends had been "constantly accused of a purpose to destroy the Union and bespattered with every imaginable odious epithet; and some who were friends, as it were but yesterday have made themselves active in this." (Douglas had faced the same hardships, but he would not go on record as admitting to feeling any pain.) 21

It was a moment of attractive honesty, but was Lincoln sharing all of his pain? Would any well-adjusted human being not have felt twinges doing what these two men had done, or what any political candidate running for office must do? Most of us would, as Lincoln admitted, flinch a little bit at being called a hypocrite in newspapers that our neighbors, friends, and families could read. Wouldn't it hurt to get zinged by another person (who happened to be your competitor for a job, a *job*) while hordes of people laughed at your foe's wit? Wouldn't it also hurt to have to explain repeatedly to your spouse and children why you could not take part in some important family event because you had to woo voters in some swing precinct? And would it not hurt, just a little, to look at the human being who is your opponent, with perhaps their own equally valid claim to be treated with dignity and respect, (even if you didn't like them that much) and deliver your *own* zinger, sending the blood rising to that person's face as the crowds laughed or even bayed in delight? Who would want to do this, not just at some part-time, local level, but as their life's work?

Lincoln would, God help him.

"Ambition has been ascribed to me," he said, and if the Springfield crowd was hoping for a red-meat attack on Douglas, they would be disappointed. 22

Instead . . .

"God knows how sincerely I prayed from the first that this field of ambition might not be opened." But the cup had not passed Lincoln in this vast prairie Gethsemane, and the candidate took this occasion to admit a truth that Billy Herndon would affirm, famously, years later. 23

"I claim no insensibility to political honors. . ." He probably paused, looked out into this crowd, saw familiar faces, some of whom he may have known since he came to town over a quarter century ago, all his belongings stuffed into saddle bags, a lanky Rube on a Rube's nag. Somehow, that unpromising piece of work on his unpromising piece of horseflesh had overcome pennilessness, depression, ruthless ambition, social clumsiness, suicidal moments, political disappointments, and an erratic marriage to challenge the greatest political leader in the land, to give him a run for his substantial money. But even then, even after all the miles, all the bad food and uncomfortable lodging, all of the argument, all of the pain, Lincoln announced that, "today could the Missouri restriction be restored, and the whole slavery question replaced on the old ground of 'toleration['] by *necessity* where it exists, with unyielding hostility to the spread of it, on principle, I would, in consideration, gladly agree, that Judge Douglas should never be *out*, and I never *in*, an office, so long as we both or either live." 24

Such an odd, bittersweet way to end a campaign. Maybe it was being home, maybe it was all that pain, maybe he was more exhausted than anyone thought. (Douglas, despite what the Chicago *Times* reported as he readied to make his final appearances up in Chicago, was by all accounts an absolute wreck by this time.) Maybe he had answered his own question— why have I done this?—by answering, "I'm no longer sure." Victory would come with its own costs; back into the meat grinder in far-off Washington with adversaries every bit as tough as Douglas and the Illinois Democratic press. The Senate floor had become an especially rancorous place; one could ask Charles Sumner. Did he really want this?

The *Tribune's* November 2 coverage of the speech put the best face on it, explaining that the crowd was so enthusiastic to start with that "speaking was out of the question. Lincoln tried it, and though he held at all times an audience of 5,000 or more, something more demonstrative than his convincing and unimpassioned oratory was needed to satisfy the eager crowd." The noisy torch-light procession through the city that followed made for better press. 25

Billy Herndon had if anything worsened Lincoln's anxiety over the final weeks, unintentionally jerking his friend around, making optimistic predictions only to follow these with the "'brute forecast'" that *all is NOT safe."* Until Tuesday nothing would be certain. But more than once, as Lincoln's most trusted friend heard reports from his contacts in the Republican party and among the Danites, Billy muttered that it all *"feels right in our bones."* 26

"I Expect Everyone to Desert Me Except Billy"

Torrential rains fell over much of the sodden Illinois landscape Tuesday. The foot soldiers of democracy faced one last challenge in this exercise in popular government: getting to the polls over swollen streams and roads churned to oatmeal. But the Illinois voters--who along with disenfranchised women and children had injected themselves so enthusiastically into this campaign--would not be denied.

The ballots that they cast were not issued by the state of Illinois, which lacked a statewide voter registration law. The Democrats would print and distribute their ballots, the Republicans their own; it was not uncommon for local party organizations to run off "bogus opposition tickets" to dupe those intending to vote for their foes. 27

All the advantages of incumbency aside, the race was Douglas's to lose. The most recent reapportionment of the state had been undertaken in 1852, before there was a Republican party, and a subsequent effort had been judged no better, dooming its enactment. What this meant was that the Republican North was somewhat underrepresented and the Democratic South rather overrepresented in the Illinois State General Assembly, which consisted of a 25-man Senate and a 75-member House of Representatives. Adding to Republican fears, 13 state senators did not stand for reelection this time around, and eight of them were Democrats. 28

The names Douglas and Lincoln did not appear as ballot choices. You could not cast a vote for either man directly; instead, if you were a Douglas supporter you would pick up a color-coded Democratic Party ballot and vote for your local Democratic legislative candidate (after ascertaining that he was a Douglas Democrat, and not a Danite.) Then you trusted that candidate, should he win, to do your bidding. The vote that would officially determine Illinois' senator for the next six years would not take place until January 6, 1859. (You could vote directly for the state treasurer and for the state superintendent of education, as well as for your Congressman.) 29

The rain, Republicans would later complain, caused 10,000 voters to stay home, and that may have been the case, although were that so, probably 4,500 would have voted Republican, the same number Douglas

Democrat, and perhaps 1,000 for a Danite. What the rain did do was to hold down the much-dreaded street violence that often marked Election Day in the state capital. The *Illinois State Journal* wrote on Wednesday that "We are gratified to state that the election . . . passed off as usual, without any disturbance. The rain fell almost incessantly throughout the entire day, and the streets were in horrid condition." Nonetheless, by supper time the jailers at the Springfield city prison had filled nearly every cell. 30

By day's end, Lincoln, a discerning reader of returns, knew he had lost.

The most important result was this: in the new State Assembly, there would be 54 Democrats and 46 Republicans. The voters chose 46 Democrats to go to Springfield, and 41 Republicans. The 13 Senate holdovers would only lengthen the odds that Republicans could persuade any Democrats to vote for Lincoln in the Senate race come the January legislative ballot on the grounds that the Republicans had won the "popular vote." 31

It would have been a hard argument to sustain, for it wasn't immediately clear which party represented the will of the majority. True, Lincoln's party had won the state treasurer race, with 125,430 votes for the Republican, 121,609 votes for the Douglas Democrat, and 5,071 for the Buchanan Democrat. Republican candidates for the U.S. House of Representatives had won 49.9% of the statewide vote, to 48.5% for Douglas Democrat candidates. Voters had been reminded that their votes for General Assembly would determine the Senate winner, and Allen Guelzo argues persuasively that Lincoln "won" close to 52% of the votes cast for seats in the state legislature's lower house to Douglas' 45%, and that Lincoln "won" close to 54% of the Senate votes. 32

What about the districts where Lincoln and Douglas had debated? The Ottawa district, the Freeport district, the Charleston district and the Galesburg district elected Republicans to both the state Senate and the House. The Quincy, Alton, and Jonesboro districts sent Democrats to Springfield. (Douglas' home base, Chicago, sent Republicans to both houses. Lincoln's neighbors in the Springfield district sent a Republican to the Senate and two Democrats to the House.) Lincoln "won," debate districts, four to three. 33

This analysis allows us to declare a winner, and (best of all) the winner we wanted all along. But it can get in the way of the fact that Lincoln faced: he was not the winner, and he knew it. He would not go to the Senate. Douglas would.

On November 4, Lincoln took up his pen to write to the Honorable John J. Crittenden. Crittenden had written Lincoln on the 27th of October, to both complain of and disavow a reference made in the Missouri *Republican* to "private correspondence" between Lincoln and the Kentucky senator, and Lincoln—who surely was not the source of the pro-Douglas leak—magnanimously apologized if this "has given you any pain." 34

"The emotions of defeat, at the close of a struggle in which I felt more than a merely selfish interest, and to which defeat the use of your name contributed largely, are fresh upon me," wrote Lincoln. Defeat hurt. Defeat to Douglas, whom Lincoln liked and respected less and less through the campaign, hurt a little more. Defeat at the hands of a man whom Lincoln truly believed to have gone over to the slave power conspiracy; defeat brought about by malapportionment; by the assumed "colonization" of Irish voters in swing districts; defeat due to rains. It stung. But defeat due also to the endorsement of Douglas by the Senator who claimed the mantle of the man that Lincoln had called "my *beau ideal* of a statesman"-- defeat under those conditions was almost too much to bear, especially after Billy Herndon had felt victory in his bones; especially since Lincoln himself, sometime around the time he found his moral voice at Galesburg had told a friend, "I think we may have the gentleman." 35

They hadn't. And now Lincoln was admitting to an influential and respected figure--who had contributed to that defeat--that defeat really hurt.

Yet "even in this mood, I can not for a moment suspect you of anything dishonorable." 36

Lincoln had again fallen short. He had in 1848 wanted to return to Congress, but that had been denied him. In 1855, he had been the insider among the anti-Douglas forces for the US Senate seat, and that seat had gone to Trumbull. In 1856, his name had been placed in nomination as the

Republican candidate for vice president, but the nod had gone to someone else. Now this. After all that work, all those miles, all that pain. Now this.

In the weeks following the election, as the sheriff released pugilists from the Springfield jail and meaningless late returns came in, his supporters wrote to their man; most wrote in genuine pain. "I don't think it possible for you to feel more disappointed than I do," wrote Horace White, who had been with Lincoln almost literally every step of the way as the lead correspondent for the Chicago *Press and Tribune*. Lawyer Henry P.H. Bromwell wrote from Charleston, "I know it would be impossible for me to feel worse over any political defeat whatever . . ." "The result in Illinois," wrote David Davis, "has both astonished and mortified me beyond measure," and he added, "Some of you may forgive" Lyle Dickey and Crittenden, and for that matter the at best tepid support from William Henry Seward and Horace Greeley, "but I cannot." Bloomington's David Brier confessed that the loss had hit him harder than "any since that of Mr Clay in 1844." And party leader Norman Judd wrote from Chicago to ask for Lincoln's help in retiring the party's $2,500 debt, adding, "If you feel as blue as I have since the election I do not blame you." Judd added a sprightly, "The future looks gloomy to me." 37

Lincoln sent out letter after letter from home and office in response. Still the leader, Lincoln refused to whine. This election was over; now it was time to get back to business, both personal and political. To Judd he confessed that he had wanted keenly to go to the Senate, but "I am convalescent and hoping these lines may find you in the same improving state of health." Lincoln figured that "We have some hundred and twenty thousand clear Republican votes" in the state. "That pile is worth keeping." Looking to the next race, in 1860, Lincoln cautioned Judd, "In that day I shall fight in the ranks, but I shall be in no ones way for any of the places. I am especially for Trumbull's reelection," and this brought him to the topic of a reapportionment bill. "Unless something can be done Trumbull is eventually beaten two years hence. . ." A day later, on November 16, he responded to Judd's request for financial help in retiring the state Republican party's debt. Because of "my loss of time and business," over the past five months, "I am absolutely without money now for even household purposes" and "am the poorest hand living to get others to pay." But Judd should put him down for $250. 38

"You are feeling badly" about the defeat, noted Lincoln. *"'And this too shall pass away.'* Never fear." 39

For someone who had taken a painful defeat, Lincoln's correspondence shows an almost unnatural lack of anger, with the exception of his November 17 response to a demand from an annoying client in a messy real estate case: "You perhaps need not be reminded how I have been personally engaged the last three months . . . I will have no more to do with this class of business . . . I would not go through the same labor and vexation again for five hundred [dollars]". 40

But by November 19, he seemed to have revived. Lincoln assured Henry Asbury that "Douglas had the ingenuity to be supported in the late contest as the best means to *break down* and *uphold* the Slave interest. No ingenuity can keep those antagonistic elements in harmony long. Another explosion will soon come." The same day, he wrote to Anson G. Henry, "I am glad I made the late race. It gave me a hearing on the great and durable question of the age, which I could have in no other way; and although I now sink out of view, and shall be forgotten, I believe I have made some marks which will tell for the cause of civil liberty long after I am gone." That day's letter to Anson Miller asserted that, "I hope and believe seed has been sewn that will yet produce fruit. The fight must go on." And he wrote on that same day to Eleazar A. Paine that "the fight must go on. Let no one falter. The *question* is not half settled. New splits and divisions will soon be upon our adversaries; and we shall [have] fun again." 41

A day later, responding to M.M. Inman's query--"if Douglas can spend fifty to a thousand hundred dollars to get men elected to the Legislator, why can not the whole Republican party rais[sic] 50 or 60 thousand dollars to get them out,"-- Lincoln explained to this resident of "Annan, " as Inman spelled it, that he would "duly consider" the point. Then he added, "The fight must go on. We are right and we cannot fail. There will be another blow-up in the democratic party before long.

"In the mean time, let all Republicans stand fast by their guns." 42

Lincoln repeated these themes again and again through November and December. On December 8, he answered a letter from H.D. Sharpe: "I think we have entered upon a durable struggle as to whether this nation is to ultimately become all slave or all free, and though I fall early in the contest, it is nothing if I shall have contributed, in the last degree, to the final rightful result." On December 12, he wrote to Alexander Sympson, "I expect the results of the election went hard with you. So it did with me, too, perhaps not quite as hard as you supposed. I have an abiding faith that we shall beat them in the long run." He added, "I write merely to let you know that I am neither dead nor dying." 43

Turning down entreaties from Trumbull that he seek a seat in the House of Representatives opened by the death of Douglas's friend Thomas Harris, he noted Douglas's trip to the South, "seeking to re-instate himself in that section. The majority of the democratic politicians of the nation mean to kill him; but I doubt whether they will adopt the aptest way to do it." If the Democrats were to push a territorial slave code on the Little Giant at the Democratic National Convention in Charleston, South Carolina in 1860, "he will bolt at once," and "claim that all Northern men shall make common cause in electing him President. . ." Should that happen the North would face the problem Illinoisans faced last summer: "whether the Republican party can maintain it's [sic] identity or be broken up to form the tail of Douglas' new kite." He permitted himself a little bitterness: "Some of our great Republican doctors will then have a splendid chance to swallow the pills they so eagerly prescribed for us last Spring . . .and although I do not feel that I owe the said doctors much, I will help them, to the best of my ability, to reject the said pills." He still had his eye on Douglas. Accordingly, he sent appeals to friends at the *Press and Tribune* in Chicago for copies of the debate texts in hopes of making a scrapbook. Such control of the first draft of history might be useful should he renounce his own stated preference for private-citizen status at some undetermined point in the future. It also suggested that he felt pride in the campaign he had waged; people do not generally keep scrapbooks of their disasters. 44

He seemed to be on the mend. The letters that he wrote show Lincoln making the most of the messages of consolation sent him. When he told

Asbury or Judd or the southern Illinoisan who misspelled his own town's name to keep up the fight, to watch for the next split in the Democratic ranks, to continue the struggle, Lincoln reinforced his own inner voice, a voice that counseled resiliency and vigilance, and endurance. The fight must go on.

The letters were helpful in another way. In writing back Lincoln sometimes did what a lot of us might be excused for doing in the situation: he wrote that he was finished, he was through, that someone else would need to pick up the standard for the next, inevitable fight. Although he may have at some level believed this—Lincoln could get pretty discouraged—when you write things like this you invite people to say: no; you're not finished by half; you'll win next time. Lincoln, being only human, probably needed those reassurances.

As a financially-strapped Lincoln did self-therapy by letters written to political friends, Mary, herself part of "a political partnership" that had been defeated, medicated the hurt in her own way. Starting in April and lasting through July she presided over the making of a dress by Springfield's Irish-born dressmaker, Mrs. LaBarthe (the French surname really helped business) to the tune of $38, a lot of money in 1858. In fact, writes Mary's biographer, in 1859 "she spent $196.55 for her clothes, and the cost of just one of her dresses represented two months' pay for a typical Springfield family. . ." Purchases such as these "established a pattern of buying undertaken . . . to make restitution for personal and political defeats." (In short, Lincoln could not afford to lose many more elections.) 45

As he mended from the loss to Douglas, however, one dreaded day loomed before him: January 6, 1859. When the newly-elected General Assembly met that day in the State Capitol a few blocks from Lincoln's home on Eighth and Jackson, one of their first orders of business was the appointment of the man who would serve with Trumbull in the United States Senate.

The Capitol building and Lincoln were old friends; he and other members of the Sangamon County "Long Nine" had deftly conspired decades ago to move the state capital from Vandalia northwest to Springfield. Lincoln had himself served as a state legislator there; he had argued cases before the state Supreme Court within its stone walls. He had spent a fair amount of time in its alcoves and corridors bonding with the other male attorneys and legislators when he could not stay in the same house with Mary. He had embarked upon his greatest journey to date with a speech given in the House chamber, on a house that Lincoln warned could not remain forever divided. Workplace, clubhouse, and site of some of the most important moments of Lincoln's professional life, the Capitol building, a mere walk from Lincoln's home, was a place that he would normally have looked to for assurance and stability.

But not today. Inside it went as expected: 54 votes for Douglas, 46 for Lincoln. 46

The Democrats took to the streets. Raucous celebrations broke out (not that spontaneously of course, for everyone had known what would happen.) But poor Lincoln had not the luxury of being cross state in Charleston, or up in Chicago, or even down in Jonesboro. Try to imagine how he felt. This would be similar to interviewing for a coveted job at the same time that a neighbor whom you have come to like less and less interviews for the same job. The neighbor gets it, and then throws a loud party to celebrate. 47

Lincoln met this excruciating ordeal—humiliation piled atop humiliation—with humor and resolve. A Kentucky journalist found the Republican in good enough spirits to admit that he felt like the Kentucky boy who had stumbled running up a hill: *"I am too big to cry about it, but it hurts too much to laugh."* And he later told a friend that, hitting a slick spot as he walked to the office, his foot had slipped, "but I recovered myself & lit square and I said to myself, 'It's a slip and not a fall.'" 48

Nonetheless, later that day Henry C. Whitney found Lincoln in the Lincoln and Herndon law office, just around the corner from home and across the way from the Capitol building. Lincoln was "gloomy as midnight," remembered Whitney. Convinced he was finished in politics, Lincoln croaked "I expect everyone to desert me except Billy." 49

For his part, Billy had played a vigorous role in the campaign, loyally traveling east in the late winter and early spring of 1858 to meet prominent abolitionists such as Theodore Parker, Wendell Phillips, and the great William Lloyd Garrison to line up what support he could from them. He had also paid courtesy calls on Greeley and Douglas. Back in Illinois, Herndon had worked like mad to "woo the Know-Nothing vote" and stoke the fires of the feud in the Democratic party. (He functioned as a key intelligence operative, for his father and brother were leading Danites.) The campaign sent Billy to "smaller villages in the Sangamon region" and even if he didn't draw Lincoln-sized crowds, he served his friend's cause well. He made it his job to go after the "lazy or indifferent voter" by setting up a "'*Stump*' or goods-box, right at their door so that they had to listen." (How would this go over in *your* neighborhood?) They loved Billy in Menard County, and one citizen of Petersburg urged Herndon to run for Congress after hearing him speak on behalf of Lincoln. 50

He obsessively clipped and pasted into notebooks newspaper items that Lincoln could have used (but generally didn't) on the stump against Douglas. He did what his biographer called the "dirty work" of the campaign, plying dad and brother Elliott for inside information from the Danite camp, largely because someone had to do it, and "it was not the kind of thing that suited Lincoln's tastes." 51

When it ended in defeat, Billy wrote yet another letter in a long correspondence to Boston's Theodore Parker, an odd couple if ever there was one. Parker was a Brahmin Unitarian minister, Herndon a volcanic frontier lawyer. Billy wrote:

> We are beaten in Illinois, as you are aware; but you may want to know the causes of our defeat. Firstly, then, I have more than once said our State represents three distinct phases of human development: the extreme north, the middle, and the extreme south. The first is intelligence, the second timidity, and the third ignorance on the special issue [slavery]. . .If a man spoke to suit the north—for freedom, justice—this killed him in the center and in the South. . .Lincoln tried to stand high and elevated, so he fell deep. 52

Secondly, a little unfairly, Herndon charged, "Greeley never gave us one single, solitary, manly lift. . .his silence was his opposition." In fact, "we never got a smile or a word of encouragement outside of Illinois from any

quarter during all this great canvass. The East was for Douglas *by silence.*"
Third, "Thousands of Whigs dropped us just on the eve of the election,
through the influence of Crittenden." Fourth the pro-slavery men "threw
into this State money, men, and speakers." 53

Billy seemed to be getting more agitated as he wrote. (Parker must
have found these letters entertaining.) Fifth, "thousands of roving, robbing,
bloated, pock-marked Catholic Irish were imported upon us from Philadelphia, New York, St. Louis, and other cities. I myself know of such by their
own confession. [And he didn't mean confession to a priest.] Some have
been arrested, and are now in jail awaiting trial." 54

Which in Billy's mind was a good place for them. He'd probably dam-
aged his friend's candidacy back in October when as the Chicago *Press and
Tribune's* unnamed "special correspondent" he had opined that what with
Election Day "colonization" of these "pock-marked," "Ishmaelite" Irish
voters a likely possibility, "a general and terrific row over the Irish," was
imminent. And he was "not at all sure but that the Republicans should
rise and cut their throats." And when a drunken Irishman disrupted a
Danite meeting in Springfield, Billy the Republican jumped up, hollering, "'God damn the Irish, I want it distinctly understood that *we*"—the
Republicans—"are willing to have war with them." So saying, Billy gave
the Irishman the bum's rush down the stairs. Needless to say it had not
helped Lincoln with anyone but the most vigorous of Know Nothings. 55

So there sat Lincoln on a January day, the long prairie winter stretched
out before him, Springfield Democrats baying over his defeat, convinced
that only his erratic partner would stand by him, and strapped for funds to
boot. A short stroll away sat home, and his sons, and a wife whose love and
political savvy lived uneasily next to some pretty disturbing (and costly)
behaviors. And from where he now sat, it looked as though he would be in
Springfield for an indefinite period of time. Maybe forever.

Meanwhile, Douglas had been writing his own letters, thanking
Virginia governor Henry Wise on November 7 for his "eloquent and admi-
rable address to the Illinois Democratic State Central Committee," which
had "aroused every Democrat. . .to renewed exertions." He added, "Pardon
me for saying that it was a noble, patriotic letter and has done its work."

Looking to 1860, Douglas assured Wise, "Whatever may be the result in the other Northern states you may always rely upon Illinois as being faithful to the Democracy against the assaults and treasonable purposes of the Abolitionists and their allies." In early December he thanked a Louisiana committee headed by the expansionist Pierre Soule for their congratulations on "the glorious triumph achieved [sic] by the Democracy" against "the Enemies of the Constitution and the Union." Planning a convalescent trip back home to Washington by way of New Orleans, Cuba and New York, he accepted the Louisianians' invitation to speak on December 6 at the New Orleans Odd Fellows Hall. 56

Arriving down river days later, Douglas began the speech, "When I determined to visit New Orleans, it was only on private business of an imperative character; and it was my desire to arrive and depart as quietly as possible, and without, in any way, connecting myself with politics. I approached your city, as I supposed, unheralded and unknown, and I was amazed at the magnificent reception extended to me on the levee, by so vast a concourse of people. . .This was a compliment which filled my heart with gratitude, and did not leave me at liberty to decline the first request you might make of me. I have, therefore, yielded to your solicitations, to make a few remarks. . ." Nearing the end of the speech, he responded to shouts from the audience of "Cuba! Cuba!" by asserting that "it is our destiny to have Cuba, and it is folly to debate the question. . .The same is true of Central America and Mexico." Gosh it was good to talk about *important* issues again. 57

By the day of Lincoln's final rejection by the legislature of Illinois, Douglas had nearly reached the nation's capital. In Baltimore, he received a wire from Charles Lanphier:

Glory to God and the Sucker Democracy. Douglas 54, Lincoln 46. Announcement followed by shouts of immense crowd present. Town wild with excitement. Democrats firing salute. . .Guns, music, and whiskey rampant. 58

As Lincoln sat, defeated and "abandoned" in Springfield, muskets popping, whiskey bottles spattering, bands playing, crowds singing, the delighted Lanphier received the Senator's response:

"Let the voice of the people rule." 59

The Little Giant, one scholar has argued, won a "great personal and political triumph," for "Against enormous odds Douglas had beaten his two most powerful political enemies: the Republican Party and James Buchanan." In fact, the biggest loser in the race was Buchanan. The Danites pulled few votes, even in Egypt where John Logan won handily over all challengers. And that was only in Illinois. In Pennsylvania, New York, and New Jersey, "twenty-five antiadministration congressmen" won their races. And Douglas would not go away anytime soon. 60

In faraway Manhattan, Horace Greeley must have chuckled in delight at the results: Southern Democrats would never permit Douglas to get the 1860 nomination. Greeley believed that, "As he is doomed to be slaughtered at Charleston it is a good policy to fatten him meantime." That meant that whomever the Republicans nominated in 1860 had an excellent chance of winning the presidency. 61

This was especially the case after the disastrous late April Democratic national convention of 1860. Quincy's William Richardson, aided by Linder and Logan and countless other Illinois Democrats, scrambled over the floor of Charleston's Institute Hall, trying mightily to hold the national party together and secure Douglas's nomination. But when a Southern-sponsored platform plank calling predictably for a federal fugitive slave code for the territories failed to get the supermajority that it needed, slave state delegations under the leadership of men like William Lowndes Yancey and Jefferson Davis and Douglas's old nemesis John Slidell led their delegations out of the convention in a well-choreographed bit of political theater. Douglas would get the nomination all right, but not in South Carolina. It would come weeks later, at Baltimore, in a hastily called attempt to salvage the race. Southern Democrats, some anxious to lose the presidential election and take their states out of the Union, nominated Buchanan's vice president John Cabell Breckinridge for president. Eventually, another Henry Clay acolyte--Whig Senator John Bell of Tennessee--would throw in, too. 62

Two years earlier, on a June night in Springfield, Lincoln had tested his House Divided speech on Billy Herndon, and over the objection of others

Herndon had practically ordered Lincoln to deliver the speech as written; "it will make you President." At the close of a Senate campaign that had begun with Lincoln quoting Jesus Christ, a campaign in which Lincoln had extended the great Douglas to the late innings, a campaign in which Lincoln had nearly toppled the Little Giant, a campaign in which Lincoln could not have failed to notice that he had physically outlasted his famous opponent *and* proved himself on a national stage, the Republican would not have been human if he did not grow in confidence. That confidence that would stay with him. In August, just after the Ottawa debate, a Philadelphia journalist had predicted that Lincoln, "the most used-up man in the United States," would not survive; "there will scarcely be anything left of him." Reporting that Lincoln "exhibits the appearance of great mental and bodily suffering," the Easterner noted that six debates remained: "*I don't believe he will fill them all.*" But Lincoln had to take slightly guilty satisfaction—as well as encouragement and no small pride--in his physical state relative to that of Douglas by campaign's end. He could have gone many more rounds. Douglas could not have done so. 63

Correspondents, some of them hard-to-please Easterners, reinforced this. The New York *Evening Post's* Chester P. Dewey had written even before the vote that, "the N.Y. Republicans who were in love with Douglas, are rather more inclined to take a different view now. They find much to admire & praise in your conduct of the campaign & be assured that you have made hosts of warm friends at the East." Massachusetts Republicans had in late August admitted initial misgivings over Lincoln's challenge to the great Douglas, but now confessed that "the success which has attended his forensic efforts have exceeded their most sanguine expectations." New York's Rochester *Democrat* proclaimed that "Mr. Lincoln has now a reputation as a statesman and orator, which eclipses that of Douglas as the sun does that the twinklers of the sky." The once lukewarm New York *Tribune* hailed Lincoln's speeches as "pungent without bitterness and powerful without harshness." Boston's George W. Searle wrote to ask for copies of those speeches. And New Yorker H.D. Sharpe wrote from Broadway, comparing Lincoln to Franklin and Jefferson in his "advocacy of the rights of man, as understood by those sages." Sharpe hoped that "as it is an attribute of Providence to help the weak & defenseless," that his note would "encourage you and every one in future endeavors to extend the blessings of Liberty, until equal rights . . . may be enjoyed by all, in our beloved Country." 64

For their part, Illinoisans told Lincoln what those future endeavors needed to be. Horace White predicted "your popular majority in the state will give us the privilege of naming our man on the national ticket in 1860—either President or Vice Pres't. Then, let me . . . assure you, Abe Lincoln . . . shall be an honored name before the American people." Charleston's Henry Bromwell confessed that in the course of the 1858 race, "I had come to regard you personally with feelings such as I never had toward any man except Henry Clay," so the "disappointment and chagrin I feel are very bitter." But "you come out of the fight with Laurals as the champion of those principles for which the free states contend, with the applause of the whole Republican Host. The way seems paved for the presidential victory of 1860." Douglas and the Democrats would not this time be able to "skulk behind gerymandered District lines to deprive you of the fruits off honest victory." One letter from Bloomington assured Lincoln that "you have planted the seed that will germinate & ripen in to glorious fruit," pledging, "I give you my hand on the next great fight and when it comes shall not fail to be with you." David Davis wrote five days after the vote that, "You have made a noble canvass" which "has earned you a National reputation & made you friends every where." David Brier of Bloomington wrote that having conversed with "quiet men, who listened calmly," he could report that "You stand at this moment amongst men of sense as much higher than Douglass mentally and physacally." Newspaper publisher Benjamin C. Lundy, son of one of the great abolitionists, wrote from Magnolia on November 22, 1858, "we have hoisted the names of Seward and Lincoln as our choice for Presidential & Vice Presidential candidates in '60." Lundy hoped that Lincoln would "bare the Republican standard either as candidate for President, Vice President, or Governor of the State." Herndon's July prediction no longer seemed so outlandish. And the Chicago *Daily Democrat*, noting that "it is not only in his own State that Honest old Abe is respected" called on Illinois Republicans to "present his name to the next National Republican Convention, first for President and next for Vice President." Although this seemed like hedging bets, the *Democrat* proclaimed, "the Great Man of Illinois is Abraham Lincoln. . ." 65

Billy Herndon had in fact not been alone in resenting the lack of support from Eastern Republicans. Many Illinois Republicans had come to distrust the Eastern Republican leaders, especially the man most likely to be the Republican presidential nominee, New York Senator William Henry Seward. That same bitter January of 1859, a bunch of the boys, including David Davis, Leonard Swett, Jesse Fell, and Lincoln, were sitting around Springfield shooting the breeze about alternatives to Seward. And, recalled Davis, Lincoln, seemingly back from the depths said, in effect, what about me? (Greeley had heard the same thing in his visit to Quincy.) When, in the summer and fall of that year, speaking invitations started coming in from all over Illinois, as well as Iowa, Indiana, Wisconsin, Kansas, and most importantly, Ohio (where he would again follow Douglas around the state, arguing for Republican candidates in a much-watched off year election), Lincoln began to look and feel like a hot property. 66

He had by this time become accustomed to speaking invitations, especially since receiving the Republican nomination for Senate in June of 1858. From August 10 to September 30 of that year, Lincoln received at least 27 letters requesting that he speak in various corners of Illinois. (Many were accompanied with reports on Douglas' doings in these neighborhoods; these pieces of local intelligence were designed in some cases to leverage a Lincoln visit, in others to build the Republican's confidence by noting the Little Giant's lack of popularity.) And it must have been flattering to know that the Republicans of Rockford, Highland, Magnolia, Newton, Danville, Princeton, Petersburg, and Edwardsville longed to hear and see their Senate candidate. But the requests from outside the state, after the defeat, had to encourage him even more. 67

And then came the big one, an invitation in early 1860 to go to the big city and deliver an address at Brooklyn's Plymouth Church. This allowed him to successfully raid Seward's backyard and take a side swing through New England, important stops on the road to the Republican nomination. Practically ordered by Horace White to address Wisconsin Republicans on the 28ᵗʰ of February, 1860 (this would offer, wrote White, "training for the Presidency") Lincoln cheerfully declined, "with a hint of pride," for he had to be in Brooklyn. (Organizers later moved the speech to Manhattan's Cooper Union.) The prospect of going into unfamiliar terrain, especially to New York City, might have intimidated some. But Lincoln had by this time given Douglas a terrific scare; he had won accolades from fellow Illinoisans and from around the free states, and he had been told by people whom he respected that he was presidential timber. Speaking to a New York audience might not be just the same as taking the stump in Jasper County, but could it be more daunting than appearing with Douglas in hostile Jonesboro? 68

In March, 1860, Follett, Foster, and Company published Lincoln's scrapbook of the debate transcripts. On May 10, the Republican state convention instructed the Illinois delegation to vote for Lincoln as the party's nominee as President of the United States at the approaching Republican National Convention in Chicago. 69

Lincoln was in Springfield on May 18 when the telegram came from upstate.

"He Would Invite the Whole Crowd"

Douglas won the debates, of course; he returned to his Senate seat, and despite some buffeting gained the presidential nomination of a badly-fractured Democratic party in the summer of 1860. When early local elections in Ohio, Indiana, and Pennsylvania resulted in Republican victory, he made a brave and historic decision. To James Sheridan (who along with Henry Binmore had gotten jobs with Senator Douglas at least in part for their stalwart "phonography" in the '58 campaign) he said, "Mr. Lincoln is the next President. We must try to save the Union. I will go South." And off he went, pugnacious as ever in the face of hostile crowds. In Raleigh, in answer to a question, he vowed that as President he "would hang any man higher than Haman" who attempted disunion. When the Union broke up, he stood by his president and erstwhile defeated foe. Legendarily, he held Lincoln's hat when the President rose to give his 1861 inaugural address. 70

But in early June, 1861, his health, never great to start with and probably not helped by the 1858 race, gave out. On his death bed, he ordered Adele to tell his sons Robby and Stevie, "to obey the laws and support the Constitution of the United States." What was left of the American nation mourned. He was forty-eight years old. 71

In the summer of 2004, Barack Obama, the African-American Demo-crat and state legislator seeking Douglas' old Senate seat, recalled visit-ing his own father's gravesite in Kenya. There, he came to the realization that "the best in him wasn't all that different from the best in my white grandfather from Kansas; you know, that the values that connected my mother and my father were values that I could embrace, that I didn't have to choose between them." And so it is with Douglas and his nemesis, Lincoln. It's comparatively easy to identify the "best" in Lincoln, for we've been weaned on it. But even if Douglas had truly dreadful racial views, the "best" in him is well worth celebrating: his love of self-government, his passion for the Union of the states, his love of this nation. Couple that with Lincoln's commitment to the doctrine of human equality and to the natural right to work hard and advance oneself, and you have a set of principles upon which to rebuild and sustain a nation. [72]

But can we as a nation mobilize those principles while suffering from a form of political amnesia? Sure, the battlefield re-enactors and The History Channel and the vast military history section at our gigantic bookstores keep us well-attuned to our nation's brave military past. But how do we keep from falling into the trap exemplified by this "eye-witness" remem-brance of the Freeport debate?

> Will say I have heard them debate. They both were out for President. The debate was, shall we crush slavery by force? Lincoln wanted slavery abolished by force. Douglas wanted to buy all the slaves and free them. Lincoln claimed there always would be some to buy and would cost too much. Lincoln claimed they could crush the South in a few days and free the negro race all at once. I remember well Lincoln had a voice like a roaring lion. Douglas could say more in a minute than Lincoln could in a half hour. I was a boy 13 years of age. My father took me along. He was deeply interested, as his father was a slaveholder in North Carolina at the time. . . [73]

An amusing and harmlessly inaccurate account of the second debate, as amusing and harmless as the local Freeport legend that Jane Addams may have been the "beautiful young lady" riding in the carriage with "Fred" Douglass; she was not born until 1860, so this would have been some trick on Douglass's part. [74]

But our political amnesia, our political Alzheimer's if you will, is not always so harmless. Don't we need to know that there was a time when serious, mainstream candidates in an important northern state competed for office in part by denying racial equality, and were cheered for it? That racial (and religious) attitudes in the free states were a lot more complex before the Civil War than we assume, and that they remained that way for a good long time afterward, and that 50 years after debates that turned on the issue of racial equality, white supremacy still drove violence in the home city of the nation's most famous white advocate of freedom, when whites slaughtered blacks in the 1908 Springfield race riots? Likewise, isn't it important for us to know that there was a time in American life when average people endured real discomfort to hear the candidates who competed for their votes, and that the many women who endured those discomforts were listening even though they could not vote at all?

A year before Douglas' death, on May 18, 1860, a crowd had gathered in front of the respectable house at the corner of Eighth and Jackson in Springfield, to cheer the newly-nominated Republican candidate for President.

Lincoln, too, had won the debates, even in failing to gain the Senate seat. Something like the perfect storm had occurred. Had Lincoln not lived in Illinois, had he not lost the Senate seat to Trumbull, he would not have been able to take on Douglas, the man whose very presence drew the newspaper coverage, and without that coverage, the race would have truly been a "non-event." Had Douglas allotted Lincoln only a single debate, or a best-of-three series, not the seven encounters, would Lincoln have found his voice in time? And had the people of Illinois not responded so enthusiastically to the prospect of this showdown, had there been only a sparse turnout to witness the debates, there would have been little news value to what was still Douglas' race to lose. At the same time, had Lincoln defeated Douglas, he might have had a harder time winning the presidency; American presidential history is littered with the corpses of Senators who tried and failed to make it to the White House. Similarly, had Greeley and the eastern Republicans not attempted to persuade Illinoisans that as Easterners they knew what was best for the people of Illinois, there might not have been such interest in de-railing Seward's candidacy in Chicago.

But all these things had happened. And Lincoln had learned that he at the very least belonged in Douglas' league; that he could do well by doing good—that voters would respond to the sorts of passionate moral arguments against slavery that Lincoln had sounded, especially from Galesburg to Alton; and that the narrow defeat represented perhaps not so much an ending as a beginning. In a political sense, Lincoln had come of age, as a young person comes of age as they near the end of high school, or of college; he could answer those questions--*who am I as a politican?* and *where do I fit into this political culture?*--with confidence now. The narrow defeat represented commencement, the opening of new challenges, new opportunities. The 1858 campaign toughened and sharpened Lincoln for what lie ahead.

As the crowd noise rose that May day in 1860, the candidate emerged to cheers. He seemingly had no prepared text, and Lincoln was never at his best when called on to speak extemporaneously. The friendly *Illinois State Journal* reported that Lincoln "did not suppose that the honor of such a visit was intended particularly for himself, a private citizen, [which it certainly was] but rather to the representative of a great party." [Which it also was.] Not quite sure what a presidential nominee was supposed to say on such occasions, he referred the crowd "to his previous public letters and speeches," an utterance which would not make anyone forget Daniel Webster or Patrick Henry. 75

Just prior to the end of the speech, Lincoln "said he would invite the whole crowd into his house if it was large enough to hold them." 76

One of those ever present voices called out, "We will give you a larger house on the fourth of next March."

But since the crowd was so large, Lincoln continued, "he would merely invite as many as could find room."

They cheered wildly, and reported the *Journal*, "Mr. Lincoln's house was invaded by as many as could 'squeeze in!'" No word on Mary's reaction. 77

Five years later they would bring Lincoln back to Springfield in mourning. It is said that Booth decided on murder after hearing Lincoln, in another otherwise undistinguished response to a joyous crowd outside his residence, endorse voting for blacks who had served in the Union armed forces and for "the very intelligent." The President had two years earlier indicated his esteem for the black soldiers serving in the wake of his issuance of the Emancipation Proclamation, soldiers serving "with silent tongue, and clenched teeth, and steady eye, and well-poised bayonet;" and he had recommended to Louisiana's reconstruction governor that some blacks be allowed to vote; and he had written to Senator Sumner requesting full death benefits for the widows of black soldiers massacred at Fort Pillow, even though many of these marriages had not been recognized as legal under Southern state law, the sorts of local laws of which Douglas was so enamored. Of course he had rejoiced at Illinois' ratification of the Thirteenth Amendment, ending slavery, "a King's cure for all our evils." Five weeks before Booth got to him, Lincoln had given an inaugural address in which he had said that this bloodiest war in American history was a just God's reward for the sin of American—not Southern, American—Slavery. It was as though the Lincoln of October, 1858, the Lincoln of Galesburg and Quincy and Alton, had won a struggle with the Lincoln of September, the Lincoln of Charleston. 78

And perhaps the outcome of that struggle was never in doubt. A Springfield builder and contractor named John Armstrong told Billy Herndon of a conversation he'd witnessed in Lincoln's office only days after the House Divided speech. As Lincoln, wrote, head down, one Doctor Long walked in to let Lincoln know what a disaster the speech had been. Too abolitionist by far. "Well, Lincoln," he said, "that foolish speech of yours will probably kill you—will defeat you in this Contest—and probably for all offices for all time to come." Having shared that happy analysis, Long pronounced himself "sorry—very sorry." He "wished it was wiped out of existence," and added, "Don't you wish so."

Lincoln stopped writing. He put his pen down.

He lifted his eyeglasses and looked at the doctor. Looked at him, said Armstrong, "with a look of insulted dignity."

Well, Doctor, began Lincoln, "If I had to draw a pen across and erase my whole life from Existence & all I did; and I had one poor gift or choice left, as to what I should Save from the wreck, I should choose that speech and leave it to the world unerased." 79

Lincoln began growing in important ways after Charleston, and through to Alton. Of course that development, that growing confidence, that more focused moral sense was but a critical early stage in the internal strengthening of the man who would defend the Union, issue the Emancipation Proclamation, recruit and speak up in defense of black servicemen, become the first president to call for black suffrage and endorse the final destruction of slavery.

How did a man of Lincoln's background pull this off? "Education: Deficient," he wrote of himself in a brief set of campaign biography notes just prior to delivering the House Divided speech. He spent his early years in notoriously anti-black regions, slave-state Kentucky, southern Indiana, and Egypt, where some of his fellow Illinoisans would come to rue the day he was born. Given all that, Knox College historian Rodney Davis told me, "he should have been a Jacksonian Democrat. He should have been Stephen Douglas."

Why didn't Lincoln go that way?

Professor Davis looks you in the eye.

"I don't have the answer. That's the great mystery." 80

I sit on a July evening on a wooden bench within the deserted confines of the Abraham Lincoln National Historical Park, mere blocks from where Lincoln gave and defended that fiery anti-slavery acceptance speech, the park vacant but for the squirrels skittering around Lincoln's unpretentious corner lot. The campaign that he made in 1858, his friend Joseph Gillespie thought, "first inspired him with the idea that he was above the average of mankind." But that realization, undeniably true though it was, needed a number of things to happen before it could emerge. Lincoln needed to take on a giant; Lincoln's challenge to the giant needed to capture the attention of his fellow Illinoisans; and his challenge needed to catch the eye of people outside of his state and his region. Retrospectively, we can almost say that Lincoln needed to bravely *lose* the election, and to take time to reflect on what he had done on the way to his impressive defeat. So that by August of 1864, with Grant and Sherman bloodily grinding it out, Republican leaders and Lincoln himself expecting electoral defeat in the fall, wise men telling the President to abandon emancipation and thus salvage a second term, Lincoln would answer the demand that he return to slavery the black heroes of the battles of Port Hudson and Olustee: "I should be damned in time & eternity for so doing. The world shall know that I will keep my faith to friends and enemies, come what will." There were worse things than losing an election. 1858 had taught him that, and that made all the difference. 81

He came of age on the roads and rails and rivers he'd traveled and on the speakers' platforms with Douglas, especially after that dismaying five minutes at Charleston, especially in autumn in the Mississippi Valley. High summer abstractions hardened into commitment, to conviction. In July, he confessed in writing that "I have never professed an indifference to the honors of official station, and were I to do so now, I should only make myself ridiculous." There was nonetheless, "a higher aim than that of mere office." Britain's century-long fight to abolish the slave trade "had it's open fire-eating opponents; it's stealthy 'don't care' opponents, it's dollar and cent opponents; it's inferior race opponents; it's negro equality opponents; and it's religion and good order opponents," and these people "got offices, and their adversaries got none." But although "they blazed, like tallow-candles for a century, at last they flickered in the socket, died out, stank in the dark for a brief season" and were forgotten, "except for the smell." But our schoolchildren, he wrote, know the names of William Wilberforce and Granville Sharpe, who struggled to end the wrong. The "higher object" of Lincoln's own struggle "may not be completely attained within the term of my natural life," but "it will come in due time." And "I am proud, in my passing speck of time, to contribute an humble mite to that glorious consummation, which my own poor eyes may not last to see." 82

Noble words; but July words, easily drafted, harder to speak before Douglas and his hecklers and his writers in the central counties whose voters would decide this election. Any one of us might excuse ourselves from asking the hard question: *but do you really mean it?* Not until he turned west from Charleston and set his face for the decisive showdowns with Douglas would Lincoln be able to answer *Yes, I do.* Why did he commit, when so many of his friends had all along counseled caution as the means to victory?

Once, in 1841, in the midst of an especially dark depression, Lincoln had offered reassurance to his friend Joshua Speed that he would not take his own life, despite his deep sadness, for "I have an irrepressible desire to live until I can be assured that the world is a little better for my having lived in it." 83

A sultry July evening; you sit on a bench in Springfield, sizing up the light brown house, a respectable home but no Monticello, no Mount Vernon; the picket fence, the squirrels capering, and you think about that rage to live, at least until such time as he could feel *that the world is a little better for my having lived in it.* Blocks away he had begun his campaign with Christ's words: a house divided against itself cannot stand. And from Ottawa to Jonesboro, from Sullivan to Oquawka, to Alton and back to Springfield he had grown more assured and less inhibited in a moral sense. An ongoing democratic conversation before the people of Illinois had forced this change. The invitations to speak all over the north, to accept the Republican nomination, to lead the nation at a time of maximum crisis came to him in the months and years after the devastating final vote that January day over at the state capitol. These drove away the pain of the loss, strengthening further his sense that he was above the common run of humanity; but none would have come without the inner change, the migration of the generous spirit from the private into the public man, the learning of and the commitment to a new, more confident, more moralistic language on slavery in the summer and especially in the fall of 1858. He found that voice under wide Illinois skies in front of thousands of his fellow citizens, some of whom spoke that same language, many more of whom were not at all sure about such ideas, and some of whom angrily and loudly disagreed, and this in a tight race which—for all Lincoln knew—might be his own last, best chance to leave the world a little better place.

An Illinois friend—one of the generous-spirited small-town heroes that I met in the towns and cities of Lincoln's Illinois--contends that he aims to "get right with Lincoln," to understand him as fully as possible. And you sense that Lincoln--a work in progress as are we all, as individuals and as a nation—was himself trying all along to get right with someone, whether consciously or subconsciously trying to exercise "a little more courage and self-restraint," to become at least in a political sense the person he really was, to become more truly human. 84

NOTES

Notes for Prologue: "He Don't *Care* Anything About It"

1 See, for instance, Don E. Fehrenbacher, *Prelude to Greatness: Lincoln in the 1850s*, (Stanford: Stanford University Press, 1962); David Potter, *The Impending Crisis: 1848-1861*, (New York: Harper Torchbooks, 1976.) See also Richard Allen Heckman, *Lincoln v. Douglas: The Great Debates Campaign*, (Washington: Public Affairs Press, 1967), p. iii. Heckman writes that, "One trap into which the lay reader may fall is a tendency to believe those who are obsessed with the idea that the debates were one of the greatest pivotal moments in history." The three most important works on the 1858 debates are Allen Guelzo, *Lincoln and Douglas: The Debates That Defined America*, (New York: Simon & Schuster, 2008) David Zarefsky, *Lincoln, Douglas, and Slavery: In the Crucible of Public Debate*, (Chicago: University of Chicago Press, 1990), and Harry V. Jaffa, *Crisis of the House Divided: An Interpretation of the Issues in the Lincoln-Douglas Debates*, (Chicago: University of Chicago Press, 1982.)

2 Lincoln has been the subject of an enormous number of books. Among the more recent works consulted for this sketch are David Herbert Donald, *Lincoln*, (New York: Simon and Schuster, 1995); Douglas Wilson, *Honor's Voice: The Transformation of Abraham Lincoln*, (New York: Alfred A. Knopf, 1995); William Lee Miller, *Lincoln's Virtues: An Ethical Biography*, (New York: Alfred A. Knopf, 2002); Michael Burlingame, *The Inner World of Abraham Lincoln*, (Urbana: University of Illinois Press, 1994) and Richard J. Carwardine, *Lincoln*, (Edinburgh, Pearson Education Limited, 2003). On the reactions of those who newly encountered Lincoln, see Harold Holzer, *Lincoln at Cooper Union: The Speech That Made Abraham Lincoln President* (New York: Simon and Schuster, 2004); New York *Evening Post*, August 27, 1858, in Edwin Erle Sparks, *The Lincoln-Douglas Debates of 1858: Collections of the Illinois State Historical Library*, Vol. III, Lincoln Series,

Vol. I, (Springfield: Trustees of the Illinois State Historical Library, 1908), p. 130. (Hereafter known as "Sparks."). For Lincoln's evocation of the "ancient faith, see "Speech at Peoria, October 16, 1854," in Roy P. Basler, ed., *The Collected Works of Abraham Lincoln,* Volume II, The Abraham Lincoln Association, Springfield, Ill., (New Brunswick: Rutgers University Press, 1953), pp. 247-283. (Hereafter known as *CW*). For Eric Foner, *Free Soil, Free Labor, Free Men: The Ideology of the Republican Party Before the Civil War,* (New York: Oxford University Press, 1970), especially pp. 11-39, pp. 261-300. For Lincoln's application of "the right to rise" to both whites and blacks, see Boritt, *Lincoln and the Economics of the American Dream,* pp. 155-174. On Lincoln's House Divided Speech, see "Draft of a Speech," c.late December, 1857, in Don E. Fehrenbacher, ed., *Abraham Lincoln: Speeches and Writings, 1832-1858,* (New York: Literary Classics of the United States, 1989), pp. 412-418; David Herbert Donald, *Lincoln's Herndon,* (New York: Alfred A. Knopf, 1948), pp. 118-119. Lincoln first raised the question of whether the nation could exist permanently "half slave, half free" in an 1855 letter to George Robertson. See Gabor Boritt, *"This Government Cannot Endure Permanently, Half Slave, Half Free": Lincoln and the "House Divided,"* (New York: Gilder Lehrman Institute of American History, 2005), p. 5.

3 The standard work on Douglas is Robert W. Johannsen, *Stephen A. Douglas,* (New York: Oxford University, 1973.) See also Johannsen, *The Frontier, the Union, and Stephen A. Douglas,* (Urbana: University of Illinois Press, 1980); Johannsen, *The Letters of Stephen A. Douglas,* Urbana: University of Illinois Press, 1961; and Damon Wells, *Stephen Douglas: The Last Years, 1857-1861,* (Austin: University of Texas Press, 1971.)

4 Lorman A. Ratner and Dwight L. Teeter, Jr., *Fanatics and Fire Eaters: Newspapers and the Coming of the Civil War,* (Urbana: University of Illinois Press, 2003), pp. 1-10. For the New York *Tribune's* lukewarm response to the Lincoln candidacy, see Horner, pp. 142-143; Donald, *Lincoln's Herndon,* (New York, Alfred A. Knopf, 1948), pp. 112-117. For Lincoln's reaction to Greeley, see Abraham Lincoln to Lyman Trumbull, 28 December, 1857, *CW* II, p. 430; Lincoln to Charles L. Wilson, 1 June, 1858, *CW* II, pp. 456-457; Hoyt, *Lincoln and Herndon,* pp. 141-142. By nominating Lincoln, Illinois Republicans were in effect taking the choice of U.S. Senator out of the hands of the state legislature in the event of a Republican victory, an early challenge that would later bear fruit in the Seventeenth

Dear Stan,

The book that you've just received, *The Prairies on Fire: Lincoln Debates Douglas, 1858*, developed from an interest in Lincoln that began for me in graduate school. Abraham Lincoln was not perfect, but the book makes the argument that his race against the incumbent US Senator Stephen A. Douglas in 1858 taught him some lessons that stayed with him at crunch time, during the latter years of his first term as President, when he made tough decisions, especially as regarded African American freedom. Those decisions saved and bettered the nation.

Although I wrote and published *The Prairies on Fire*, I'm not chiefly responsible for it arriving at your door. A generous benefactor conceived of and provided the support for the project of sharing the book within our group of former NC State lacrosse players and friends

Being reunited with so many great teammates and friends at Duke's induction into the North Carolina Lacrosse Hall of Fame in early June brought home for me, and maybe for you too, a realization: what a wonderful shared experience we had as young guys. At the heart of it all—the practices, the van rides, the motels, the meals, the parties, the wins, the losses—were memorable friendships. I thank each of you for making those four years so great for me.

Sincerely,

Rich (Beaver) Schwartz

Amendment. On the historic nature of the nomination, see Fehrenbacher, *Prelude to Greatness,* pp. 48-49. On party ties to the press, see Johannsen, *Stephen A. Douglas,* pp. 448-449; Ratner and Teeter, p. 10; Fehrenbacher, *Prelude to Greatness,* p. 11. Quoted in Harold Holzer, *The Lincoln-Douglas Debates: The First Complete, Unexpurgated Text,* (New York, HarperCollins, 1993), pp. 10-11. (Hereafter referred to as *LD.*)

5 The standard history of Illinois is Robert Howard, *Illinois: A History of the Prairie State* (Gtrand Rapids: William B. Eerdmans, 1972); see also Fehrenbacher, *Prelude,* pp. 4-17.Johannsen, *Stephen A. Douglas,* pp. 365-368; on Buchanan's motivation, see Johannsen, *Stephen A. Douglas,* pp. 645-650. For discussion of the complexities of the formation of the Republican Party, see Eric Foner, *Free Soil, Free Labor, Free Men: The Ideology of the Republican Party Before the Civil War,* (New York: Oxford University Press, 1970), especially pp. 11-39, pp. 261-300. For the ups and downs of the formation of the Republican party in middle-1850s Illinois, see William Gienapp, *The Origins of the Republican Party, 1852-1856,* (New York: Oxford University Press, 1987), especially pp. 122-127, 179, 286-295, 414-417, and 425-433. For material on Union County racial attitudes, see George Smith, *When Lincoln Came to Egypt* and John Y. Simon, *With Lincoln in Southern Illinois* (Herrin, Illinois, Crossfire Press, 1993), especially pp. xxiv-xxv.

6 For a colorful description of the scene in and around the Illinois State House that day, see Allan Nevins, *The Emergence of Lincoln: Douglas, Buchanan, and Party Chaos, 1857-1859,* (New York: Charles Scribner's Sons, 1951), p. 358.Richard Carwardine's *Lincoln* suggests that evangelical Protestants played a critical role in the Republican party of the 1850s: ". . . evangelical perceptions. . .brought into politics a more positive stress on conscience, Calvinistic duty, and social responsibility—a creed which reached its apogee in the early Republican party. For some this meant securing the slaves' liberty above all else; but others linked this to emancipating white freemen from the despotism of the slave power. . . Ministers who in the campaigns of 1856 and 1860 took part alternately in revival meetings and Republican rallies gave notice that religion and politics had fused more completely than ever before in American politics." Carwardine, *Lincoln,* pp. 129-130. Thus the use of the "house divided" language carried special meaning for a segment of Lincoln's audience. All quotes in this segment are taken from Lincoln, "A House Divided": Speech at Springfield, Illinois, June 16, 1858,

CW II, pp. 461-469. Modern-day scholarship suggests that a "second *Dred Scott* ruling could have come in the case of *Lemmon v. The People of New York.* Paul Finkelman, *An Imperfect Union: Slavery, Federalism, and Comity*, (Chapel Hill: University of North Carolina Press, 1981), cited in James McPherson, *Battle Cry of Freedom: The Civil War Era,* (New York: Oxford University Press, 1988), pp. 180-181. David Zarefsky concludes that Lincoln believed that such a conspiracy did exist, although the Republican admitted that he could not prove the existence of the conspiracy. Zarefsky, *Lincoln Douglas and Slavery*, p. 87, 104-106. Billy Herndon, Lincoln's law partner urged Lincoln to give the speech over the objections of conservative Republicans whom Lincoln had invited to a rehearsal, and Lincoln listened to Herndon. For Herndon's role see Donald, *Lincoln's Herndon,* pp. 117-119.

7 Stephen A. Douglas, "Speech of Senator Douglas On the Occasion of His Public Reception at Chicago, Friday Evening, July 9, 1858 (Mr. Lincoln Was Present)" http://www.bartleby.com/251/1002.html 9 August, 2004. Johannsen, *Stephen A. Douglas,* pp. 641-644 offers a good overview of Douglas' Chicago speech; David Davis to Abraham Lincoln, 3 August, 1858, Abraham Lincoln Papers at the Library of Congress Online version, http://memory.loc.gov. 13 July, 2005.

8 Douglas, Chicago speech, 9 July, 1858, www.bartleby.com 9 August, 2004.

9 Lincoln, "Speech at Chicago, Illinois, July 10, 1858," *CW* II, p. 485.

10 Lincoln, "Speech at Chicago, Illinois, July 10, 1858," *CW* II, pp. 500-501.

11 Lincoln, "Speech at Chicago, Illinois, July 10, 1858," *CW* II, pp. 500-501.

12 Lincoln, "Speech at Chicago, Illinois, July 10, 1858," *CW* II, p. 501.

13 Lincoln to Gustave Koerner, July 15, 1858, *CW* II, pp. 502-503. Koerner wrote back that he would do what he could, but that Hecker must not be offered travel expenses: "He would feel very indignant," for although having lost his fortune in the German revolutions, Hecker had struggled

to recover, and "he is a man of wealth, and even if he were not, he is so disinterested that he would never claim any compensation." Still, "I am not inclined to think that his presence will do much good.. . .amongst the Catholicks and even orthodox Protestants he is considered as the very Anti-Christ." Gustave P. Koerner to Abraham Lincoln, July 17, 1858, Abraham Lincoln Papers at the library of Congress, Online version, http://memory.loc.gov, 12 August, 2006.

14 Abraham Smith to Abraham Lincoln, July 20, 1858, Abraham Lincoln Papers at the Library of Congress, Online version, http://memory. loc.gov, 12 August, 2006; and Timothy D. Lincoln to Abraham Lincoln, July 17, 1858, Abraham Lincoln Papers at the Library of Congress, Online version, 12 August, 2006.

15 W.M. Chambers to Abraham Lincoln, July 22, 1858; Augustus H. Chapman to Abraham Lincoln, July 24, 1858; Jediah Alexander to Abraham Lincoln, August 5, 1858; Hiram M. Tremble to Abraham Lincoln, August 4, 1858, all in Abraham Lincoln Papers at the Library of Congress, Online version, 14 August, 2006.

16 "1858 Campaign Strategy," *CW* II, pp.476-481. This entry in *The Collected Works* consists of six pages of 1856 election result analysis for the counties in which Lincoln expected close races against Douglas. See also Lincoln to Joseph Gillespie, July 16, 1858, *CW* II, pp. 503-504 and, for instance, Henry C. Whitney to Abraham Lincoln, July 31, 1858, Abraham Lincoln Papers at the Library of Congress, Online version, http://memory. loc.gov, 14 August, 2006. In this, one of many letters written to Lincoln on important local political developments, Whitney of the Chicago *Press and Tribune* decried the "greediness of the stinking abolitionists" of LaSalle County, who seemed to determined to run committed anti-slavery candidates locally at the same time as erstwhile Republican Lyle Dickey was committing to Douglas. David Davis weighed in, suggesting that the best way for Republicans to win in LaSalle was "to nominate unexceptional men for the [state] Legislature." See David Davis to Abraham Lincoln, August 2, 1858, Abraham Lincoln Papers at the Library of Congress, Online version, http://memory.loc.gov, 14 August, 2006. On the Lincoln-Crittenden exchange of letters, see Lincoln to John J. Crittenden, July 7, 1858, *CW* II, pp. 483-484, and Crittenden's response to Lincoln indicated his tendency

to support Douglas in common cause against Buchanan, while offering regards to Lincoln. See John J. Crittenden to Abraham Lincoln, July 29, 1858, Abraham Lincoln Papers at the Library of Congress, Online version, http://memory.loc.gov, 14 August, 2006.

17 Johannsen, *Stephen A. Douglas*, p. 655; Lincoln, "Speech at Springfield, Illinois, July 17, 1858," *CW* II, p. 506.

18 Lincoln, "Speech at Havana, Illinois, August 14, 1858," *CW* II, pp. 541-542. When a Douglasite is the crowd offered to stand in for the Senator, Lincoln called back, "If my fighting Judge Douglas would not prove anything, it would certainly prove nothing for me to fight his bottle-holder."

19 Chicago *Press and Tribune*, 22 July, 1858, quoted in Fehrenbacher, *Prelude*, p. 94; Lincoln to Stephen A. Douglas, July 24, 1858, *CW* II, p. 522.

20 "Douglas' letter of the 24th," *CW* II n., pp. 528-529.

21 "Douglas' letter of the 24th," *CW* II n., pp. 528-529.

22 Lincoln to Douglas, July 29, 1858, *CW* II, pp. 528-529; on Danite efforts see Johannsen, *Stephen A. Douglas*, p. 649; Lincoln to Douglas, July 29, 1858, *CW* II, p. 529-530.

23 Chicago *Press and Tribune*, 28 July, 1858, quoted in Fehrenbacher, *Prelude*, p. 100; *Illinois State Journal*, 3 August, 1858, quoted in Fehrenbacher, p. 100.

24 Johannsen, *Stephen A. Douglas*, p. 664; "Douglas' letter of July 30, 1858," *CW* II, n., pp. 530-532.

25 Lincoln to Douglas, July 31, 1858, *CW* II, p. 531.

26 Fehrenbacher, *Prelude*, pp. 100-101; Johannsen, *Stephen A. Douglas*, p. 659; Fehrenbacher, *Prelude*, pp. 102-103.

27 The two best known editions of the debate transcripts are Paul Angle, *Created Equal? The Lincoln-Douglas Debates of 1858*, (Chicago:

University of Chicago Press, 1958) and Harold Holzer, *The Lincoln-Douglas Debates: The First Complete, Unexpurgated Text,* (New York: HarperCollins, 1993.) Holzer employs the "opposition" transcripts, using Democratic transcriptions as the Lincoln text, and Republican transcriptions as the Douglas text, reasoning that this will eliminate partisan "improvement" of the debaters' words.Harry V. Jaffa, *Crisis of the House Divided: An Interpretation of the Issues in the Lincoln-Douglas Debates,* (Chicago and London: University of Chicago Press, 1982) is the great intellectual history of the debates. David Zarefsky, *Lincoln Douglas and Slavery: In the Crucible of Public Debate* is a masterful examination of the rhetorical strategies employed by the two contenders.   The most recent narrative histories of the debates are Allen Guelzo, *Lincoln and Douglas: The Debates That Defined America* (New York: Simon and Schuster, 2008), Richard Allen Heckman, *Lincoln V. Douglas: The Great Debates Campaign,* (Washington: Public Affairs Press, 1967) and Saul Sigelschiffer, *The American Conscience: The Drama of the Lincoln-Douglas Debates,* (New York: Horizon Press, 1973.) Norman Corwin, *The Rivalry* (New York: Dramatists Play Service, 1957.) The play's first performance in New York City was at the Bijou Theatre on February 7, 1959. In the film *Abe Lincoln in Illinois,* the one set piece scene of the debates happens at night (all of the debates took place during the afternoon), and the blazing torches combine with a menacing interpretation of Douglas by Gene Lockhart to suggest that Lincoln was fighting a sort of American fascism in 1858, especially when Douglas raves that America should become "the terror of the world." Lincoln's House Divided speech comes at the conclusion of the debate, not as the formal kick-off to the campaign. Horace Greeley, mightily impressed, vows to make the American newspaper public know the name of Lincoln.

28 I thank Professor Mary P. Sheridan-Rabideau, Professor Carol Bork, JoAnn Price and all participants in a 2006 New Jersey Council for the Humanities Seminar on "Coming of Age Literature," for helping me to apply the notion of "coming of age" to Lincoln.

29 Alton *Daily* Courier, October 16, 1858, in Sparks, p. 500.

30 Paul Gagnon, "Educating Democracy: Are We Up To It?" *National Council for History Education Occasional Paper,* March, 2005, p. 1.

Notes for Chapter One: "I Am Yet Alive"

1 Harold Holzer, *The Lincoln-Douglas Debates: The First Complete, Unexpurgated Text,* (New York: Harper Collins, 1993), pp. 40-45. Unless otherwise noted, all direct and indirect quotes of Lincoln's and Douglas' debate remarks are taken from Holzer's invaluable edition of debate transcripts. Hereafter, Holzer's compilation will be abbreviated as *LDD*.

2 *LDD*, p. 45.

3 The pitched battle in the House ran from 1836-45, and is described skillfully in William Lee Miller, *Arguing About Slavery: The Great Battle in the United States Congress* (New York: Alfred A. Knopf, 1996.); Don Fehrenbacher, *Slavery, Law, and Politics: The Dred Scott Case in Historical Perspective* (Oxford: Oxford University Press, 1981), p. 67.

4 David Potter and Don Fehrenbacher, *The Impending Crisis, 1848-1861* (New York: Harper Torch Books, 1976), p. 90-120.

5 Holzer's edition of the debate transcripts attempts to get at the truth of what the two men said by using the opposition newspaper's word-for-word transcriptions (the Chicago *Times* for Lincoln, the Chicago *Daily Press and Tribune* for Douglas.) Holzer includes both newspapers' reports of crowd reaction, and where the reported words of the two candidates differ, the "friendly" newspaper's version in brackets.

6 *LDD*, pp. 40-42; Herbert Mitgang, *Lincoln As They Saw Him* (New York: Rinehart & Co., 1956), p. 108.

7 *LDD*, p. 41.

8 *LDD*, p. 41.

9 *LDD*, p. 46. All press descriptions of crowd reaction and of the candidates' behavior on the debate platforms in the seven towns come from Holzer, *LDD* unless otherwise noted.

10 Don Fehrenbacher, *Prelude to Greatness: Lincoln in the 1850s* (Stanford: Stanford University Press, 1962), p. 101-102. Hereafter referred to as *Prelude.*

11 For reaction to Douglas' Kansas-Nebraska Act, see Johannsen, *Stephen A. Douglas*, pp. 447-464.

12 For instance, see Bernard Bailyn, *The Ideological Origins of the American Revolution* (Cambridge, Mass.: Belknap Press, 1967) pp. 144-159.

13 Johannsen, *Stephen A. Douglas* (New York: Oxford University Press, 1973), p. 660. Hereafter referred to as *SAD.* The letter to Lanphier is quoted in Robert W. Johannsen, *The Letters of Stephen A. Douglas* (Urbana: University of Illinois Press, 1961), pp. 426-427.

14 In *Prelude,* Fehrenbacher provides frequent references to these important voting districts; see, for instance, p. 71. On Lincoln's central Illinois orientation, see, for instance, William Lee Miller, *Lincoln's Virtues: An Ethical Biography* (New York: Alfred A. Knopf, 2002), especially p. 346.

15 *LDD,* p. 50.

16 For material on Douglas' plantation attachments, see *SAD,* p. 337.

17 *SAD,* p. 660.

18 Interview with Leonard Lock, Ottawa, Illinois, July 2, 2003. On "free labor ideology," see Eric Foner, *Free Soil, Free Labor, Free Men: The Ideology of the Republican Party Before the Civil War* (New York, Oxford University Press, 1970), pp. 11-39.

19 Roy Basler, ed., *CW* III, p. 20.

20 Don E. Fehrenbacher and Virginia Fehrenbacher, *Recollected Words of Abraham Lincoln* (Stanford: Stanford University Press, 1996), p. 455-456. On the term "nigger" in niddle ninettenth-century America, see Randall Kennedy, *Nigger: The Strange Career of A Troublesome Word,* (New York: Pantheon Books, 2002), pp. 5-6. "In *A Treatise on the Intellectual*

Character and Political Condition of the Colored People of the United States: and the Prejudice Exercised Toward Them (1837), Hosea Easton wrote that nigger 'is an opprobrious term, employed to impose contempt upon [blacks] as an inferior race. . .'" Kennedy writes that, "Easton averred that the earliest instruction white adults gave to white children prominently featured the word *nigger*. Adults reprimanded them for being 'worse than niggers,' for being 'ignorant as niggers.' For having 'no more credit than niggers'; they disciplined by telling them that unless they behaved they would be carried off by 'the old nigger' or made to sit with 'niggers' or consigned to the 'nigger seat,' which was, of course a place of shame."

21 *LDD*, p. 41

22 Mitgang, p. 108.

23 David Herbert Donald, *Lincoln*, (New York: Simon and Schuster, 1996), p. 217.

24 Mitgang, pp. 108-109.

25 Mitgang, p. 109.

26 *LDD*, p. 43.

27 Mitgang, p. 109. David Herbert Donald agrees with the *Times* that Lincoln came in second at Ottawa. See Donald, *Lincoln*, p. 217.

28 Mitgang, pp. 111-112; *LDD*, p. 43.

29 Johannsen, *Letters of Stephen A. Douglas*, p. 427.

30 For Douglas' characterizations of Trumbull during the Jonesboro debate, for instance, see *LDD*, pp. 142-148; Lyman Trumbull to Abraham Lincoln, 24 August, 1858, Abraham Lincoln Papers at the Library of Congress, Online version, http://memory.loc.gov 13 July, 2005.

31 Don Fehrenbacher, ed., *Abraham Lincoln: Speeches and Writings, 1832-1858*, (NewYork: Literary Classics of the United States, 1989), p. 536.

32 Fehrenbacher, *Speeches and Writings,* p. 536; Donald, *Lincoln*, p. 217; J. H. Jordan to Abraham Lincoln, 25 July, 1858, Abraham Lincoln Papers at the Library of Congress, Online version, http://memory.loc.gov 13 July, 2005; Henry C. Whitney to Abraham Lincoln, 26 August, 1858, Abraham Lincoln Papers at the Library of Congress, Online version, http://memory. loc.gov 13 July, 2005.

33 Potter and Fehrenbacher, *The Impending Crisis, 1848-1861,* p. 338. Fehrenbacher raises similar points in *Prelude,* as on p. 109.

34 Potter and Fehrenbacher, p. 329, quoted in Miller, *Lincoln's Virtues,* p. 347.

35 Miller, *Lincoln's Virtues,* pp. 489-490, n.

36 Harold Holzer, *Lincoln As I Knew Him: Gossips, Tributes, and Revelations From His Best Friends and Worst Enemies,* (Chapel Hill: Algonquin Books, 1999), pp. 78-80.

37 Basler, ed., *CW* II, pp. 546-547. Historian Pauline Maier suggests that, "In many ways, Douglas' history was more faithful to the past and to the views of Thomas Jefferson. . .Lincoln's view of the past, like Jefferson's in the 1770s, was a product of political controversy, not research, and his version of what the founders meant was full of wishful suppositions. . .But Lincoln was the greater statesman. . .In Lincoln's hands, the Declaration of Independence became first and foremost a living document for an established society, a set of goals to be realized over time. . ." *American Scripture: Making the Declaration of Independence* (New York: Alfred A. Knopf, 1997), pp. 206-207.

Notes for Chapter Two: "The Scurviest of All Possible Heresies"

1 *Freeport's Lincoln: Exercises Attendant Upon the Unveiling of A Statue of Abraham Lincoln; Freeport, Illinois, August 27, 1929, The Seventy-First Anniversary of the Freeport Lincoln-Douglas Debate Containing Addresses Delivered at Unveiling, List of Exhibits Displayed, Account of Lincoln-Douglas Debate, Etc.* (Freeport: W.T. Rawleigh, 1930; Re-issued, 1988, Freeport Lincoln-Douglas Society.), p. 135. Hereafter referred to as *FL*.

2 *LDD*, p. 87.

3 *FL*, pp. 147-149.   .

4 *FL*, pp. 198-204.

5 *FL*, pp. 142-145.

6 *FL*, p. 163.

7 *FL*, p. 163.

8 *FL*, pp. 202-203.

9 *FL*, pp. 198-204.

10 *LDD*, PP. 86-87.

11 Fred L. Holmes, "The Fate of the Nation Was Decided at Freeport That Day," (Madison, Wisconsin), reprinted in *FL*, pp. 87-88.

12 *FL*, pp. 193-195.

13 "The Wagon" in the Freeport *Weekly Bulletin,* http://lincoln.lib. niu.edu/lincolndouglas/commentary.html , 21 September, 2003. "The Illinois Historical Digitalization Projects of the Northern Illinois University" website features a wealth of sources, including many accounts of the debates from Illinois newspapers, as well as debate transcripts, maps, and other information relating to the Lincoln-Douglas race of 1858. Hereafter referred to as *NIU.*

14 *LDD*, pp. 87-88; Mitgang, p. 113; Sparks, pp. 79-82.

15 *LDD*, p. 6. George Buss and Rich Sokup confirmed the story, interview of July 2, 2003, Freeport, Illinois.

16 *LDD*, p. 88. Holzer's recounting of the incident includes the line, "Ain't Hitt here yet?" On Hitt's advance to the platform, see Sparks, p. 79.

17 *FL*, p. 54; *LDD*, p. 90; *LDD*, p. 113.

18 On Lincoln's cadence, see Ronald C. White, *Lincoln's Greatest Speech: The Second Inaugural* (New York: Simon and Schuster, 2002), esp. p. 165.

19 Allen Guelzo, *Abraham Lincoln: Redeemer President* (Grand Rapids: William R. Eerdmans, 1999) p. 221.

20 Rodney O. Davis, "Dr. Charles Leib; Lincoln's Mole?" *Journal of the Abraham Lincoln Association* 24:2, 2003, pp. 20-35.

21 Mitgang, pp. 114-115.

22 Mitgang, pp. 114-115.

23 Mitgang, pp. 114-115.

24 Chicago *Journal*, September 2, 1858, *NIU*, 21 September, 2003.

25 Chicago *Press and Tribune,* September 9, 1858, *NIU*, 21 September, 2003; Galesburg *Semi-Weekly Democrat*, September 1, 1858, *NIU*, 21 September, 2003; Rockford *Republican,* September 2, 1858, *NIU,* 21 September, 2003.

26 Freeport *Weekly Bulletin,* September 2, 1858, *NIU*, 21 September, 2003.

27 Freeport *Weekly Bulletin,* September 16, 1858, *NIU*, 21 September, 2003.

28 Mitgang, pp. 119-121.

29 Mitgang, pp. 119-121.

30 Mitgang, pp. 119-121.

31 Mitgang, pp. 115-117.

32 Frankfort *The Commonwealth*, September 7, 1858, p. 524, Sparks; Wilmington *Journal*, in Washington *Union*, September 16, 1858, pp. 525-526, Sparks; *The Mississippian*, September 14, 1858, in

Washington *Union*, September 22, 1858, p. 543, Sparks; Georgia *Federal Union*, September 7, 1858, p. 578 in Sparks.

33 Holmes, in *FL,* p. 74.

34 See Fehrenbacher, *Prelude*, p. 122. For the traditional explanation, see Alan Nevins, *The Emergence of Lincoln.*(New York: Charles Scribner and Sons, 1951) pp. 381-382.

35 Quoted in Holmes, *FL*, p. 74.

36 Fehrenbacher presents the most persuasive attack on what he considers the overblown Freeport story. See *Prelude*, pp. 122-140. See also David Potter and Don Fehrenbacher, *The Impending Crisis: 1848-1861* (New York: Harper Torchbooks, 1976), pp. 331-338. Potter refers to the Freeport question as "one of the great nonevents in American history."

37 Quoted in Johannsen, *SAD*, p. 670.

38 Quoted in Robert Johannsen, "Douglas and the South," in *The Frontier, the Union, and Stephen A. Douglas* (Urbana and Chicago: University of Illinois Press, 1980), p. 195; see also *SAD*, p. 686; Johannsen, "Douglas at Charleston," in *The Frontier, the Union, and Stephen A.* Douglas, p. 148.

Notes for Chapter Three: "Why Didn't You Shoot Him?"

1 *LDD*, p. 138; Johannsen, *Stephen A. Douglas*, p. 553, p. 602.

2 I've followed Lincoln's speaking schedule during this period chiefly through *CW* III, pp. 76-96. Thomas F. Schwartz, "You Can Fool All of the People: Lincoln Never Said That," *For the People: A Newsletter of the Abraham Lincoln Association* Winter, 2003 5:4, pp. 1-3.

3 Stephen W. Sears, *George B. McClellan: The Young Napoleon* (New York: Ticknor and Fields, 1988), pp. 58-59.

4 "Douglas on the Stump," *Weekly North-Western Gazette,* September 14, 1858, *NIU,* 4 January, 2004.

5 *CW* III, p. 77-78.

6 *CW* III, pp. 78-80.

7 *CW* III, pp. 83-84.

8 *CW* III, p. 91.

9 *CW* III, pp. 89-90.

10 *CW* III, p. 89.

11 *CW* III, pp. 92-95.

12 *CW* III, p. 95.

13 Smith and Simon, p. xxxii; *LDD,* p. 137; Darrel Dexter, *A House Divided: Union County Illinois, 1818-1865,* (1994), pp. 77-82; reprint from files of Geof Skinner, Union County *Gazette and Democrat,* 3 July, 2003.

14 Dexter, *A House Divided*, p. 80; Sears, *George McClellan,* pp. 58-59.

15 " 'Great Debate' Between Lincoln and Douglas at Jonesboro" *Illinois State Journal*, 20 September, 1858, *NIU,* 28 December, 2003; *LDD*, p. 137.

16 *LDD*, p. 156.

17 Dexter, p. 86. Dexter quotes an eyewitness's memory that Douglas rose and said, "My friends, I want you to listen to my friend Mr. Lincoln. . .I want to say that there is no better man than Mr. Lincoln." But neither Chicago newspaper transcription reported any such interjection. It is hard to imagine it happening and neither team of phonographers picking it up.

18 Shelby Foote, *The Civil War, A Narrative: Fort Sumter to Perryville,* (New York: Random House, 1958), p. 15.

19 "'Great Debate' Between Lincoln and Douglas at Jonesboro"' *Illinois State Journal,* 20 September, 1858, *NIU,* 28 December, 2003.

20 Abraham Lincoln to Elihu B. Washburne, September 16, 1858, *CW* III, pp. 144-145.

21 Abraham Lincoln to Martin P. Sweet, September 16, 1858, *CW* III, p. 144.

22 *CW* III, p. 144.

23 Abraham Lincoln to Joseph Gillespie, September 16, 1858, *CW* XI, Second Supplement (New Brunswick: Rutgers University Press, 1990), p. 16. For Herndon's involvement, see David Donald, *Lincoln's Herndon,* (New York, Alfred A. Knopf, 1948), pp. 112-122.

24 Lincoln to Gillespie, *CW* XI, p. 16.

25 *Illinois State Journal,* 20 September, 1858, *NIU,* 28 December, 2003.

26 *LDD*, p. 135; p. 370. This result must have represented a setback for Phillips, who had on July 24 written enthusiastically of his address to "a Court house full of people at Pinkneyville in reply to Dougherty & Logan especially to Logan. My friends think I did it with perfect success, as Logan was greatly stirred and replies to me to-day. I think he cannot do it to any purpose, as I managed to avoid any personalities, and told no filthy yarns." David L. Phillips to Abraham Lincoln, July 24, 1858, Abraham Lincoln Papers, Online version, http://memory.loc.gov, 14 August, 2006. Once the Civil War came, Logan surprised some of his neighbors by siding with the Union. He became one of the most gifted of the "political generals" in either army, winning accolades at the Battle of Atlanta and acquiring the nickname "Black Jack" as a subordinate to Grant and Sherman. See Shelby Foote, *The Civil War, A Narrative: Red River to Appomattox,* (New York: Random House, 1974), pp. 482-485. Phillips, appointed a US Marshal for southern Illinois, would abuse his authority, jailing Dr. Israel Blanchard under suspicion of disloyalty. Logan would use his influence with Lincoln to secure Blanchard's release. Logan campaigned for Lincoln in 1864, and became a key figure in post-war Republican politics, championing the cause of freedmen and Union veterans. See Mark Neely, *The Fate of Liberty: Abraham Lincoln and Civil Liberties.* (New York: Oxford University Press, 1991), pp. 53-55. Neely writes that, "Perhaps the poorest sense of judgment in

the field belonged to David L. Phillips, United States marshal for the Southern District of Illinois. . .Phillips tended to find traitors lurking in almost any gathering of Democrats."

Notes for Chapter Four: "I Will Stand By the Law of This State"

1 *LDD*, p. 185.

2 Lincoln-Douglas Museum wall text, 4 July, 2003; "Lincoln and Douglas at Charleston," *Prairie Beacon News*, Paris, Ill., September 24, 1858, *NIU*, 3 April, 2004; David Kent Coy, *Recollections of Abraham Lincoln in Coles County, Illinois: Stories About His Family and Friends.* (Charleston, Illinois: Looking For Lincoln Committee, 2000), p. 9; *LDD*, p. 186. Holzer contends that it was 32 young women. Local sources divide it, 16 young men, 16 young women.

3 Lincoln-Douglas Debate Museum wall text, 4 July, 2003; Lincoln-Douglas Debate Festival Booklet. (Charleston, Illinois: WEIU-TV, 1994.) Also, *LDD*, p. 186; Lincoln-Douglas Debate Museum, wall text, 4 July, 2003; Lincoln-Douglas Debate Museum, 4 July, 2003; *Prairie Beacon News*, September 24, 1858, *NIU*, 3 April, 2004.

4 *LDD*, p. 186; Lincoln-Douglas Debate Museum wall text, 4 July, 2003; *Prairie Beacon News*, September 24, 1858, *NIU*, 3 April, 2004.

5 Lincoln-Douglas Debate Museum wall text, 4 July, 2003; *Prairie Beacon News*, September 24, 1858, *NIU*, 3 April, 2004; Thomas A. Marshall to Abraham Lincoln, 22 July, 1858, Abraham Lincoln Papers at the Library of Congress, Online version http://memory.loc.gov 13 July, 2005.

6 *Prairie Beacon News*, September 24, 1858, *NIU*, 3 April, 2004; Lincoln-Douglas Debate Museum wall text, July 4, 2003.

7 *LDD*, p. 189.

8 David Zarefsky contends that this was actually an important juncture in the debates, at least insofar as Lincoln's furtherance of the "slave power conspiracy" charge first articulated in the House Divided speech.

Trumbull charged that Douglas had attempted to deprive Kansans of the chance to vote on whether the territory would be slave or free by deleting language to that effect from the so-called "Toombs Bill." Zarefsky calls Lincoln's lengthy Charleston discussion of the Trumbull-Douglas dispute "a masterful exercise of refutation. He never advanced the conspiracy charge himself. He stated only that Trumbull had done so and he would vouch for Trumbull's integrity." Zarefsky, *Lincoln Douglas and Slavery,* esp. pp. 60, 97-103.

9 *CW* II, p. 405.

10 Gabor S. Boritt, *Lincoln and the Economics of the American Dream,* p. 159. The Charleston opening speech received special attention in Lerone Bennett's anti-Lincoln screed, *Forced Into Glory: Abraham Lincoln's White Dream* (Chicago: Johnson Publishing Company, 2000.)

11 Mario Cuomo and Harold Holzer, eds., *Lincoln on Democracy: His Own Words, With Essays by America's Foremost Civil War Historians.* (New York: Harper Perennial, 1991), p. 129; Interview with Professor Rodney O. Davis, Galesburg, Illinois, 5 July, 2003.

12 Lincoln-Douglas Debate Museum wall text, 4 July, 2003.

13 New York *Evening Post,* September 21, 1858, in Sparks, p. 319.

14 "Abraham Lincoln," *Weekly Belleville Advocate,* September 29, 1858, *NIU,* 3 April, 2004; "The Charleston Debate" *Weekly North-Western Gazette,* Galena, Illinois, September 23, 1858, and September 28, 1858, *NIU,* 3 April, 2004; *LDD,* "The 1858 Popular Vote—Debate Counties."

15 "Dred Scott Decision Endorsed," *Freeport Weekly Bulletin,* September 30, 1858, *NIU,* 3 April, 2004.

Notes for Chapter Five: "A Monstrous Heresy"

1 *CW* III, P. 202. Also, see *The Lincoln Log: A Daily Chronology of the Life of Abraham Lincoln,* 5 June, 2004. http://www.stg.brown.edu/projects/lincoln. Hereafter known as *LL;* Henry C. Whitney to Abraham Lincoln,

23 September, 1858, Abraham Lincoln Papers at the Library of Congress, Online version http://memory.loc.gov 13 July 2005.

2 Paul M. Angle, *Created Equal? The Complete Lincoln-Douglas Debates of 1858* (Chicago: University of Chicago Press, 1958), p. 276. Angle quotes a "Letter From Sullivan," Chicago *Times*, September 20, 1858. The Missouri *Republican* clipped significant portions of this article for its September 23 edition; see Sparks, pp. 557-562.

3 Angle, *Created Equal?* pp. 276-277.

4 Angle, pp. 277-278.

5 Chicago *Times*, September 20, 1858, in Angle, p 278.

6 Chicago *Times*, September 20, 1858, in Angle, pp. 278- 279.

7 Chicago *Times*, September 20, 1858, in Angle, p. 279.

8 Chicago *Times*, September 20, 1858, in Angle, p. 279-280.

9 Angle, pp. 280-281.

10 Chicago *Press and Tribune*, September 26, 1858, in Angle, pp. 280-281.

11 Chicago *Press and Tribune,* September 26, 1858, in Angle, pp. 280-281; the Missouri *Republican*, a pro-Douglas newspaper, offered a nearly identical account; see Sparks, pp. 557-562; Quincy *Whig and Republican*, October 11, 1858, in Sparks, pp. 562-563. It would be useful to know what Lincoln said in his speech that followed the incident, but no known copy exists; neither White nor Hitt were on hand.

12 Chicago *Times*, September 26, 1858, quoted in Angle, pp. 282-283.

13 Chicago *Times*, September 26, 1858, quoted in Angle, pp. 282-283.

14 *LL,* 5 June, 2004; *CW* III, p. 202-203.

15 *LL*, 5 June, 2004; *Illinois State Journal*, October 2, 1858, quoted in *LL*, 5 June, 2004.

16 *CW* III, p. 203.

17 *CW* III, p 204.

18 Jesse K. DuBois and Ozias M. Hatch to Abraham Lincoln, 7 September, 1858, Abraham Lincoln Paper at the Library of Congress, Online version, http://memory.loc.gov 13 July 2005.

19 *CW* III, pp. 204-205.

20 *LL*, 5 June, 2004; Angle, pp. 283-284.

21 St. Louis *Democrat* quoted in Galena *Weekly North-Western Gazette*, September 21, 1858, *NIU*, 31 May, 2004; Galena *Weekly North-Western Gazette*, September 28, 1858, *NIU* 31 May, 2004; Washington *Union*, September 15, 1858, quoted in Galena *Weekly North-Western Gazette*, September 28, 1858, *NIU*, 31 May, 2004; Galena *Weekly North Western Gazette*, October 5, 1858, *NIU*, 31 May, 2004.

22 Quincy *Daily Whig and Republican*, September 25, 1858, *NIU*, 31 May, 2004.

23 Freeport *Weekly Journal*, quoted in the Freeport *Weekly Bulletin*, September 23, 1858, *NIU*, 31 May, 2004; Freeport *Weekly Bulletin*, October 7, 1858, *NIU*, 31 May, 2004. On Lincoln's flap with the Illinois Central (which ended amicably), see David Herbert Donald, *Lincoln* (New York: Simon and Schuster, 1995), p. 156.

24 Jacksonville *Sentinel*, September 24, 1858, *NIU*, 31 May, 2004.

25 Chicago *Press and Tribune*, October 1, 1858, quoted in Angle, p. 284.

26 *Central Illinois Gazette*, September 29, 1858, *NIU*, 31 May, 2004.

27 *LDD*, p. 234; Galesburg *Semi-Weekly Democrat*, October 9, 1858, *NIU*, 17 June, 2004.

28 Galesburg *Semi-Weekly Democrat*, October 9, 1858, *NIU*, 17 June, 2004; *LDD*, p. 235.

29 Galesburg *Semi-Weekly Democrat*, October 9, 1858, *NIU*, 17 June, 2004.

30 Galesburg *Semi-Weekly Democrat*, October 9, 1858, *NIU*, 17 June, 2004.

31 Galesburg *Semi-Weekly Democrat*, October 9, 1858, *NIU*, October 9, 1858, 17 June, 2004.

32 Galesburg *Semi-Weekly Democrat*, October 9, 1858, *NIU*, 17 June, 2004.

33 *LDD*, p. 235; Ralph Gary, *Following in Lincoln's Footsteps: A Complete Annotated Reference to Hundreds of Historical Sites Visited by Abraham Lincoln* (New York: Carroll and Graf, 2001), p. 71. I appreciate Professor Rodney O. Davis' clarification of this development.

34 *LDD*. p. 235.

35 Allan Nevins, *The Emergence of Lincoln: Douglas, Buchanan, and Party Chaos* I (New York, Charles Scribner's Sons, 1951), pp. 386-387.

36 *LDD*, p. 236.

37 The first two quotes are from Lincoln's Peoria speech of October 16, 1854, *CW* II, p. 266. The second comes from Lincoln's Chicago speech of July 10, 1858, *CW* II, p. 500.

38 *CW* II, p. 255.

39 Douglas L. Wilson, *Honor's Voice: The Transformation of Abraham Lincoln.* (New York: Alfred A. Knopf, 1998), pp. 206-209. Throughout Wilson's book the Lincoln of the 1830s and 40s emerges as a young man prone to political attack, serious bouts of depression, and social missteps. See also Michael Burlingame, *The Inner World of Abraham Lincoln* (Urbana:

University of Illinois Press, 1994.) Burlingame includes in this collection essays on "Lincoln's Midlife Crisis: From Party Hack to Statesman," and "Lincoln's Anger and Cruelty."

40 Quoted in Kent Gramm, *November: Lincoln's Ellegy at Gettysburg* (Bloomington: Indiana University Press, 2001), pp. 126-127.

41 Pauline Maier, *American Scripture: Writing the Declaration of Independence.* (New York: Alfred A. Knopf, 1997.)

42 Wilson, *Honor's Voice.* See especially pp. 265-323.

43 Robert V. Bruce, "The Riddle of Death," in Boritt, ed., *The Lincoln Enigma*, pp. 130-145.

44 The admonition that fatalities could occur is taken from the Quincy *Whig and* Republican, October 11, 1858, in Sparks, p. 563; for Mary Lincoln's plight see Jean H. Baker, *Mary Todd Lincoln: A Biography* (New York: W. W. Norton, 1987), pp. 152-154.

45 Freeport *Weekly Journal*, October 14, 1858, *NIU*, 17 June, 2004; Bloomington *Daily Pantagraph*, October 13, 1858, *NIU*, 17 June, 2004; Chicago *Times*, quoted in *LDD*, pp. 236-237; *LDD*, p. 237. The quotes come from the New York *Herald*, whose editor James Bennett Gordon, was proud that he published a Northern paper that stood up for Southern principles. See Ratner and Teeter, *Fanatics & Fire Eaters*, pp. 10-11.

46 *FL,* pp. 137-138.

47 *FL*, p. 167-169; p. 180; pp. 138-139; p. 144; p. 168; p. 180.

48 *FL*, p. 142.

Notes for Chapter Six: "The Successive Acts of A Drama"

1"The Lincoln Log," http://www.stg.brown.edu/projects/lincoln. 5 June, 2004.

2 "The Lincoln Log," 5 June, 2004; Committee from the Advisory Commission to the Board of Directors of the Illinois State Historical Library, *Semi-Centennial of the Lincoln-Douglas Debates in Illinois, 1858-1908: Circular of Suggestions for School Celebrations.* (Springfield, Illinois: Phillips Brothers, 1908), p. 36. Historical Society of Quincy and Adams County, 7 July, 2003.

3 *Semi-Centennial of the Lincoln-Douglas Debates*, p. 36.

4 Interview with Phil Germann and David Costigan. Historical Society of Quincy and Adams County, 7 July, 2003; William Mussetter, "Black history display teaches about Lincoln's view," Quincy *Herald Whig*, 8 October, 1994. Historical Society of Quincy and Adams County, 7 July, 2003.

5 Terrell Dempsey, *Searching for Jim: Slavery in Samuel Clemens' World.* (Columbia: University of Missouri Press, 2003), pp. 30-33; pp. 102-104.

6 Germann and Costigan interview, 7 July, 2003. Historical Society of Quincy and Adams County, 7 July, 2003.

7 "Down on the Irish," Freeport *Weekly Bulletin*, 26 August, 1858, *NIU*, 31 May, 2004; "Republican Combinations," Freeport *Weekly Bulletin*, 23 September, 1858, *NIU*, 31 May, 2004.

8 "The Two Despotisms—Catholicism and Slavery—Their Union and Identity." Illinois *State Journal*, 30 August, 1858, *NIU*, 31 May, 2004.

9 Illinois *State Journal*, 30 August, *NIU*, 31 May, 2004.

10 Illinois *State Journal,* 30 August, 1858, *NIU*, 31 May, 2004.

11 Illinois *State Journal*, 30 August, 1858, *NIU*, 31 May, 2004.

12 William E. Gienapp, *The Origins of The Republican Party, 1852-1856* (New York, Oxford University Press), p. 287.

13 Both accounts of Lincoln's Monmouth speech appear in a single entry in *CW* III, pp. 244-245.

14 *CW* III, pp. 244-245.

15 *LDD*, p. 278.

16 "The Quincy Debate," in *Freeport's Lincoln*, pp. 151-154. Spencer's recollection of the existence of the Wide Awakes may also have been flawed. Most of Lincoln's biographers have tended to date the Republican marching clubs to the 1860 presidential campaign, and have established Hartford, Connecticut as the place of origin. See, for instance, Richard Carwardine, *Lincoln*, pp. 113-114, and Allan Nevins, *The Emergence of Lincoln: Prologue to Civil War, 1859-1861* (New York: Charles Scribner's Sons, 1851), pp. 304-305. For Douglas' drinking, see Bryon Andreasen, "A Little Known Eyewitness Account From The 1858 Lincoln-Douglas Senate Campaign," *For The People: A Newsletter of the Abraham Lincoln Association,* Vol. 10: 2, Summer, 2008, pp. 1-2. Allen Guelzo reports that at Quincy, Douglas' remarks "meander[ed] alcoholically from pillar to post." Guelzo, *Lincoln and Douglas: The Debates That Made America,* p. 248.

17 "Pen Pictures of the Central Part of the City of Quincy As It Was When Douglas and Lincoln Met in Debate." *Journal of the Illinois State Historical Society,* XVIII, July, 1925. Springfield: Illinois State Historical Society, p. 393. Originally published in Quincy *Daily Herald*, 13 October, 1908. Historical Society of Quincy and Adams County, 7 July, 2003.

18 "Pen Pictures. . ." Historical Society of Quincy and Adams County, 7 July, 2003.

19 "Pen Pictures. . ." Historical Society of Quincy and Adams County, 7 July, 2003.

20 "Pen Pictures. . ." Historical Society of Quincy and Adams County, 7 July, 2003.

21 *LDD*, pp. 277-279.

22 Mike Cashman, quoted in untitled article, Quincy *Herald-Whig*, 1936. Historical Society of Quincy and Adams County, 7 July, 2003.

23 Ronald White, *Lincoln's Greatest Speech: The Second Inaugural Address,*(New York, Simon and Schuster, 2002), p. 48. White asserts that in his set-piece addresses Lincoln spoke about "one hundred words per minute." In debate he can be assumed to have spoken faster, but not radically so.

24 For a short discussion of the many uses of the word, see Randall Kennedy, *Nigger: The Strange Career of A Troublesome Word,* (New York: Pantheon Books, 2002.)

25 David Herbert Donald, *We Are Lincoln Men: Abraham Lincoln and His Friends,* (New York: Simon and Schuster, 2003), p. 107; *LDD*, p. 322.

26 New York *Herald*, October 13, 1858, in Sparks, p. 540; Norfolk *Argus*, in Washington *Union*, September 2, 1858, in Sparks, p. 542; Cincinnati *Commercial*, September 23, 1858, in Sparks, pp. 540-541; Boston *Daily Advertiser*, in Sparks, pp. 536-537; Cincinnati *Gazette*, September 9, 1858, in Sparks, pp. 542-543; New York *Evening Post*, October 18, 1858, in Sparks, p. 540.

Notes for Chapter Seven: "It is The Eternal Question"

1 *LDD*, p. 322.

2 Paul Simon, *Freedom's Champion: Elijah Lovejoy*. (Carbondale and Edwardsville: Southern Illinois University Press, 1994), pp. 61-63. Simon may have been drawn to the Lovejoy case in part because of his own experiences as a courageous Illinois newspaperman.

3 Paul Simon, *Freedom's Champion,* p. 97.

4 Simon, *Freedom's Champion*, pp. 110-117.

5 Simon, p. 115-116.

6 The description of Lovejoy's death draws on Simon, pp. 129-133. After the murder, Hope is alleged to have hollered, "I would like to kill every damned Abolitionist fanatic in town!" Quoted in Simon, p. 134.

7 Henry Mayer, *All on Fire: William Lloyd Garrison and the Abolition of Slavery*. (New York: St. Martin's Griffin, 1998), pp. 237-239.

8 John Splaine, *A Companion to the Lincoln Douglas Debates*. (Washington: National Cable Satellite Corporation, 1994), p. 4; Simon, p. 140. No one was ever convicted for the Lovejoy killing.

9 Shelby Foote, *The Civil War: A Narrative; Fort Sumter to Perryville*. New York: Random House, 1958, p. 459; David Herbert Donald, *Lincoln*, pp. 90-91; Simon, p. 141; Ralph W. Gary, *Following in Lincoln's Footsteps*. (New York: Carroll and Graf, 2001), p. 9.

10 Donald, *Lincoln*, p. 91; Foote, *The Civil War*, p. 459.

11 Jean Baker, *Mary Todd Lincoln: A Biography*. (New York: W.W. Norton, 1987), p. 154.

12 Johannsen, *Stephen A. Douglas*, pp. 541-544; *Congregational Herald*, quoted in "The Proof is Here," Freeport *Weekly Bulletin*, 14 October 1858. *NIU*, 7 July, 2004.

13 Donald, *Lincoln*, pp. 158-160; see also Michael Burlingame, "The Lincolns' Marriage," *The Inner World of Abraham Lincoln*. (Urbana: University of Illinois Press, 1994), p. 277. Burlingame's account has Mary chasing her husband a little less threateningly with a broom; on the Trumbull relationship, see Burlingame, *The Inner World of Abraham Lincoln*, pp. 309-310.

14 Quoted in Carl Landrum, "Debates took toll on Douglas' voice, health," Quincy *Herald-Whig*, 16 October, 1994; Alan Nevins, *The Emergence of Lincoln: Douglas, Buchanan, and Party Chaos*. (New York: Charles Scribner's Sons, 1951), p. 390; *LDD*, p. 322; "Six-Pounder." Dixon *Republican and Telegraph*, 14 October, 1858. *NIU*, 7 July, 2004.

15 Baker, *Mary Todd Lincoln*, p. 154.

16 *LDD*, pp. 321-322.

17 "Response to the Bulletin," Freeport *Weekly Journal*, 14 October, 1858, *NIU*, 7 July, 2004; "Abe Lincoln." Freeport *Weekly Bulletin*, 14 October, 1858, *NIU*, 7 July, 2004; "The Proof is Here." Freeport *Weekly Bulletin*, 14 October, 1858, *NIU*, 7 July, 2004; "Douglas Coming to His Milk," Dixon *Daily Republican and Telegraph*," 14 October, 1858, *NIU*, 7 July, 2004.

18 *LDD*, p. 322.

19 *LDD*, p. 322.

20 "Senator Brown Upon Douglas," *The National Era*, Washington, D.C., 30 September, 1858, Accessible Archives, http:www.accessible.com/accessible/text/freedom/ 12 April, 2004.

21 See, for instance, Bernard Bailyn, *The Ideological Origins of the American Revolution*; on republicanism and the founding of the Whigs, see Harry L. Watson, *Liberty and Power: The Politics of Jacksonian America,* (New York: Noonday Press, 1990), pp. 158-159, 171.

22 Martin Luther King, Jr., "Letter From Birmingham City Jail," in James Melvin Washington, *A Testament of Hope: The Essential Writings and Speeches of Martin Luther King, Jr.* (San Francisco: Harper San Francisco, 1986), p. 295.

23 Lincoln quoted his speech at Springfield, June 26, 1857; *CW* II, pp. 405-406.

24 See Potter, *The Impending Crisis*, pp. 223-227, and William Lee Miller, *Arguing About Slavery: The Great Battle in the United States Congress* (New York: Alfred A. Knopf, 1995), p. 28-29.

25 Fehrenbacher, ed., *Abraham Lincoln: Speeches and Writings, 1832-1858*, pp. 810-811.

26 Charles H. Ray to Abraham Lincoln, July 27,1858, Abraham Lincoln Papers at the Library of Congress, Online edition, http://memory.loc.gov, 14 August, 2006.

27 Missouri *Democrat*, October 16, 1858, in Sparks, p. 497; *Illinois State Register*, October 18, 1858, in Sparks, p. 503.

Notes for Chapter Seven: "It is The Eternal Question"

1 *LDD*, p. 322.

2 Paul Simon, *Freedom's Champion: Elijah Lovejoy*. (Carbondale and Edwardsville: Southern Illinois University Press, 1994), pp. 61-63. Simon may have been drawn to the Lovejoy case in part because of his own experiences as a courageous Illinois newspaperman.

3 Paul Simon, *Freedom's Champion*, p. 97.

4 Simon, *Freedom's Champion*, pp. 110-117.

5 Simon, p. 115-116.

6 The description of Lovejoy's death draws on Simon, pp. 129-133. After the murder, Hope is alleged to have hollered, "I would like to kill every damned Abolitionist fanatic in town!" Quoted in Simon, p. 134.

7 Henry Mayer, *All on Fire: William Lloyd Garrison and the Abolition of Slavery*. (New York: St. Martin's Griffin, 1998), pp. 237-239.

8 John Splaine, *A Companion to the Lincoln Douglas Debates*. (Washington: National Cable Satellite Corporation, 1994), p. 4; Simon, p. 140. No one was ever convicted for the Lovejoy killing.

9 Shelby Foote, *The Civil War: A Narrative; Fort Sumter to Perryville*. New York: Random House, 1958, p. 459; David Herbert Donald, *Lincoln*, pp. 90-91; Simon, p. 141; Ralph W. Gary, *Following in Lincoln's Footsteps*. (New York: Carroll and Graf, 2001), p. 9.

10 Donald, *Lincoln*, p. 91; Foote, *The Civil War*, p. 459.

11 Jean Baker, *Mary Todd Lincoln: A Biography*. (New York: W.W. Norton, 1987), p. 154.

12 Johannsen, *Stephen A. Douglas*, pp. 541-544; *Congregational Herald,* quoted in "The Proof is Here," Freeport *Weekly Bulletin*, 14 October 1858. *NIU*, 7 July, 2004.

13 Donald, *Lincoln*, pp. 158-160; see also Michael Burlingame, "The Lincolns' Marriage," *The Inner World of Abraham Lincoln.* (Urbana: University of Illinois Press, 1994), p. 277. Burlingame's account has Mary chasing her husband a little less threateningly with a broom; on the Trumbull relationship, see Burlingame, *The Inner World of Abraham Lincoln*, pp. 309-310.

14 Quoted in Carl Landrum, "Debates took toll on Douglas' voice, health," Quincy *Herald-Whig,* 16 October, 1994; Alan Nevins, *The Emergence of Lincoln: Douglas, Buchanan, and Party Chaos.* (New York: Charles Scribner's Sons, 1951), p. 390; *LDD*, p. 322; "Six-Pounder." Dixon *Republican and Telegraph,* 14 October, 1858. *NIU*, 7 July, 2004.

15 Baker, *Mary Todd Lincoln*, p. 154.

16 *LDD*, pp. 321-322.

17 "Response to the Bulletin," Freeport *Weekly Journal*, 14 October, 1858, *NIU*, 7 July, 2004; "Abe Lincoln." Freeport *Weekly Bulletin*, 14 October, 1858, *NIU*, 7 July, 2004; "The Proof is Here." Freeport *Weekly Bulletin,* 14 October, 1858, *NIU*, 7 July, 2004; "Douglas Coming to His Milk," Dixon *Daily Republican and Telegraph*," 14 October, 1858, *NIU*, 7 July, 2004.

18 *LDD*, p. 322.

19 *LDD*, p. 322.

20 "Senator Brown Upon Douglas," *The National Era,* Washington, D.C., 30 September, 1858, Accessible Archives, http:www.accessible.com/ accessible/text/freedom/ 12 April, 2004.

21 See, for instance, Bernard Bailyn, *The Ideological Origins of the American Revolution*; on republicanism and the founding of the Whigs, see

Harry L. Watson, *Liberty and Power: The Politics of Jacksonian America,* (New York: Noonday Press, 1990), pp. 158-159, 171.

22 Martin Luther King, Jr., "Letter From Birmingham City Jail," in James Melvin Washington, *A Testament of Hope: The Essential Writings and Speeches of Martin Luther King, Jr.* (San Francisco: Harper San Francisco, 1986), p. 295.

23 Lincoln quoted his speech at Springfield, June 26, 1857; *CW* II, pp. 405-406.

24 See Potter, *The Impending Crisis*, pp. 223-227, and William Lee Miller, *Arguing About Slavery: The Great Battle in the United States Congress* (New York: Alfred A. Knopf, 1995), p. 28-29.

25 Fehrenbacher, ed., *Abraham Lincoln: Speeches and Writings, 1832-1858,* pp. 810-811.

26 Charles H. Ray to Abraham Lincoln, July 27,1858, Abraham Lincoln Papers at the Library of Congress, Online edition, http://memory. loc.gov, 14 August, 2006.

27 Missouri *Democrat*, October 16, 1858, in Sparks, p. 497; *Illinois State Register*, October 18, 1858, in Sparks, p. 503.

28 *LDD*, pp. 8-15.

29 *LDD,* pp. 25-26.

30 "180 Mutilations of Lincoln's speech," Bloomington *Daily Pantagraph*, 13 October, 1858, *NIU,* 17 June, 2004. The mystery on this excerpt lies in its date. The Alton debate, referred to ostensibly on the 13th of October by the *Pantagraph*, would not take place for two days. The paper may have been guilty of a typo; the description of Lincoln's last half-hour at Alton appears to have been drawn from the debate itself.

31 Letter from Henry Wise to Stephen A. Douglas, via John Moore, quoted in Robert Johannsen, *The Letters of Stephen A. Douglas*. (Urbana: University of Illinois Press, 1961), p. 429.

29 *LDD,* pp. 25-26.

30 "180 Mutilations of Lincoln's speech," Bloomington *Daily Pantagraph*, 13 October, 1858, *NIU,* 17 June, 2004. The mystery on this excerpt lies in its date. The Alton debate, referred to ostensibly on the 13th of October by the *Pantagraph*, would not take place for two days. The paper may have been guilty of a typo; the description of Lincoln's last half-hour at Alton appears to have been drawn from the debate itself.

31 Letter from Henry Wise to Stephen A. Douglas, via John Moore, quoted in Robert Johannsen, *The Letters of Stephen A. Douglas*. (Urbana: University of Illinois Press, 1961), p. 429.

Notes for Chapter Eight: "But It Hurts Too Much to Laugh"

1 "Conclusion of the Joint Debates Between Lincoln and Douglas," Rockford *Republican*, 28 October, 1858. *NIU,* 11 August, 2004; Chicago *Press and Tribune*, 29 October, 1858, in Angle, *Created Equal?* p. 404; Burlington *State Gazette*, October 29, 1858, in Sparks, p. 533; Washington *National Era*, 28 October, 1858, http://www.accessible.com/ accessible/text/freedom 12 April, 2004; J.H. Jordan to Abraham Lincoln, 25 July, 1858, Abraham Lincoln Papers at the Library of Congress, Online version http://memory.loc.gov 13 July, 2005.

2 "$52,000 for Douglas!" Dixon *Republican and Telegraph*, 28 October, 1858. *NIU,* 11 August, 2004; F. C. Fay to Abraham Lincoln, 3 September, 1858, Abraham Lincoln Papers at the Library of Congress, Online version http://memory.loc.gov_13 July, 2005.

3 Lincoln to Norman Judd, 20 October, 1858, *CW* III, pp. 329-330.

4 Angle, *Created Equal?* pp. 403-411; Chicago *Times*, 2 November, 1858, quoted in Angle, p. 408; Chicago *Times*, 31 October, 1858, quoted in Angle, p. 405-406.

5 "How to Vote for Lincoln," Freeport *Weekly Journal,* 14 October, 1858. *NIU,* 13 August, 2004.

6 Chicago *Press and Tribune,* 28 October, 1858, quoted in Angle, pp. 403-404.

7 Henry C. Whitney to Abraham Lincoln, 14 October, 1858, Abraham Lincoln Papers at the Library of Congress, Online version http://memory. loc.gov 13 July, 2005; Lincoln to Judd, *CW* III, p. 330.

8 Lincoln to Judd, *CW* III, p. 330. J. Rowan Herndon to Abraham Lincoln, 25 October, 1858, Abraham Lincoln Papers at the Library of Congress, Online version http://memory.loc.gov 13 July, 2005.

9 Jacksonville *Sentinel,* 22 October, 1858, *CW* III, pp. 328-329.

10 Lincoln to Judd, 24 October, 1858, *CW* III, p. 332; Lincoln to John Moses, 24 October, 1858, *CW* III, p. 332.

11 Lincoln to Alexander Sympson, 24 October, 1858, *CW* III, p. 332.

12 Lincoln to Edward Lusk, 30 October, 1858, *CW* III, p. 333; quoted in David Herbert Donald, *Lincoln's Herndon,* New York: Alfred A. Knopf, 1948, p. 122.

13 Lincoln to Thomas Henderson, 18 October, 1858, Roy P. Basler, ed., *The Collected Works of Abraham Lincoln: First Supplement, 1832-1865,* (New Brunswick, Rutgers University Press, 1990), p. 33.

14 Chicago *Journal,* in Rockford *Republican,* 28 October. *NIU,* 11 August, 2004.

15 Johannsen, *SAD,* p. 676; Bruce Catton, *The Coming Fury: The Centennial History of the Civil War,* Vol. I, (New York: Pocket Books, 1971), p. 3.

16 Fehrenbacher, *Prelude,* p. 118. See also Fehrehbacher, ed., *Abraham Lincoln: Speeches and Writings, 1832-1858,* (New York: Literary Classics of the United States, 1989), p. 875.

17 "Crittenden on Douglas," Washington *National Era,* 4 November, 1858. http://www.accessible.com, 12 April, 2004. Crittenden, upon learning that the letter had been published, wrote to Lincoln that, "I have had no act or part, agency or privity in respect to it, or its publication—it is wholly unauthorized by me. I should have considered myself dishonored, if I could ever have consented to, or permitted any use to be made of our correspondence, that would have been injurious or embarrassing to you . . ." John J. Crittenden to Abraham Lincoln, 27 October, 1858, Abraham Lincoln Papers at the Library of Congress, Online version, http://memory.loc. gov 13 July, 2005.

18 Allan Nevins, *The Emergence of Lincoln: Douglas, Buchanan, and Party Chaos, 1857-1859,* (New York: Charles Scribner's Sons, 1951), p. 396.

19 "The Lincoln Log," Thursday, October 28, 1858. http://www.stg. brown.edu/projects/lincoln, 5 June, 2004.

20 "Fragment: Last Speech of the Campaign at Springfield, Illinois," 30 October, 1858, *CW* III, pp. 334-335.

21 30 October, 1858, *CW* III, pp. 334-335.

22 *CW* III, p. 334.

23 *CW* III, p. 334.

24 *CW* III, p. 334.

25 For Douglas' physical condition, see, for instance, Angle, p. 405; Chicago *Press and Tribune,* 2 November, 1858, quoted in Angle, pp. 406-407.

26 Quoted in Donald, *Lincoln's Herndon,* p. 125.

27 Fehrenbacher, *Prelude,* p. 114.

28 Fehrenbacher, *Prelude,* p. 115.

29 Fehrenbacher, *Prelude,* pp. 118-119.

30 Saul Sigelschiffer, *The American Conscience: The Drama of the Lincoln-Douglas Debates,* (New York: Horizon Press, 1973), p. 383; *Illinois State Journal,* quoted in "The Lincoln Log," Tuesday, 2 November, 1858. http://www.brown.edu, 5 June, 2004.; "The Lincoln Log," Tuesday, 2 November, 1858. http://www.brown.edu, 5 June, 2004.

31 "The Lincoln Log," Thursday, 4 November, 1858. http://www.brown.edu, 5 June, 2004; Fehrenbacher, *Prelude*, pp. 118-119.

32 Fehrenbacher, *Prelude*, p. 115; Guelzo, *Lincoln and Douglas,* pp. 285-286; Holzer, "The 1858 Popular Vote—Debate Counties," in *LDD*, p. 373.

33 "Lincoln vs. Douglas: Election Results of the 1858 Campaign for U.S. Senator from Illinois," Peter Siczewicz, Abraham Lincoln Historical Digitization Project, *NIU*, 14 August, 2004.

34 Lincoln to John J. Crittenden, 4 November, 1858, *CW* III, pp. 335-336.

35 Lincoln to Crittenden, 4 November, 1858, *CW* III, pp. 335-336.

36 Lincoln to Crittenden, *CW* III, pp. 335-336.

37 Horace White to Abraham Lincoln, 5 November, 1858, Abraham Lincoln Papers at the Library of Congress, Online version http://memory.loc.gov 13 July, 2005; Henry P.H. Bromwell to Abraham Lincoln, 5 November, 1858, Abraham Lincoln Papers at the Library of Congress, Online version http://memory.loc.gov 13 July, 2005; David Davis to Abraham Lincoln, 7 November, 1858, Abraham Lincoln Papers at the Library of Congress, Online version http://memory.loc.gov 13 July, 1858; David Brier to Abraham Lincoln, 7 November, 1858, Abraham Lincoln Papers at the Library of Congress, Online version http://memory.loc.gov 13 July, 1858; Norman B. Judd to Abraham Lincoln, 15 November, 1858, Abraham Lincoln Papers at the Library of Congress, Online version http://memory.loc.gov 13 July, 1858.

38 Lincoln to Judd, 15 November, 1858, *CW* III, pp. 336-337.

39 Lincoln to Judd, 15 November, 1858, *CW* III, pp. 336-337.

40 Lincoln to Samuel C. Davis and Company, 17 November, 1858, *CW* III p. 338.

41 Lincoln to Henry Asbury, 19 November, 1858, *CW* III, p. 339; Lincoln to Anson G. Henry, 19 November, 1858, *CW* III, p. 339; Lincoln to Anson S. Miller, 19 November, 1858, *CW* III, p. 340; Lincoln to Eleazar A. Paine, 19 November, 1858, *CW* III, p. 340.

42 Exchange of letters, Lincoln and M.M. Inman, 9 November, 1858 and 20 November, 1858, *CW* III, p. 341.

43 Lincoln to H.D. Sharpe, 8 December, 1858, *CW*, p. 344; Lincoln to Alexander Sympson, 12 December, 1858, *CW* III, p. 346.

44 Lincoln to Lyman Trumbull, 11 December, 1858, *CW* III, pp. 344-345; Lincoln to Charles H. Ray, 20 November, 1858, *CW* III, p. 341; Lincoln to Henry C. Whitney, 30 November, 1858, *CW* III, p. 343; Lincoln to Henry C. Whitney, 25 December, 1858, *CW* III, p. 347.

45 Jean Baker, *Mary Todd Lincoln: A Biography*, (New York: W.W. Norton, 1987), pp. 156-157.

46 Fehrenbacher, *Prelude*, p. 115.

47 Michael Burlingame, "The Most Ambitious Man in the World," *The Inner World of Abraham Lincoln*, pp. 247-248.

48 Quoted in Burlingame, *The Inner World of Abraham Lincoln*, pp. 247-248.

49 Quoted in Burlingame, *Inner World*, p. 248; Donald, *Lincoln's Herndon*, p. 126; Donald, *Lincoln*, p. 228.

50 Donald, *Lincoln's Herndon*, pp. 114-123.

51 Donald, *Lincoln's Herndon*, p. 122-123.

52 Quoted in Sigelschiffer, *The American Conscience*, pp. 385-386.

53 Quoted in Sigelschiffer, *The American Conscience*, pp. 385-386.

54 Quoted in Sigelschiffer, *The American Conscience*, pp. 385-386.

55 Quoted in Donald, *Lincoln's Herndon*, pp. 124-25.

56 Stephen A. Douglas to Henry A. Wise, 7 November, 1858, Robert Johannsen, ed., *The Letters of Stephen A. Douglas*, (Urbana: University of Illinois Press, 1961), p. 429; Douglas to Pierre Soule et. al., December, 1858, Johannsen, *Letters of Stephen A. Douglas*, p. 430.

57 "Speech of Senator S.A. Douglas At The Meeting in Odd-Fellows' Hall, New Orleans, on Monday Evening, December 6, 1858," Stephen A. Douglas, *Speeches of Senator Stephen A. Douglas On the Occasion of His Public Receptions By the Citizens of New Orleans, Philadelphia, and Baltimore*, (Washington: Lemuel Towers, 1858), Illinois State Historical Library, Springfield, p 1; "Speech of Senator Douglas" Odd Fellows Hall, New Orleans, 6 December, p. 9.

58 Charles Lanphier, telegram to Stephen A. Douglas, 6 January, 1859, quoted in Johannsen, *SAD*, p. 679.

59 Douglas to Lanphier, 6 January, 1859, Johannsen, *Letters of Stephen A. Douglas*, p. 433.

60 Damon Wells, *Stephen Douglas: The Last Years, 1857-1861*, (Austin, University of Texas Press, 1971), p. 137; Robert Rutland, *The Democrats: From Jefferson to Carter*, (Baton Rouge: Louisiana State University Press, 1979), p. 103.

61 Rutland, *The Democrats*, pp. 103-104.

62 There is a colorful discussion of the Charleston Democratic Convention in Bruce Catton, *The Coming Fury*, pp. 1-46.

63 Philadelphia *Press*, August 26, 1858, in Sparks, p. 126.

64 Chester P. Dewey to Abraham Lincoln, 30 October, 1858, Abraham Lincoln Papers at the Library of Congress, Online version http://memory.loc.gov 13 July, 2005; Lowell *Journal and Courier*, August 30, 1858, in Sparks, pp. 517-518; Rochester *Democrat*, November 10, 1858, in Sparks, p. 583; New York *Tribune*, October 26, 1858, in Sparks, p. 505; George W. Searle to Abraham Lincoln, 5 November, 1858, Abraham Lincoln Papers at the Library of Congress, Online version http://memory.loc.gov 13 July, 2005; H.D. Sharpe to Abraham Lincoln, 9 November, 1858, Abraham Lincoln Papers at the Library of Congress, Online version http://memory.loc.gov 13 July, 2005.

65 Horace White to Abraham Lincoln, 5 November, 1858, Abraham Lincoln Papers at the Library of Congress, Online version http://memory.loc.gov 13 July, 2005; Henry P.H. Bromwell to Abraham Lincoln, 5 November, 1858, Abraham Lincoln Papers at the Library of Congress, Online version http://memory.loc.gov 13 July, 2005; William Hanna and John H. Wickizer to Abraham Lincoln, 5 November, 1858, Abraham Lincoln Papers at the Library of Congress, Online version http://memory.loc.gov 13 July, 2005; David Davis to Abraham Lincoln, 7 November 1858, Abraham Lincoln Papers at the Library of Congress, Online version http://memory.loc.gov 13 July, 2005; David Brier to Abraham Lincoln, 7 November, 1858, Abraham Lincoln Papers at the Library of Congress, Online version http://memory.loc.gov 13 July, 1858; Benjamin C. Lundy to Abraham Lincoln, 22 November, 1858, Abraham Lincoln Papers at the Library of Congress, Online version http://memory.loc.gov 13 July, 1858; Chicago *Daily Democrat*, November 11, 1858, in Sparks, p. 587.

66 Fehrenbacher, *Prelude*, p. 117; Burlingame, *The Inner World of Abraham Lincoln*, pp. 249-250.

67 Donald, *Lincoln*, pp. 244-246. The Abraham Lincoln Papers at the Library of Congress, Online version include a large number of invitations to speak from the summer of 1858.

68 Holzer argues that the Cooper Union Address was the speech that made Lincoln President. If so, then Lincoln's 1858 campaign acquires even greater importance, as the debates raised Lincoln's visibility in such a way as to gain him the invitation to Brooklyn. Harold Holzer, *Lincoln at Cooper*

Union: The Speech That Made Abraham Lincoln President (New York: Simon and Schuster Paperbacks, 2005), see especially pp. 28-59;

69 Donald, *Lincoln*, pp. 244-246.

70 Johannsen, *SAD*, pp. 797-798; Catton, p. 102.

71 Johannsen, *SAD*, p. 872.

72 Barack Obama interview, "Fresh Air," National Public Radio, 12 August, 2004.

73 Account of Samuel Leonard, *Freeport's Lincoln*, pp. 154-155.

74 Jean Bethke Elshtain, *Jane Addams and the Dream of American Democracy: A Life,* (New York: Basic Books, 2002), p. 1.

75 Abraham Lincoln, "Response to A Serenade," 18 May,, 1860, *CW* IV, p. 50.

76 Lincoln, "Response to A Serenade," *CW* IV, p. 50.

77 *CW* IV, pp. 50-51.

78 Abraham Lincoln, Speech on Reconstruction, Washington, D.C., 11 April, 1865, pp. 697-701; Abraham Lincoln to James C. Conkling, 26 August, 1863, pp. 495-499; Abraham Lincoln to Michael Hahn, 13 March, 1864, p. 579; Abraham Lincoln to Charles Sumner, 19 May, 1864, p. 595; Abraham Lincoln, Second Inaugural Address, pp. 686-687; Response to Serenade, Washington, D.C., 1 February, 1865; all from Don Fehrenbacher, ed., *Abraham Lincoln: Speeches and Writings, 1859-1865: Speeches, Letters and Miscellaneous Writings Presidential Messages and Proclamations,* (New York, Literary Classics of the United States, 1989.)

79 William Herndon, interview with John Armstrong, in Douglas L. Wilson and Rodney O. Davis, *Herndon's Informants: Letters, Interviews, and Statements About Abraham Lincoln*, (Urbana: University of Illinois Press, 1998), p. 575.

80 Rodney O. Davis interview, Galesburg, Illinois, 5 July, 2003.

81 Quoted in Burlingame, *The Inner World of Abraham Lincoln*, p. 251; "Interview with Alexander W. Randall and Joseph T. Mills," 19 August, 1864, *CW* VII, pp. 506-508. The diary entry includes some Lincoln banter on the campaign against Douglas. Four days after the interview with Randall and Mills, on August 23, 1864, Lincoln famously asked his cabinet to sign an envelope bearing his prediction that he would not be re-elected. At about this time, the New York Republican leaders Thurlow Weed and Henry Raymond had informed Lincoln of his dire re-election prospects, urging him to begin negotiations with the South on the basis of Union alone; slavery should be negotiated. See "Memorandum Concerning His Probable Failure of Re-Election," 23 August, 1864, *CW* VII, pp. 514-515.

82 "Fragment on the Struggle Against Slavery," [c. July, 1858], *CW* II, p. 482.

83 Quoted in Burlingame, *The Inner World of Abraham Lincoln*, p. 253.

84 George Buss interview, Freeport, Illinois, 2 July, 2003; Frederich Buechner, "To Be a Saint," *The Magnificent Defeat* (San Francisco: Harper San Francisco, 1985), pp. 118-123.

ACKNOWLEDGEMENTS

This book developed from a journey to Illinois in the summer of 2003, funded by a Morris County Teacher Fellowship offered me by the Geraldine R. Dodge Foundation. The Foundation's generosity enabled me to visit the small Illinois towns that hosted the debates, to examine the ways in which those towns have kept alive the memory of the debates, and to meet with Lincoln and Douglas scholars, buffs, and presenters. I had originally hoped to braid the story of the debates with the stories of these modern-day towns and people, but a concern over focus and sheer page length forced me to rein in my ambitions.

Regretful that I could not allot them space in the text, I offer warm thanks to Leonard Lock of Ottawa; George Buss and Rich Sokup of Freeport; Geof Skinner of the Union County *Gazette-Democrat,* Anna-Jonesboro; Dr. and Mrs. B.F. McClerren and Connie Russell of Charleston; Professor Rodney O. Davis of Knox College, Galesburg; Phil Gerhmann of the Historical Society of Quincy and Adams County and Professor Dave Costigan of Quincy University, Quincy; Charlene Gill, Don Lowery, John Meehan, and Kelly Miller of Alton; and Rudy Davenport of the Springfield area NAACP, Springfield. The generosity and kindness extended me by each of these Illinoisans will always remain a fond memory, and I hope their enthusiasm for a critical chapter in the nation's life lives on in the pages of this book.

The esteemed Lincoln scholar Thomas F. Schwartz of the Illinois Historic Preservation Agency helped in two important ways. First, he generated a list of people to contact, many of whom are represented above. Second, he read the manuscript and offered useful criticisms. I owe Dr. Schwartz immense gratitude for his encouragement of this project. I have also benefited from the critical reading of individual chapters by three other prominent Lincoln scholars: Harold Holzer of the Metropolitan Museum of Art, New York; Professor Kent Gramm; and Professor Rodney O. Davis, Knox College, Galesburg, Illinois. I have appreciated their willingness to read and comment on my writing. Larry D. Mansch, teacher, lawyer, soldier, and Lincoln scholar also read the manuscript and offered timely encouragement. Of course, any errors are of my own doing.

I thank also the Gilder Lehrman Institute for American History, which provided me and other teachers the opportunity to study Lincoln under Professor Gabor Boritt of the Civil War Institute of Gettysburg College in the summer of 2005, the Abraham Lincoln Presidential Library and Museum and the Horace Mann Insurance Company, which awarded me a Horace Mann-Abraham Lincoln Fellowship in the summer of 2006, and the Civil War Institute, which extended me a teacher scholarship for its one-week seminar on Lincoln in the summer of 2007. All enabled me to try to "get right with Lincoln" in the presence of talented scholars and gifted educators from across the nation. I also offer sincere thanks to Professor Herman Belz of the University of Maryland, College Park, whose graduate seminar in constitutional history introduced me to Lincoln's writings.

A number of people have contributed in ways large and small to this book. They include Douglas Downen, Lee Perry, Susan Pilshaw, Pat and Gene Maynard, Dick Smullen and Carol Petersen, Howard Saretan, Dan Smith and Michael Gross. I also thank Don Patterson, John Manning, Don Guida, Tom Callanan, Joe Righetti, Doreen Guzo and Michelle Kowalsky of Whippany Park High School.

My students have strengthened my commitment to this project, encouraging me to keep trying. They have been able companions in the annual springtime classroom journey back into Lincoln's life and times. I thank them, my colleagues, our staff, our administration, and the people of Hanover Township, New Jersey for their interest and support.

I thank as well my brother, Jim Schwartz, and my sister, Susan Drew, for their support of my lifelong interest in history.

I thank also Rosemary G. Schwartz, formerly a school librarian in the South Orange-Maplewood school district, for reading closely an early draft of the book. Her love and support have helped me to bring the project to conclusion, and she has kept faith with the memory of my father in this and in so many other ways.

Lastly, I thank my wife Trink and my daughters Anne and Erin for their love and for their patience, without which I would not have started, sustained, nor finished this book.

Richard Schwartz
Morristown, New Jersey, 2010

INDEX